# THE
# PSYCHOANALYSIS
# OF WAR

Franco Fornari

# THE
# PSYCHOANALYSIS
# OF WAR

Translated from the Italian
by Alenka Pfeifer

INDIANA UNIVERSITY PRESS
Bloomington & London

*The Psychoanalysis of War (Psicanalisi Della Guerra)* was originally published in Milan by Giangiacomo Feltrinelli Editore in 1966.

Indiana University Press edition published by arrangement with Doubleday & Company, Inc., 1975.

Also available in paperback from Doubleday & Company, Inc., Anchor Books Line.

Published in Canada by Fitzhenry & Whiteside Limited, Don Mills, Ontario
Manufactured in the United States of America


Library of Congress Cataloging in Publication Data

Fornari, Franco.
   The psychoanalysis of war.
   Translation of Psicoanalisi della guerra.
   Bibliography
   1. War—Psychological aspects.  I. Title.
U22.3.F6713   1975       355.02'019   74-17458
ISBN: 0-253-34632-0

# CONTENTS

# INTRODUCTION

This book is an elaboration, with some additions and revisions, of a paper I presented at the Twenty-fifth Congress of Romance Language Psychoanalysts, held in Milan in the spring of 1964. It was translated into French by Madame Pape-Scognamiglio and published, in conjunction with the Congress, by the Presses Universitaires de France. In France, therefore, in contrast with the course of events in Italy, this book was published before my *Psychoanalysis of Nuclear War*, the French translation of which is presently being published by Gallimard.

In a certain sense it would have been preferable if the present volume had been published first in Italy as well. In it I discuss the fundamental dynamics psychoanalysis detects in the war phenomenon, setting them, however, against the background of sociological and ethnological studies of the same problem, and without neglecting the contributions of other psychoanalytic authors. The book thus presents not only the results of my own investigation but—given the extreme gravity and complexity of the problems—also the testimony of a number of scholars in this field.

While *The Psychoanalysis of Nuclear War* is a specific investigation of the *war crisis created by the nuclear era, and consequently of the crisis of the sovereign state,* as a type of state organization closely associated with the war phenomenon, in this book I intend to apply the psychoanalytic instrument of investigation to the study of the war phenomenon in general.

The reader who has kindly followed my former endeavors will find in this book broader cultural references serving as a frame to the thesis of the individual responsibilities for war which is here understood *not* as something vague and mystical but as an empirical psychoanalytic disclosure and as a presupposition for allowing the individual to escape from his alienation in the state.

In fact, I believe that in our times when, owing to the advent of the nuclear era, the state, "the industrialist of the violence saved by the citizens," is becoming (to use the language of the Kanachi tribes whom we shall discuss later) "the sorcerer who kills us," the crucial problem is that of abolishing the monopolization and capitalization of violence by the state.

The first question which the man in the street would ask of a psychoanalyst concerned with war might be the following: What right has a psychoanalyst to occupy himself with these matters which are not in his competence? My answer is that the psychoanalyst, analyzing persons experiencing political problems, finds himself in a privileged position to observe *the individual modes*, that is, the internal mechanisms through which political and social experiences in general are elaborated. He is, therefore, in the best of positions to observe both the influence exerted by the unconscious on men's political preferences and the ways in which war is fantasied in the unconscious. The psychoanalyst is particularly able to observe, through symbolic language and the affective dialectic (which has its own specific laws different from those of dialectic understood as a purely cognitive experience), that individuals' political preferences as well as their experiences in war —in addition to containing realistic motives—are influenced by systems of defense against psychotic anxieties (i.e., against obviously illusory fears). It is this last observation that seems to justify psychoanalytic research in an area which, if investigated with an appropriate instrument, reveals factual peculiarities and massive distortions of reality approaching the modes of psychopathological experience.

We shall later have occasion to go deeply into the context of the psychotic anxieties and defenses that participate in the war phenomenon. Here I should like only to call attention to certain symbolic peculiarities regarding two protagonists of the atomic situation—the commander of the B-52 that dropped the bomb on Hiroshima, who named the airplane after his mother, Enola Gay and General Leslie Groves, director of the Manhattan Project and father of the atomic bomb, who, after a successful first experiment, cabled President Truman: "Baby is born."

What is the meaning of these symbolic peculiarities whereby the emergence of an all-destructive reality is associated with the symbols of procreation and preservation of the species, through a primary love relationship such as that between mother and child?

Of course one may think that questions of this sort, regarding symbolic peculiarities, are idle and senseless. According to a new cynico-scientific attitude considered realistic, the things that count are discussions on megatons, overkill, and the cold-blooded count of the number of millions of people America can afford to lose (fifty million? one hundred million?). Are psychoanalysts who concern themselves with the symbol of Enola Gay projected into the airplane that bombed Hiroshima and with "baby is born" used to announce the creation of the atomic bomb merely chasing butterflies? I do not raise these questions only because the student of the unconscious ascribes great importance even to little things. The truth is that clinical experience teaches us that *when a destructive reality is covered with symbols of love, this may constitute a maneuver destined to conceal deep depressive or persecutory anxieties, and that such concealment is very likely to predispose him who makes it to grave distortions in reality-testing and so render him unable to correctly foresee the possible consequences of his actions.*

At this point the contribution that psychoanalysis can bring to the study of the war phenomenon would appear to concern not so much the problem of the desirability or non-desirability of war, as the rationally correct manner of evaluating it.

One could contest the right of psychoanalysis to occupy itself with military matters on the grounds that these have their own objective laws that have nothing to do with psychoanalysis, which should concern itself with treating neurotic and psychotic disorders—and perhaps war neuroses—in a minority of sick people. However, some psychoanalysts maintain that the nuclear situation is in itself a war neurosis.

In order to reply to those who would contest the right of psychoanalysis to occupy itself with the neurotic or psychotic[1] situations that interfere in the war phenomenon, I should like to examine a specific politico-military doctrine—namely, the so-called MacNamara's doctrine, also known as the doctrine of escalation. Reduced to its simplest formulation this doctrine is *a practice of dissuasion.* Its starting point is the presupposition that the United

[1] *Psychotic:* adjective of psychosis. To be differentiated from the adjective "neurotic" of neurosis. In psychosis, serious disorders are present of the capacity to test reality correctly; namely, disorders of ideation (delusions), of perception (hallucinations), alterations of the time-space experience, etc., which are not recognized as such by the subject. In neurosis, the prevailing disorders are emotional or behavioral (behavior may be abnormal), but they are always recognized as such by the subject.

States is a peace-loving nation which somehow regards itself as the guardian of world peace. As we know, the motto of the Pentagon is "Peace is our profession." MacNamara's doctrine is based on a practice of dissuasion of the aggressors through successive, aggressive/punitive interventions which increase in violence until the aggressors no longer find it "convenient" to attack and, consequently, desist from further aggression.

Personally I believe that this doctrine is more psychological than military and that it is based on considerable distortions of reality and on a remarkable lack of information on the singular mechanisms which operate in war. MacNamara's doctrine would be valid only if applied to a dispute between two individuals or two groups whose actions would be governed exclusively by concrete utility.

A doctrine based on the idea that a nation can perform the function of *defensor pacis* by virtue of its ability to retaliate with progressively deadlier attacks aimed at intimidating the opponent is in fact *absurd*, because the nations against whom such dissuasion is directed consider it a provocation to war. The inefficiency of such a doctrine in achieving its stated aims is explained on the basis of its obvious faith in the principle of violence and on the basis of the lack of scientific information on the psychic mechanisms that operate in war.

Although polemologists believe, as we shall see, that war is deeply rooted in man's masochosadistic[2] universe, and that it is, specifically, an agency that inflicts martyr-

---

2 *Sadomasochism; masochosadism:* These terms signify human behavior characterized by erotic pleasure in attacking, humiliating, or destroying others (sadism), or in being attacked, humiliated, or destroyed by others (masochism). The tendency is to use one or the other of the above terms depending on whether sadism or masochism is considered primary. Freud was at first inclined to regard sadism as primary; later on, however, after his elaboration of the doctrine of the death instincts, he regarded masochism as primary.

dom, MacNamara's doctrine seems to be ignorant of the fact that the technique of escalation, rather than being a technique of dissuasion, could be *an ideal technique of mutual arousal of fanaticism in the antagonists* and that it has, in fact, a great capacity for arousing, in those whom it should dissuade, the wish for sacrificing themselves in order to attest to the justice of their cause. On the basis of this situation of bearing witness through sacrifice, war renders men blind to their own interests. In clumsily bringing the mentality of "convenience" into a territory that is deeply rooted in the irrational, MacNamara seems to have been totally ignorant of the fact that in addition to fighting for practical convenience, man fights for other mysterious, apparently illusory conveniences.

In this manner the lack of information on the interference of certain illusory functions in men's actions—and the inadequacy in dealing with such functions—may cause an operation initiated by a nation in the genuine belief of being a *defensor pacis* (which in itself indicates a dose of Manicheism verging on the pathological), to be transformed into war pure and simple. The technique of dissuasion thus achieves the very opposite of the desired situation—namely, it arouses an increasingly masochosadistic fanaticism in those who were to be dissuaded from it, as has been abundantly proved by the Christian martyrs, by the victims of the Inquisition (the function of which was dissuasion from heresy—*defensor fidei*), and finally by the victims of torture in modern war.

Accordingly, the problems of dissuasion from aggression would not appear to be purely military ones. They cannot be left in the hands of just any general who may, perhaps, be concerned about impotence and yet know nothing at all about the unconscious anxieties which such problems of impotence may determine, or about the influence these anxieties may exert, especially in the field of military decision-making.

To be sure, those who have command positions often find themselves forced to make decisions while caught in the whirlwind of events. However, it may perhaps be worth remembering here that psychology has often been called "the science of decisions."

In American reviews of *The Psychoanalysis of Nuclear War*, I was criticized for not having taken sufficiently into account the sociological contributions to the study of war. This happened because I preferred to include the broader cultural references into the paper I wrote for the Congress, the purpose of which was, as is usual, to inform my colleagues of the contributions of other investigators and to explore the possible relationships between psychoanalytic investigation and the contributions of other disciplines.

Intending, at first, merely to present the results of the sociological research on war, I was soon persuaded by my reflection on these results that they would constitute the ideal starting point for a psychoanalytic exploration of the war phenomenon. Let us take, for example, the demographic factor of war to which Bouthoul attributes a particular importance in determining the deep bellicose disposition, and which he elaborates in such a way as to define war as "deferred infanticide" acting "unconsciously" in men. I doubt it very much that the man in the street (or even a scientist who is not familiar with psychoanalytic discoveries) could easily accept this thesis. The psychoanalyst on the other hand, who is familiarized with the whole realm of unconscious intrafamilial destructive impulses, finds this thesis stimulating and in accordance with many unconscious fantasies.

If we were to trace Bouthoul's thesis to the unconscious, therefore, we would not be permitted to consider the demographic factor of war as a purely arithmetico-quantitative datum. What becomes operative in the unconscious would seem to be the fantasy repercussions of the intrafamilial destructive impulses (the Oedipus complex), whereby fathers experience fantasies of killing their sons and sons harbor fantasies of killing their fathers. In this manner the fantasy repercussions of the demographic factor would appear to be connected in the unconscious with the destructive fantasies of children who are too numerous and are frustrated because they are receiving an insufficient amount of mothering.

An analogous exploration with psychoanalytic instruments may be carried out with regard to Bouthoul's other conclusions about the economic and psychological factors of war. In the same manner as the psychoanalyst feels that he cannot understand a form of adult behavior unless he traces it to its infantile sources, the psychoanalytic investigation of the social phenomena cannot disregard the so-called primitive forms of society. With regard to this, it will be sufficient to remember the example given us by Freud in *Totem and Taboo* where the psychoanalytic method was employed to investigate the problem of the origin of civilization and the laws of man. For this reason, the second chapter of this book deals with war among primitive peoples. Here again, intending at first only to present a summary of ethnographic data, I then had the stimulating surprise of discovering, with singular clarity, *the mechanism of paranoid elaboration of mourning:* an unconscious mechanism which I believe to be central to the war phenomenon and which shall be the running thread in our investigation of the relations between mourning, war, and social phenomena in general.

Since mourning constitutes a depressive and also a persecutory experience (as is shown for example by the fear that the dead will return to haunt us, or by the primitive custom of placing a heavy stone on the tomb in order to prevent the dead from returning), war as a paranoid elaboration of mourning would appear to represent essentially and simultaneously a defense against depressive and persecutory anxieties.

War was initially interpreted by psychoanalysis as a periodic discharge of repressed criminal impulses, a peri odic return to barbarity. This theory of war (which does not, after all, bear a particularly psychoanalytic stamp), however, has had the merit of calling attention to the fact that in the unconscious, these repressed criminal impulses are directed against the parents (the father) and that the killing of the enemy would therefore appear to be the exportation into a foreign country of a criminal product originally intended for the father. Since this hostility against the father is in turn connected, in the child, with a conflict of rivalry for the possession of the mother, the problem of war, according to the classical psychoanalytic theory, is unconsciously connected with the dramas of impotence and fantasies of potency of infantile sexuality; this is so much the more so inasmuch as in dreams intrusive weapons are usually sexual symbols.

Subsequently war—understood as a system of security rather than a return to barbarity, that is, considered mainly in relation to the anxieties and defenses which it mobilizes and controls—was interpreted as a true paranoia,[3] i.e., as a mental illness.

Personally I believe that war represents a social institution the aim of which is to cure the paranoid and depressive anxieties existing (in a more or less marked de-

---

[3] *Paranoia:* Paranoia is a mental illness characterized by various delusions, the most typical of which is the delusion of persecution. Thus the terms "paranoid" and "persecutory" are often used synonymously.

gree and more or less resolved in terms of integration with reality) in every man.

This organization serves two security functions and may be pictured as an iceberg, one part of which is visible and the other hidden in deep waters. The first part corresponds to the defense against external danger (i.e., the real flesh-and-blood enemy), while the other, the hidden part, corresponds to an unconscious security maneuver against terrifying fantasy entities which are not flesh and blood but represent an absolute danger (as experienced, for example, in nightmares) which we could call the "Terrifier."

If we remain on the purely politico-military level, i.e., on the external part of the iceberg, the most obvious and generally held opinion is that war protects us from enemies who threaten our security, that is to say, from *external aggressors.*

If, however, we employ the psychoanalytic instrument of investigation, the instrument invented specifically for the exploration of the unconscious, we find that the submerged part of the iceberg—the invisible part of war as a security organization—serves to defend ourselves against the "Terrifier" as an internal, absolute enemy similar to a nightmare, through *a maneuver which transforms this terrifying but ultimately unaffrontable and invulnerable entity into an external, flesh-and-blood adversary who can be faced and killed.* If we now pause to reflect on the singular relation between these two systems of security that are coinvolved in war, we arrive at the paradoxical conclusion that *war is a security organization not because it permits us to defend ourselves from real enemies, but because it succeeds in finding, or in extreme cases, in inventing, real enemies to kill; and that if it were not for war, society would be apt to leave men defenseless before the emergence of the Terrifier as a purely internal foe.* (As we shall see later, this did happen in the case of the Kanachi tribes.)

In this manner we arrive at the incredible paradox that the most important security function is not to defend ourselves from an external enemy, but *to find a real enemy.*

Accordingly it would seem that, more profound than the anxieties caused by the external world, there exist in men deep anxieties created by the purely illusory, fantasy dangers of the internal world. We need only to fall asleep and each of us can experience, in the safe immobility of sleep (from which all external danger is eliminated), terrifying nightmares of annihilation of ourselves or of a person or thing we hold dear. Thus if we succeed in finding something bad (an enemy) to destroy in the external world, we are able to reassure ourselves both against the fear that this bad something may hurt us (reassurance against persecutory anxieties) and against the danger of our destructive attacks being directed toward what we love (reassurance against depressive anxieties).

It was precisely *outward deflection of the death instinct* that Freud called the process through which the original bad presence (the Terrifier as the emergence of the death instinct in the nightmare) is projected into the dangers of the external world, in order that it may be attacked and that the nightmare-anxiety situation, which may be regarded as the original emergence of the death instinct in our consciousness, may thus be avoided.

The fact that every man, while sleeping, may feel threatened by imminent destruction—a situation that the nightmare has in common with the attack of anxiety in waking life—may be considered the emotional nucleus of an innate paranoia. Accordingly, war could be seen as an attempt at therapy, carried out by a social institution which, precisely by institutionalizing war, increases to gigantic proportions what is initially an elementary defensive mechanism of the ego in the schizo-paranoid phase.

In clinical paranoia (understood as individual paranoia), the Terrifier is projected into a reality of the external world which is usually only imagined to be dangerous. In war, however, the Terrifier is projected into a really dangerous enemy, who may really kill and be really killed. From this point of view, war would not seem to be a mental illness, but rather an attempt to control the fear of an absolute destruction, such as that expressed by the Terrifier, through a system which, ritualizing and relativizing the destroying and the being destroyed, would appear to constitute a costly and tragic system of security, involving an intricate interplay between the inner and the outer world, between illusion and reality. The most enigmatic aspect of this system would seem to be its desire to control the uncontrollable by translating internal psychotic anxieties into real external dangers.

I have called *paranoid elaboration of mourning* that group of maneuvers through which the Internal Depressive Terrifier, emerging in the form of a sense of guilt for the death of the love object (a particularly painful part of the crucial experience of mourning), is eluded in an ambiguous manner. In other words, we imagine that the love object has died not because of our own fantasy sadistic attacks against it, but because of the evil magic of the enemy. The experience of mourning then becomes not sorrow for the death of the loved person, but the killing of the enemy who is falsely thought to be the destroyer of the loved object.

The security organization of war, expressed as a defense against psychotic anxieties, rests, as we have seen, on the fact that the external enemy is merely a relative danger in contrast with the absolute danger of the Internal Terrifier. However, from the moment that war, as atomic war, becomes a potentially absolute external danger, the security maneuver of which we have spoken, and which was based on *the contrast between the absolute character of the illusory internal danger and the relative character of the real external danger,* tends to become impossible. Consequently war would appear to have lost its curative functions with regard to basic psychotic anxieties, that is to say, it seems that *we can no longer cure our madness with war.*

On the other hand, the prospect of having to renounce war altogether could lead to the mobilization of anxieties more serious than those associated with the real dangers of a traditional war. The new element, however, introduced by the nuclear situation, seems to be connected with the fact that the tendency of the Illusory Internal Terrifier and the Real External Terrifier (the atomic bomb) to coincide creates unexpected difficulties at the level of integration between illusion and reality. Thus, the particularly difficult problem arises of finding new security organizations which would permit us to control the psychotic anxieties that are going to be mobilized whether war is perpetuated or abandoned.

In the distinction between war of the traditional type as a particular dialectic between the Absolute Terrifier (illusory) and the relative (real) danger, and the nuclear situation as a tendency of the Illusory Terrifier and the Real Terrifier to coincide, we may perhaps find the premise for the justification of the psychoanalytic investigation of war and its crisis.

If the current nuclear situation is really weakening man's ability to distinguish between nightmare and reality, it seems only logical to employ, along with the more traditional methods of investigating political phenomena, and in particular war, the instruments of investigation offered by the science whose task it is to study the causes and the modes of expression of mental disorders.

If war, in addition to providing an outlet for repressed impulses (a thesis first advanced by Freud), also provides a security system for the purpose of defending man against deep-seated anxieties which are congenital to him, it is easy to understand why it has prospered—like religion— throughout human history, regardless of the different cultural, economic, and political situations of the societies which practiced it. This could indicate that *the defense against psychotic anxieties lies at the origin of, or at least plays an important role in, the formation of society and its institutions.* This thesis would also explain why among many primitive peoples war often has the significance of a rite rather than the aspect of industrialized destruction which prevails in modern wars.

The forces of nature, as the dangers and threats that the external world has always posed to men, seem to be well on their way to an "unconditional surrender" to the rule of man. We have been familiarized quite some time ago with the condemnation of man's domination by man. It could not have been foreseen, however, that even the conquest of the forces of nature would bring us to a condition of alienation whereby our nature-transforming scientific labors, as well as the man-dominated nature itself, now confront us as "a foreign and enemy power." Did Bacon's axiom that "knowledge is power" anticipate, then, from its very beginnings, the sadistic nature of the advent of the scientific era in Western culture?

When Oppenheimer declares that what is "technically sweet" exerts an irresistible attraction on him, or when Fermi remarks that guilt feelings are irrelevant because it is a question of "a physics that is too beautiful," the psychoanalyst suspects that the scientists vaguely feel that they are doing something wrong, but that they elude bad conscience by deceiving themselves. Actually, rather than serving science in the most authentic and humanistic manner, they seem to be intoxicated by the vice of epistemophilia[4] as if by a drug. Thus sadistic impulses may hide behind the human desire for knowledge; and it seems that we are even disposed, in the name of a "beautiful physics" to take the world apart—as a child does with his toys—to see how it is made.

To be sure, science is not an evil; on the contrary, it is our hope. Nevertheless, it is necessary to realize that it can also be pursued with a certain sadistic perversion. Just as an authentic relationship is based on our capacity to identify with the other, so the possibility of avoiding that our domination of nature transform it into a foreign and enemy power rests on our capacity to identify with nature. But if we ourselves are the nature we wish to dominate (and the poets and mystics have always intuited such a basic oneness with nature), then our transforming nature is truly meaningful only because we are obligated, in symmetrical reciprocity, to transform ourselves as well. In the realm of interhuman domination, a revolt of the oppressed classes creates the conditions for the establishment of new relations between men. In the same manner, the relationship between dominant man and dominated nature (now suffering a crisis because the forces of the conquered nature have turned against man) creates the conditions for the expansion—and perhaps for the shift—of the crisis of the realm of domination from interhuman relations to the relations between man and

---

4 *Epistemophilic:* from epistemophilia—love of knowledge. Epistemophilia, in the form of inquisitive curiosity, is considered to be a specific component of infantile sexuality. In the child, epistemophilia may assume a sadistic character through fantasies of violent penetration of the mother's body in order to discover its secrets. Children's tendency to break toys in order to see "how they are made," or "what's inside," is connected with such fantasies.

nature, and between man and the products of his work. It is easy to predict that the birth of a future humanism will depend on the modes of solution of the crisis of man's power over nature (nature understood as the life-giving environment and therefore as a mother symbol) and of the crisis of man's power over the products of his work.

If, as it appears, war can no longer be used to control deep psychotic anxieties, and the war crisis determines the emergence of such anxieties, a new problem arises, namely, how to create institutions that would control collective psychotic anxieties without recourse to war. It would be logical to think that the rise of a great pacifist ideology could accomplish this task. However, it is necessary to recognize that, until now, pacifism has always been an expression of individual good will, and that it has never given rise to social institutions capable of performing the security functions (against deep-seated anxieties) served by war.

What, then, is to be done?

Naturally, when faced with such a question, one immediately thinks of the functions of religious institutions and of the relation that such institutions have, among primitive peoples, to gods, ancestors, and the dead in general. In reality, however, the religious institution among primitive peoples is intimately associated with the war institution, and this chiefly through the mechanism of paranoid elaboration of mourning, as we shall later have ample occasion to show.

Political ideologies, which have partly taken the place of religion, also perform the task of controlling the paranoid and depressive anxieties of mourning. As ideologies are easily militarized, however, we cannot but tend to consider them a part of the war phenomenon rather than its substitute. As an introduction to the discussion of the need for new institutions (a topic I have already discussed elsewhere but would like to take up again here, with renewed vigor), I deem it important to insist on the thesis that in tracing the war phenomenon to the unconscious of each man we arrive at considering each man responsible for war.

I realize that this thesis may be misunderstood—as indeed it has been misunderstood—as a mystical thesis. During a public debate held before a select audience of Italian intellectuals, the thesis presented in this book elicited two opposite objections. First, it was accused of mysticism on the grounds that it did not properly show the importance of the realistic motives for war, *in primis* economic factors; second, it was charged with cynicism because my discussion was understood by some as a veritable attack on man's tendency to fight for ideal values.

I have often noted that the most common type of anxiety aroused by a psychoanalytic discussion of war is the fear of an "ideological demobilization" vaguely perceived as a betrayal of one's political beliefs, whatever they may be. The defense against such anxiety is a *true accrochement à l'objet*, a typical occurrence when profound anxieties are mobilized, but also a sign of a very strong ambivalence toward the love object one fears to betray. In my opinion, however, the thesis that each individual is responsible for war, derived from the acknowledgment of the unconscious motivations for war, represents an attempt to formulate in a new manner the dialectic between the internal and the external world, between the illusory and the real, or, if you will, an attempt to formulate in a new manner the problem of how the psychotic anxieties relative to the Internal Terrifier may be resolved.

To return to the iceberg analogy, since the psychoanalytic discussion of war concerns more the submerged, invisible part of the iceberg than its external, visible part, it may be considered by some a metahistorical, metapolitical, or even astral discourse, generic and lacking in specificity. Thus it may be affirmed that psychoanalysis can explain, at the most, some of the mechanisms of war in general but not why war breaks out at a certain historical moment; for example, why World Wars I and II broke out precisely when they did. While a criticism of this sort is partly valid, historical facts also exist that refute it. In reference to this I should like to point out that neither the phenomenology of mourning nor its paranoid elaboration was extraneous to the beginning of World War I (the assassination at Sarajevo) or World War II (Hitler's protests to Ambassador Henderson that—and whether this was true or not is of little importance in an investigation of unconscious processes—in 1939, prior to the invasion of Poland, the Polish had castrated a number of German soldiers). In both instances we find, in actual, concrete historical situations, solid evidence which permits us to see the relation between mourning and its paranoid elaboration in war not as a generic factor but as a specific precipitating factor.

A striking example of how the paranoid elaboration of mourning affected a particular period of European history in a decisive manner may be found in Czar Alexander's role in the politics of repression of liberal movements and in the formation of the Holy Alliance after the defeat of Napoleon. Bertrand Russell, in his *History of the Ideas of the Nineteenth Century*, proposed that there is a relationship between the fact that young Prince Alexander, instigated, perhaps, by his mother, was involved in the assassination of his father, and the fact that following his accession to the throne he progressively repudiated every liberal tendency until he reached a reac-

tionary, mystic involution which led him to promote the
most merciless repression of the liberals whom he saw as
the very essence of evil. In this instance the paranoid elaboration of mourning was expressed through Alexander's
projection onto the liberals of the part of himself that
killed his father (or participated in the conspiracy, at any
rate); the liberals became the parricidal part of himself
which was alienated from the self and attacked. In fact, it
may be significant that Czar Alexander fantastically accused the liberal movements of wanting to *"écraser
l'infâme"* (i.e., the projection of killing his own infamous
father).

Another specific situation in which paranoid elaboration of mourning may be observed in a massive social phenomenon is anti-Semitism. The pre-Hitlerian anti-
Semitism, as we know, accused the Jews of two basic
crimes: 1) that they were the sons of Judas, who had
betrayed Jesus Christ; 2) that they were the descendants
of Christ's murderers.

The fact that Jews have always lived as a minority in
Christian countries has constituted a most favorable condition for the paranoid elaboration of mourning. For the
Christian, the entire world of guilt is based on the fact
that "sins are the cause of Christ's death." Every Christian, therefore, at the moment when he feels guilty, is apt
to feel that his love object has died, that it has died
through his fault, through his failure to observe the pre-
cepts of his church. Depressive anxieties of this sort are
rather hard to endure, and anti-Semitism offers Christians
a way to avoid mourning and the sense of guilt for the
death-loss of the love object by projecting into the Jews
the cause of the death and betrayal of Christ.

By reversing the thesis that the psychoanalytic thesis
of war is non-specific because it is metahistorical and

metapolitical, we could say that the economic, political, ideological, racial, etc., factors *are specifically generators of conflicts but are not specific factors of war.*

The conflicts generated by these factors exist continuously and may express themselves in a non-warlike form. When, however, the economic, political, ideological, and racial conflicts are expressed in the form of war, it means that a new fact has come into existence. I have used the expression "paranoid elaboration of mourning" to describe the appearance of this new fact, which institutionalizes a group of processes aimed at avoiding the profound human suffering which is generated in the experience of mourning. Conflicts connected with specific historical situations reactivate the more serious conflicts which each of us has experienced in infancy, in the form of fantasies, in our affective relationship to our parents. The confusion between the real historical events and these unconscious vicissitudes lies at the basis of the transference of the problems of our internal world into the external world. The exportation of the problems of the inner world into the outer world, which is an essential part of the mechanism of paranoid elaboration of mourning, may be considered the presupposition which renders it easy for certain political operators to present war as a dramatic but definitely desirable event because it allows the externalization of both the fear of being killed by what we love and the fear of killing what we love.

From a psychological point of view, then, the *aspecific factor of war* is constituted by the unconscious depressive and persecutory anxieties.[5] Their mobilization, in relation to the war phenomenon, requires the intervention of spe-

[5] *Depressive anxiety:* The principal content of a depressive anxiety is a relation to a good, protecting object of whose destruction we feel guilty; the depressive anxiety impels us to preserve the good object from the attacks of the bad self.

cific and adequate historical realities which function as elements activating the transference processes.

What distinguishes the universe of peace from the universe of war, however, would appear to be this: that while in time of peace society requires the individual to adopt realistic defenses for controlling his unconscious anxieties, in time of war it proposes as a defense the institutionalization of the expulsion of the Internal Terrifier onto the enemy. And since the enemies are now in possession of nuclear weapons, this institutionalization of the expulsion of the Internal Terrifier onto the external enemy (who has become an atomic bomb) threatens to put an end to the institutionalization of the exportation of the Internal Terrifier as a security operation.

War has always been a strange import-export agency of destruction. The new fact which comes into existence with the advent of the atomic era is the pantoclastic[6] prospect, owing to which the accumulation of aggressiveness in the state can no longer be discharged through exportation and is in danger of determining a sort of tumorous growth which would progressively absorb the energies of every nation—especially those possessing nuclear weapons. The progressive growth and inflation of military power, accompanied by the impossibility of outward discharge, is on the verge of becoming a malignant tumor which will progressively destroy the healthy tissue. The war institution, which until now could be fantasied as the powerful sorcerer who protects us, is now on the verge of becoming the sorcerer who kills us.

In this situation the abolition of the sovereignty of the state—as the attribute of the state that is most closely connected with the war institution—becomes inevitable. The reappropriation by each individual of the aggressive-

[6] *Pantoclastic*: adjective taken from psychiatric terminology. It signifies total destruction.

ness saved by him and deposited into the state, as if into a bank, thus appears to be the path that must be taken if the state is to be liberated from the accumulation of private violence which it has monopolized, capitalized, and finally increased to nuclear proportions. In turn, such a reappropriation, since it would indicate the transition from the violence *legibus solutum* of the state to the aggressiveness *legibus ligatum* of the citizens, would also indicate the transition from *an anomic situation* (i.e., the situation of war) to a *holonomic situation*[7] (the Omega Institution described in chapter 5 of this book).

I think that at the end of this book, the reader may ask the following question: Supposing that your schema is valid and supposing that the solution proposed by you is carried out, what do you think would happen? What should concretely be done? It seems to me that I have partly answered this question in the latter chapters of this book, even if only in a generic way, by proposing the foundations for the hypothesis of the Omega Institution and by raising the problem both of the mobilization of the anxieties and of how to control them. These are problems of specialized research which can be faced with appropriate techniques and which could direct and follow a practical procedure. In my final reply to the Congress I have tried to apply the schema and the concept of *the transference neurosis*,[8] bringing it from the clinical field

---

[7] *Holonomic*: adjective used by Dr. Fornari to describe that situation in which the state, whose sovereignty has been abolished, is subject to the same laws of individual ethics which are obeyed by its citizens. From *holo-*, a word element meaning "whole" or "entire," and *nomos*, the Greek word for "law." (Translator's note.)

[8] *Transference neurosis*: The transference neurosis, according to Freud, is a particular situation in the psychoanalytic treatment whereby neurotic symptoms are transformed or at times replaced by a particular type of disturbed relationship of the patient to the analyst, with whom the patient relives infantile experiences confused with the reality of his treatment.

to the field of social phenomena. On the basis of this schema, derived from psychoanalytic practice, when an attempt is made to eliminate a human ill with a given therapeutic instrument, this ill tends to reproduce itself in the very operation that should eliminate it. This is what Sartre called "counterfinality" and we shall later see how it may be understood from a psychoanalytic point of view.

I should like to end this introduction on a note of hope. Naturally, it is all too easy to become skeptical in the face of man's perverse obstinacy to commit errors. However, the psychoanalytic method has led the investigators in this field to the conviction that what appears to be an error, a *lapsus*, a neurotic or psychotic symptom, invariably has a hidden significance which must only be discovered. Thus I have attempted to show the truly essential role that social institutions play as defenses against deep psychotic anxieties. War is perhaps the most ancient and also the most fierce of these institutions—its destructive capacity *crescit eundo*. Yet one thing seems to be certain, namely, that war can exercise its function of resolving psychotic anxieties only through the recovery of a certain original ritual function which I do not think can be reestablished in Western culture. In any event, what I wish to affirm is that the antianxiety functions of the war phenomenon are not at all directly proportional to its destructive intensity. On the contrary, the growing destructive intensity of war, having reached its apex in the nuclear era, has thrown war into a state of crisis; herein lies our hope.

However, I have another, more profound reason for hope. For some time now I have been aware of changes in the air. The enthusiasm with which my thesis was greeted at the Congress in Milan by highly qualified psychoanalysts of various nationalities and political per-

suasions convinced me that the ideas contained in my
thesis must have been already present in their minds,
though perhaps not as yet clearly focused. These ideas
thus seem to be in the air. In his play *Incident at Vichy*,
Arthur Miller presents a character who has been told by
a psychoanalyst that every man is guilty of the evil in the
world. By a curious coincidence, I too have written a
novel—which I hope to see published—in which the pro-
tagonist experiences the feeling, in a dimension of guilt
that is both illusory and real, that he is the cause of the
evil in the world.

Elsa Morante affirmed, at a conference, that each and
every man must be made to bear the responsibility for
nuclear weapons. In his book *Uscita di Sicurezza* (*Emer-
gency Exit*), Silone alludes to the new frontier when he
says: "The frontiers of peace and truth are no longer geo-
graphical. They run within each nation, within each of
us." The new Papacy and the new Empire, constituted
by the two opposing power blocs, perhaps ensnare men,
the guelphs and ghibellines of today, in the old falla-
cies; but at the same time there are perhaps people in
every country, every political party, every walk of life, some
of them famous and others unknown, who need only to
find out about each other's existence in order to become
confident that what they have begun to intuit as the new
course of history can really be pursued. It is to these people, who are willing to assume full responsibility as rendered possible by our knowledge of the unconscious,
people whom I should call humanistic, that I dedicate this
book.

Thus I hope, with Thomas Mann, that one day we shall
be able to recognize in the assumption of responsibility
for our unconscious, first taught by Freud, "the corner-
stone of the edifice of a new anthropology, and so of a
new culture, which will constitute the future receptacle

of a wiser and freer humanity. . . . This doctor and psychologist will undoubtedly be honored as the pioneer of a future humanism which today we can only vaguely intuit and which will bear the stamp of experiences unknown to the humanism of yesterday. This will be a humanism that will have a different relation to the powers of the internal world, of the unconscious, of the id; a bolder, freer, more serene relation. . . . Call it, if you will, a poet's utopia, but after all it is not unthinkable that the solution to our great fear and our great hate, their conversion into a different relationship to the unconscious . . . may, one day, be due precisely to the curative effects of psychoanalysis" (Thomas Mann).

Before I conclude, I must thank my teacher Cesare L. Musatti for his invaluable criticism which helped me to gain a more thorough understanding of the problems. I should also like to thank Enzo Paci, whose thought strengthened my confidence in the heuristic, methodological, and critical fertility of my thesis. Finally, I thank Luigi Pagliarani for his invaluable collaboration in sociological investigations.

*Bonavvola, August 1965*

# THE
# PSYCHOANALYSIS
# OF WAR

# 1

# THE
# WAR PHENOMENON

The work of sociologist Gaston Bouthoul[1] may be considered the most serious attempt to date to define scientifically the problems of war. The results of his investigation can, in many respects, be profitably juxtaposed with the data of psychoanalytic investigation.

Bouthoul examines various opinions and theories about war, its morphology, its technical, demographic, economic, and psychological factors. Before attempting to outline the basic dynamic laws of the war phenomenon, Bouthoul points out some of the obstacles to a scientific study of war which can also be recognized by psychoanalysis. These consist in 1) the pseudo knowledge of war, i.e., the belief that war is a known fact, the causes of which are immediately intelligible; 2) the illusion that war depends entirely on the conscious will of men while, on the contrary, conscious motivations should be regarded merely as epiphenomena—secondary, or even accessory, motivations which prevent us from gaining a knowledge of the deep-seated bellicose tendencies and of their relation to the structural modifications in a society at war; 3) the "juridical illusionism" of war, that is to say, the sum total of those juridical rationalizations and theories that have always striven to legalize war.

[1] Gaston Bouthoul, *Les Guerres: Éléments de Polémologie* (Paris, 1951).

In the early history of international law we find the theological conception of war, in which the soldier is a terrestrial projection of a divine battle. This conception survives to this day in the form of lay mythicizations of war as an "instrument of destiny ordained to bring to completion the mysterious designs of history."

The theological mythology of war was subsequently replaced by the mythology of the state, with the apotheosis of sovereignty, the rights of conquest and first occupancy, the dynastic, aristocratic, and popular principles, and finally, with the hypostatization of nations and races. A typical mythicization of the state in relation to war is the Hegelian position, according to which war represents the moment when the state achieves its highest consciousness.

Another obstacle to the scientific study of war is the anthropomorphic conception of international law which compares war to a quarrel between individuals. Warning against the oversimplification of artificially tracing war to a single cause, Bouthoul asserts that in times of war our sensibilities are radically and sharply modified, and all moral and economic values are reversed.

According to Bouthoul, polemology, the study of war, should be based on a methodology including a description of material facts, a description of psychic behavior, "a first-level" explanation (corresponding to historians' explanations of specific wars), and a "second-level" explanation (comprising opinions and theories on war in general).

Following his examination of the technical, psychological, economic, and demographic factors of war, Bouthoul defines the real functions of war, aside from all superstructures, as *purely and simply destructive.*

The most specific characteristic of war is its being a collective phenomenon. The finality of war, on the subjective level, differs from the aims of individual aggressiveness. War is an armed conflict which requires solidarity and organization, but above all it has an ethico-legal character that is cogent for all the members of the group. According to Clausewitz, "war is an act of violence the aim of which is to force the adversary to carry out our will." Bouthoul proposes a definition of war as "an armed and bloody conflict between organized groups."

## *Technical factors of war.*

The historical sequence of the various techniques of war (i.e., the various types of weapons), as a purely objective reality datum, seems to hold little interest for the psychoanalyst. As we know, martial techniques have tended to follow and have often stimulated mankind's technical achievements. In reference to the space in which war activities unfold, the most obvious fact is that technical progress has rendered it possible to hit the enemy from an increasingly greater distance, with a rapidity and a radicality which tend to correspond to the absolute of the tales of magic. (Aladdin's lamp, for example, could destroy whole armies at one stroke.) This fact has led to an increasingly greater differentiation between the forms of the direct, body-to-body interindividual aggression and the forms in which destructive activities unfold between groups. Introducing the pantoclastic prospect, the discovery of nuclear energy has finally brought war to coincide with *the original individual fantasies of destructive sadistic omnipotence.* All this, it seems to me, merits psychoanalytic reflection. If we compare the unconscious symbolism of weapons with the technical evolution of warfare, we find that the latter—with respect to the unconscious— seems to have walked backward. The most primitive weapons (sword, spear, lance) intrude directly into the body of the other in a confrontation between two individuals and seem to be associable with *genital-sadistic fantasies.* They are in reality very close to the modes of interindividual aggression.

Firearms, on the other hand (involving the use of a projectile, that is, of something that is ejected toward the enemy), appear to be traceable to the fantasy formation of *anal sadism.*

Chemical warfare and nuclear weapons, by reason of their having introduced the pantoclastic prospect, appear to be most easily interpretable in terms of a fantasy universe dominated by omnipotence and fear of annihilation, which would seem to be typical of *oral sadism.* This disconcerting *regressive evolution of the unconscious repercussions,* whereby the technical development of warfare appears to correspond, in the unconscious, to a mobilization of successively lower regressive levels of fantasy repercussions, presents some obscure problems. If we were to use this disconcerting *regressive evolution* as a prognostic point of reference, we should be led to draw some wholly inauspicious conclusions. Psychoanalysis has made us familiar with the idea that regression characterizes the transition from individual psychology to group psychology.[2] All the same, the discovery of successively lower regressive levels, which accompany the development of war techniques, suggests an unexpected, appalling hypothesis, namely, that the technical evolution of war, measured by its paradoxically regressive unconscious repercussions, actually represents the establishment of those stages which we are by now accustomed to consider the sources of psychotic processes. Catastrophic as the prognosis derived from the levels of unconscious repercussions may be, it is nevertheless likely to agree with a diagnosis of war which man has always made but which he is only now in the position to reveal openly to himself, namely,

[2] Alix Strachey, *The Unconscious Motives of War* (London, 1957).

that war is at the same time the normality and the mental illness of man. A paradox, therefore, that becomes the more obvious the more often it is realized historically. In view of this fact, it seems as if the unexpected, appalling hypothesis mentioned above ought also to constitute the starting point for a less inauspicious prognosis: that which could finally be born of the progressive revelation of the fact that war is primarily the result of psychotic processes.

## Demographic factors of war.

The interesting chapter which Bouthoul dedicates to the demographic factors of war reveals one of the most alarming functions of the latter. Bouthoul begins with the empirical statement that every war causes an abnormal increase in mortality and that, consequently, war may appear to be a voluntary destruction of previously accumulated reserves of human capital, an act performed with the implicit intention to sacrifice a certain number of lives. Although this intention is neither explicit nor conscious, Bouthoul maintains that it is particularly operative. Proceeding from the empirical statement that every war causes the deaths of young men, Bouthoul arrives at the conception of war as *deferred infanticide.* Since the only constant and general demographic characteristic of armed conflicts is the increase in mortality, Bouthoul, disregarding any other more or less rationalized and therefore superstructural motivation, considers war *a voluntary destructive institution, the aim of which is the elimination of young men.*

War thus appears to be a recurrent social function, characterized by the accumulation of human capital, a part of which, at a given moment, is brutally ejected. Bouthoul gives the name "explosive structure" to the demo-economic structure in which there is a plethora of young men, a surplus far exceeding the basic needs of the economy. It is as if the surplus of young men constituted a disturbing force within the society. In this manner the excess of aggressiveness that constitutes the bellicose impulsion is identified with the surplus of young men. The enormous and rapid increase in European population due to Jenner's invention of vaccination, and other simultaneous progress in medicine, determined, according to Bouthoul, the replacement of biological epidemics by a disposition to war as a psychic epidemic, the purpose of which is now to eliminate the surplus population. The function of war, therefore, is *to perpetuate the species through the death of a number of individuals.*

Bouthoul considers the demographic factor of greater importance than any other, since it also absorbs the economic factor. The economic equilibrium, according to Bouthoul, is, in its most general form, constituted by two variables, one of which is population and the other the sum total of goods and means of production. In this manner, what affects the demographic factor also directly influences the economic factor. The explosive structure produced by a surplus of young men is not, however, the determining cause of war, but simply a predisposing element that reinforces other causes. The demographic factor acts *unconsciously,* determining the response to bellicose stimuli.

On the other hand, sociologist Thompson believes that it is not the demographic pressure *in se* and *per se* but the awareness of it, i.e., the extent to which the pressure is *felt* that determines the influence of the demographic factor on international problems. For example, a nation that has never experienced inflation is able to tolerate it for a considerable amount of time while a nation with previous experience of inflation will become upset at the first indication of it. In the latter case the inflation is *felt* to a greater extent, (It mobilizes anxieties more readily.)

The historical study of the relationship between demography and warlike impulses seems to confirm the existence of an intimate tie of cause and effect between the two. *"Laissez faire à Venus et vous aurez Mars,"* wrote Bergson in 1936. On the other hand, the same warlike disposition may be the cause of an increase in population, since the existence of a surplus of young men is looked upon as a means of defense. This surplus, however, in turn engenders a spirit of aggressiveness, so that the effect becomes the cause and the antinomy remains, at least for the time being, insoluble. Bouthoul sees the demographic revolution which began in the second half of the nineteenth century (prior to then, infant mortality approached 70 per cent) as closely related to the increase in warfare in Europe.

In addition to war, societies have at their disposal a number of destructive institutions that operate side by side with the natural causes of death. These institutions, as listed by Bouthoul, are direct infanticide, indirect infanticide (caused by negligence and brutality), castration, monasticism, imposed chastity, slavery, and repressive laws demanding the isolation of criminals.

Overpopulation, according to Bouthoul, does not necessarily and automatically lead to war; it simply sets in operation the destructive, eliminative institutions of which war is the extreme example and the one most blatantly institutionalized. Thus he notes that during the *Roman peace,* in the period between the end of the Punic wars and Diocletian's reign, the slaughter of millions of slaves replaced war as a destructive institution. The *Chinese peace,* in addition to being guaranteed by epidemics and internal conflicts between warlords, was also sustained by a general contempt for human life; in China, longevity was in fact considered an exceptional gift from the gods.

The *British peace* of the nineteenth century, which prevailed in spite of the great increase in population, is seen by Bouthoul as closely connected with the high mortality of the lower classes and with child labor, which cut down the younger generation. In no other country was the difference between the death rate of the rich and that of the poor so marked as in England. In Bath the average life expectancy of a gentleman was fifty-five years; that of a laborer, twenty-five.

Analogous arguments hold, according to Bouthoul, for the *Indian peace*, in effect since the end of the seventeenth century. Prior to being conquered by the British, India was one of the world's most warlike nations. Peace was attained through continuous internal struggles among princes, which were intensified by religious fanaticism. We must, however, acknowledge the existence in India of another particularly destructive institution: indirect infanticide, i.e., the extremely high infant mortality.

The means by which demographic relaxation has been achieved throughout history appear to be the following: 1) Systematic population control through abortion and infanticide. These means were adopted in ancient feudal Japan and also by some nations of Oceania and Malaysia (the insular solution); 2) creation of conditions conducive to high mortality of the young (the Asiatic solution); 3) the practice of war (the European solution).

The corollary derived by Bouthoul from the above is that *war as deferred infanticide occurs in direct proportion to the decrease in infant mortality.*

The demographic factor, then, puts into operation the destructive institutions in general; war is only one of them. The demo-economic structures are the roots of aggressiveness, while ideologies and political problems are merely superstructures or, rather, the executive forces of the basic destructive functions of war.

According to Bouthoul, Marx's prediction that capitalism would produce an increasing state of poverty in capitalist countries was not fulfilled in Europe owing to Western Europe's demographic self-limitation in the last century. An increasing state of poverty occurs, independently of political regimes, in countries which exercise no demographic control. In countries where authoritative planning is applied only to production and not to the increase in population, the results of economic planning are falsified because, by the time an adequate level of production is reached for 100 million people, a country which exercises no demographic control finds itself confronted with the fact that the 100 million people have become 130 million.

These are Bouthoul's views; I should now like to develop some psychoanalytic considerations. Although not wishing to go into the merits of the demographic theory of war, I think that Bouthoul's affirmation that the demographic factor acts *unconsciously*, in rendering men susceptible to bellicose stimuli, requires a clarification on the part of the psychology of the unconscious. The demographic factor, in fact, is not *in se* and *per se*, an element of the unconscious, rather it is an element of reality. We are therefore faced with the problem of understanding how a conscious element can act unconsciously.

The demographic situation may, in fact, be used as one of the major elements in war propaganda. It is not, however, used in the sense described by Bouthoul, that is, in the sense of "There are too many of us; some of us must die." During the two decades of fascist regime, the Italian Government exploited the image of the "proletarian" Italy in order to "justify" its war against the "rich" democracies who were accused of having a low birth rate.

According to this schema, the demographic situation makes itself felt in the unconscious mobilizing unconscious fantasies, predominantly of the oral type, in which the numerous children are equated with the child dying of hunger (i.e., deprived of his mother) who is authorized to direct his aggressiveness against his rich (i.e., loved by the mother) brother in an attack of envy.

In order to become operative in the unconscious, the demographic factor must be involved in the unconscious fantasy life. In the case of war propaganda, the demographic factor is in effect used to activate fantasies of envy.

To return to Bouthoul's statement that war is *deferred infanticide*, it must be specified that this thesis can be inserted into the context of the psychology of the unconscious only if we admit that *hostile and homicidal impulses against the children* are operative in men in general and in men who are parents in particular. Psychoanalysts became familiarized with these impulses quite some time ago through the so-called Oedipus and Cronus[3] complexes and, in the last decades, through the study of schizophrenia as one of the evolutions of the child's response to the unconscious hostility of his parents.

If we wish to consider valid the affirmation that the demographic factor acts unconsciously, then the demographic factor loses its arithmetic character and becomes

[3] *Oedipus complex:* from the Greek myth of Oedipus. The Oedipus complex consists in the son's unconscious wish to kill his father and marry his mother, which arouses a deep sense of guilt and fear of punishment by castration.

*Cronus complex:* This is the inverse of the Oedipus complex. It consists primarily in the father's unconscious hostility and rivalry in relation to his sons, and in his unconscious wish to castrate, humiliate, and annihilate them. In the Greek myth Cronus devours his sons.

instead a part of the realm of profound instinctual situations that no longer allow us to look upon war *"comme une chose,"* as a natural phenomenon belonging to objective reality. Instead, we must see war as *a human fact involving the responsibility of each man as a parent, for every parent experiences unconscious hostility against his children and unconsciously wishes their death.* If the demographic factor acts unconsciously, as Bouthoul says it does, the psychoanalytic knowledge of the unconscious leads us to the discovery of the startling fact that fathers unconsciously desire war in order that their sons may die. And this is not all. Since the Cronus complex is nothing but a transformation of the Oedipus complex, we cannot but conclude that the unconscious mode of action of the demographic factor in war is associated with the final transformation of the sons' wish to kill their fathers inverted into the fathers' wish to kill their sons.

Statements of this sort are obviously disquieting but difficult to avoid if we accept the sociological theory of the demographic factor as a function of war and, in particular, the definition of war as deferred infanticide. At this point, however, we note that in the application of the psychoanalytic knowledge of the unconscious to the war phenomenon as the final transformation of unconscious impulses, we are confronted with a problem of verification that is entirely different from that encountered in the analysis of the relations between unconscious life and individual life. When we analyze an individual, we find his Oedipus or Cronus complexes expressed in sublimated forms, or implicated in a neurosis, therefore in a sense of guilt. In such cases we are able to analyze neurotic symptoms as defensive measures against unconscious homicidal impulses, impulses merely fantasied in the unconscious; then, through reality testing, the subject is brought to verify the illusory (or at least exaggerated) character of his criminality and sense of guilt as experienced in unconscious psychic life.

But when we confront the data of the demographic theory of war with our unconscious homicidal impulses toward our fathers or toward our sons, we are forced to admit that *our unconscious homicidal impulses toward our children are verifiable in the reality of war; with the aggravating circumstance that, while on the individual level we consider ourselves guilty of infanticides we have never committed, on the collective level we commit infanticide and hold ourselves free from guilt.*

Thus the process of verification carried out by the psychoanalyst in his private practice, and the process of verification carried out by the psychoanalyst in relating unconscious life to social phenomena, are not only different, but antithetical as regards the relationship between impulses and defenses (and particularly the relationship between criminal impulses and feelings of guilt). Consequently a psychoanalytic theory of war involves a clarification of the antithetical relations existing between the psychic elements in time of war, for war is a phenomenon put into action by individuals in the politicized experience of the group. In this manner the problem of the double legality (which is one of the most striking aspects of the psychology of peace and of the psychology of war) becomes the crucial point in the description of the processes that establish themselves in men who make war. *The whole problem of war, when traced to the unconscious, does not reveal an exceptional human situation in comparison with the instinctual tendencies involved in the peace situation, but a different relation between the instincts and the defenses.* In other words, the singularity of the war phenomenon is not that it reveals to us instinctual impulses that are different from those we encounter in the unconscious of individuals, but rather that it reveals a different organization of impulses that are equally active in war, in individual life, and in peaceful life. In particular, the singularity of the war phenomenon seems to consist in a radical difference in the organization of the relations between the psychic components: the ego, the id, and the superego. The nature of the investigation of the different organization of the relations between the various psychic components will have to be clarified, but we shall, after all, be able to derive the authentic significance of such an investigation only from the criteria of verification that commonly act in our formation of reality, that is, in the relation between the psychic components on the basis of which the individual verifies the meanings of his internal world in the external world. Accordingly, if in our investigation we shall find ourselves confronted with the fact that in war we witness the coincidence of the id with the superego, we shall not be able to verify the significance of normality or abnormality by remaining on the inside of this coincidence brought about by war, but by comparing this coincidence with the normal distribution of relations between the psychic elements, which corresponds to normality, in the sense of the normality of the normal individual. We know in fact that the coincidence between the id and the superego (because the function of the superego is also the testing of reality) brings with it the impossibility of verifying reality.

The demographic factor, as a factor of war that is directly proportionate to the size of population with respect to available goods, therefore appears to be traceable to the unconscious only because it is connected, as we have already indicated, with the whole of the fantasy experiences relating to the fact that one mother must take care of too many children. The amount of maternal care received by each child in this case may easily be small enough to provoke what is commonly called early infantile frustration. All modern investigations of affective deprivation agree that an insufficient amount of mothering provokes frustration, and frustration arouses primary sadism as the mobilization of the death instinct. This mobilization may be correlated, on the one hand, to a group of destructive functions ranging from anaclitic depression to marasmus and high infant mortality, and on the other, to a group of destructive functions in the adult individual, ranging from psychic disturbances in general to criminality. (Psychic disturbances, specifically connected with the development of sexuality as a reproductive function, involve indirectly destructive functions.)

The data on early infantile frustration in relation to insufficient maternal care, which is a consequence of an excessive number of children, appear to coincide rather well with the facts connected with the destructive functions associated with the demographic factor. If, however, we connect the demographic factor with the unconscious situations attending infantile frustration in general, we must note that a certain amount of frustration is indispensable to psychic development. A certain imbalance between the needs to be satisfied and the means of satisfaction is indispensable to human evolution, for we are a species ever disposed to accept new (secondary) objects as means of satisfaction of our primary needs. A perfect equilibrium between population and goods thus appears unthinkable, except by imagining a state of things similar to that described by Huxley in *Brave New World*. With its turning round of the death instinct upon the subject, the mobilization—connected with the inevitable frustration—of primary sadism therefore plays an essential role in the development of the superego; in other words, the superego would appear to be an internalized destructive function. The problem is therefore a complex one; the princi-

pal destructive organization at man's disposal would
ultimately appear to be the superego, that is, in a broad
sense, the unconscious moral sense. It is in this direction,
I think, that the abatement of the bellicose tension should
be sought, *by following the same paths through which the
individual attains the mastery of his own destructive impulses, even if this again brings us to the problem of guilt,*
to which we will have to return later.

*Economic factors of war.*

While recognizing that a number of wars did originate
in economic conflicts, Bouthoul maintains that specific
events participating in the phenomenon of war are destructive of previously accumulated economic goods. This
empirical statement enables us to see the economic aspects of war more as destructive functions than as economic functions proper. Bouthoul stresses the fact that,
in general, the economic discussions are the ground of
bargaining and compromise *par excellence.* Davie, the
ethnologist, notes that at the moment when economic motivations arise among primitive peoples, war loses some of
its original violence. Basically war originates in the refusal
to compromise, and the refusal to compromise signals the
intervention of the bellicose impulse seeking pretexts for
satisfaction. In order for an economic factor to be transformed into cause for war, a mental state of intransigence
must supervene. The conviction, albeit erroneous, that
the economic situation is intolerable and requires war is
sufficient to determine the mental state of intransigence.
The economic theories of war a nation believes in may
themselves become, according to Bouthoul, important
factors of war. This is because war is generally provoked
not by facts but by the interpretation given to them,
especially by political leaders. When economic conflicts
degenerate into war, another factor comes into play that

renders the antagonists blind to their own economic interests and to the very instinct of self-preservation.

Following the criterion of judging the objective aspects of war by deducing them from its effects, Bouthoul finds that the principal and indisputable objective aspect of war is its destructive function. War destroys men as well as *previously accumulated goods* and is related to sacrifice and to consumption of wealth. In this manner the economic role of war is intimately related to the role of feast, understood in the sociological sense of solemn dissipation of wealth. The reversal of moral laws in war is accompanied by a reversal of economic laws. Most economic wars, according to Bouthoul, were in reality brought about by psychological factors, as a thorough investigation of their motivations would show. For this reason he criticizes the conception of war that attributes its cause to economic crises. The great majority of wars, he says, occurred without having been preceded by economic crises.

Having considered the economic circumstances that precede, accompany, and follow war, Bouthoul reaches the conclusion that the economic events of war represent *a cycle of prodigality*, which is the unconscious revival, in modern society, of rites of ostentatious consumption and destruction of wealth typical of primitive peoples. This cycle of prodigality has a specifically psychological significance and is particularly evident in the armed peace of the so-called cold war. Cold war has all the characteristics of *potlach* or the competitive donation (Marcel Mauss and Georges Bataille). Potlach is an ostentatious gift of considerable value, offered by a tribal chief to his rival. The purpose of the competitive gift is to humiliate, challenge, and obligate the recipient, who in turn must erase the humiliation, accept the challenge, and fulfill the obligation by accepting the gift; later he must retaliate with a more generous and valuable potlach. He must, in other words, return the gift with interest.

Potlach is not only a gift, however. In its most impressive form potlach consists in the solemn destruction of wealth. A tribal chief presents himself before his rival and has a number of slaves slaughtered before the rival's eyes. The rival must retaliate by slaughtering an even greater number of slaves. Potlach, then, is an act of ostentatious destruction the aim of which is to intimidate the rival and, ultimately, to give prestige to the donor or destroyer. The present frantic armaments race seems to be a cycle of prodigality-challenge in which each of the adversaries, by wasting an enormous amount of wealth on armaments, hopes to intimidate the other and prove his own superiority.[4]

The numerous theories that uphold the economic origin of war appear to be confirmed only by wars between animals (bees and ants). Bouthoul points out that bees and ants are the only animals that have an economic system in the form of accumulated goods. In some species of bees and ants we find all the characteristics of collectively organized warfare, the purpose of which is plunder. Bouthoul reminds us, however, that among these animals, *all property is strictly collective*; there is no trace of private property. This situation seems to confirm—and simultaneously to contradict in a curious manner on the ethnological level—the Marxist theories of war.

The acquisition of wealth which a victorious war determines through various forms of plunder therefore seems to be related to the problem of the tendency to appropriate wealth by violence. In this connection Glover points out that theft, at one time regarded as a form of behavior determined by economic motivations, is today considered

[4] Gaston Bouthoul, *Les Guerres*, p. 263.

a form of psychopathological behavior. It may easily be verified, through the process of reality testing, that the quantity of goods destroyed by war exceeds the quantity of goods gained by war. Both the acquisition and the loss of goods are thus a part of the reality of war. The general tendency to disregard or minimize the losses indicates that distortions of reality occur in the war phenomenon which are *to a certain extent* analogous to the distortions of reality occurring in psychopathological situations such as compulsive gambling and drug addiction.

One cannot help comparing the attitude of those who make war in the hope of economic gain to the psychology of the games of chance. Games of chance also offer a possibility of economic gain, and in the same manner as the gambler incurs the risk of losing, the nation starting a war exposes itself to defeat. It is curious to note, however, that on the conscious level, both the gambler and the nation starting a war are generally incapable of looking objectively at the loss or the defeat to which they expose themselves.

In the same manner, a drug addict is incapable of realizing the damaging effects of the drug and actually uses the drug as a defense against the damage produced by it. Strong sadomasochistic implications are operative both in compulsive gambling and in drug addiction; in the first case they are masked with the prospect of winning and in the second, with the prospect of the euphoria produced by the drug. We know, moreover, that these sadomasochistic implications are obscured in the subject by distortions of the ego, which operate in the sense of defending the subject against specific anxieties through the denial of reality. The role of the economic motivations of war therefore would appear to be that of rationalizing and obscuring its destructive functions which would, ultimately, also seem to be traceable (on the basis of Bouthoul's investigation of the economic aspects of war as a feast of solemn dissipation and destruction, potlach, etc.) to the sadomasochistic universe of man (Glover, Garma).

Those who justify war often object to those who condemn it by asking the following question: If you are faced with the problem of an oppressed, exploited nation which has no means, except the recourse to violence, of liberating itself from unjust domination, how do you solve it? A question of this sort arises from the conviction that wars are originated by the instinct of self-assertion and therefore the instinct of self-preservation. To the above question, the interlocutor usually reacts with a state of confusion and depressive feelings because the anxiety aroused by this question is related to the feeling of guilt for allowing one's brothers to die of starvation. Faced with this alternative he who condemns war ultimately feels guilty of allowing his neighbor to die of starvation. I have noted, however, that in discussions of this type it is rarely remembered that in reality war not only does not provide food for the hungry but causes a shortage of food even in countries where in time of peace there was an abundance of it. It is reasonable to think, therefore, that when we deal with the problem of war, anxieties are mobilized which tend to inhibit our critical faculties and prevent correct reality testing. We shall later examine the contents of these anxieties, chiefly in studying the war phenomenon among primitive peoples. In this manner the discussion of the economic factors of war brings us to the discussion of the psychological factors.

*Psychological factors of war.*

In the chapter dedicated to the psychological aspects of war, Bouthoul describes *the new psychological world,* i.e., the radical transformation of values brought about by war.

Apart from the initiation rites of primitive peoples which we shall discuss later, the transition to the war situation is sanctioned by a number of rites, some of which involve curses and others, accusation of the enemy. The rite of the Roman fetiales may be considered a rite of *charging the enemy with guilt*, through an authentic *litis contestatio* to which all creation (gods, men, animals, plants) was called on to bear witness. An integral part of this rite was the breaking of a cornel-berry cane —which turned red when broken—and the throwing of this cane into enemy territory.

The psychoanalytic reflection on the fetial ceremony suggests that the fantasy which is connected with it may be expressed in the following terms: "Let it be known to all—to terrestrial and celestial beings—that the enemy is in the wrong—that the enemy is bad." The ritual formula in fact runs as follows: "If my recourse to arms is unjust, may I never see my country again." The expulsion of guilt onto the enemy, so typical of the fetial rite, will appear to us in its full significance once we have shown that the mechanism of paranoid elaboration of mourning is central to the psychology of war.

The charging of the enemy with guilt seems to be of fundamental importance in escaping the sense of guilt which war provokes in man; it also marks the moment when peace turns into war, by ceremonially inaugurating the new psychological world established by war. Following this rite, homicide, pillage, and rape become legal for a given period. From that moment on, men are willing to give and receive a violent death, to appropriate by violence the enemy's goods and to lose their own, as if the sense of guilt, though eluded through projection, still involved the mobilization of self-punitive mechanisms. The instinct of self-preservation therefore suffers a crisis or, rather, becomes involved in a dramatic event governed by a radical Manicheism which is in turn regulated by the splitting of the world into friend and enemy.

The splitting of the world into friend and enemy represents an extreme simplification whereby the good and the bad are no longer integrated in the same instinctual situation and in the same object relationship, but the same situation assumes different characters according as it is consummated upon the self, or upon the other, in the paranoid aphorism of *"mors tua vita mea."* The enormous weight of human ambivalence is suddenly lifted when love and hate find two separate objects of attention.

In Bouthoul's opinion war has all the characteristics of a feast, whose principal function, according to Durkheim, is to unify the group. The most typical psychological aspects of a feast, in the sociological sense of the word, are the following: 1) It brings about a meeting of the members of a group; 2) it is a rite of expenditure and dissipation; 3) it is accompanied by a modification of certain moral laws; 4) it is a rite of collective exaltation; 5) it brings about a state of physical insensibility; 6) it is accompanied by sacrificial rites. As every one of these characteristics is found in war, war might be regarded as *the supreme feast.*

The sociological theory of war as the supreme feast agrees, as we shall see, with Abraham's interpretation of war as *a totemic feast.* However, war appears to be a subsequent elaboration of the totemic feast: in the totemic feast a tribe's own totem father is sacrificed, while in war strangers are killed. This situation is related to what we shall later have occasion to clarify as the paranoid elaboration of mourning.

The fact that among primitive peoples war is accompanied with collective dancing activities—a situation that appears to be preserved to this day in military parades— stresses the relation of war to feast. Among primitive peoples, the sacred character of war is intimately associated with the sacredness of the funeral rites. Among primitive peoples, in fact, war is intimately joined to the idea of *a human sacrifice that is pleasing to the gods,* i.e., to the cult of death and, as we shall see later, to the elaboration of mourning.

Bouthoul notes that in Western civilization, concurrently with the decline of religions, the cult of the fallen in war has been revived in the form of monuments and memorial parks. He interprets this situation as the return of archaic customs in our civilization. The cult of the fallen in war therefore tends to replace the cult of the saints.

War is a spectacular establishment of a general human situation whereby death assumes absolute value: the ideas for which we die have a right to truth, because death becomes a demonstrative process. This situation opens the chapter of the peculiar psychological problem of *death as a criterion of truth,* to which we shall have to return in order to clarify the mysterious epistemology of war, based on the postulate that *what we die for is true,* which is, however, contradicted by another postulate, namely, that *what is victorious is true,* whereby the victor is equated with what is true and right, and the vanquished with what is false and wrong.

The peculiar epistemological principles of war have curious consequences. Among primitive peoples, as we shall see, the "real" man is he who has killed an enemy. In this manner war becomes a sort of proof of one's existence and authenticity, as though man, or primitive man at any rate, waged war in order to prove to himself his own existence as a real man. The romantic glorification of heroism and the idealization of war in general are based on postulates of this kind. And it is on the basis of such postulates that war has nourished attitudes ranging from the medieval idealization of chivalry to the modern idealization of brutality.

Bouthoul also observes that in the death rite the soldier is both the sacrificer and the victim. Among the Romans, specific rites stressed the sacred character of the soldier as well as the loss of this character through desertion, a situation that is still shared at present by members of the army and the church.

Among primitive peoples as well as in our own civilization, the particular virtue of the soldier seems to lie in his *absolute dependence on the leaders,* toward whom any aggressiveness is repressed, and in the fact that all his aggressiveness is directed against the enemy.

The role of the leaders in relation to the transformation brought about by the war phenomenon is, according to Bouthoul, to follow rather than anticipate or modify the mentality of the people. The leaders have a particular talent for responding to the secret wishes of their people. Bouthoul reminds us that Machiavelli advised leaders to undertake preventive wars whenever the difficulties and conflicts within the state became too great. The role of the leaders, therefore, is not to create an aggressive tension but to deflect outward a pre-existing one. Dionysius, the tyrant of Syracuse, not only encouraged his enemies but also aided them, when necessary, to become more of a threat in order to consolidate his own kingdom.

When things turn out badly, however, the leaders serve as scapegoats for collective guilt. All leaders can exercise absolute power in war. An essential aspect of this privilege is the idealization of the leader. Soldiers fight in the name of their leader and in ancient Rome, a successful military leader acquired the attributes of Jupi-

ter. Even in our times the head of the state, in good
faith and with complete sincerity, eventually confuses his
own existence with that of his nation.

In connection with the story of Abraham, Bouthoul
notes that the culminating moment of patriarchal power
is when the father orders the sacrifice of the son. In
Bouthoul's opinion, therefore, war involves the concrete
realization on the part of the leaders of their wish to sacrifice their best citizens for the good of the nation. He
recalls, in this connection, the words spoken by an old
grenadier of Napoleon's guard after Napoleon's farewell
to his troops at Fontainebleau: "Sir, we shall no longer
have the joy of dying in your service."

The idealization of and absolute dependence on the
leader, however, are by no means a simple matter. The
need to rebel against the leader tends to manifest itself
in mutiny, considered the gravest of crimes. From a
strictly psychoanalytic point of view, the process of idealization, in effect, serves to deny strong hostile impulses and
persecutory anxieties felt in relation to the idealized
object.

Usually the hostile aspect of the ambivalence felt toward the leaders finds expression when things turn out
badly. Among the Assyrians the leaders were always the
first to be punished in case of defeat. The tendency to
punish the leaders reasserted itself in our times with the
trials of the Nazi leaders who, however, were tried and
condemned by the victors; this poses problems to which
we shall return.

One of the most obvious aspects of war, in Bouthoul's
opinion, is that it *inflicts martyrdom*. War cannot be
waged except through training for sacrifice. As the spirit
of sacrifice intensifies, it lends an enthusiasm-arousing
aspect to the warlike impulse. The spirit of sacrifice is
intimately related to the need for an ideology and pos-

sibly an ideology in the name of which one may sacrifice himself. The ideologies themselves, however, suffer a crisis when war is lost. At the end of World War I, the Germans had lost their faith in the Kaiser. Hitler re-awakened the bellicose spirit by introducing a new ideology. A similar thing happened in Russia where the spirit of sacrifice as sacrifice for the Czar, had died out but revived for the Socialist revolution as the new ideology.

In war the state becomes an organization that distributes sacrifice. Laymen who dismiss religious martyrdom with a smile are often deeply moved by political martyrdom, considering it one of the basic values of human life. In the idealization of sacrifice Bouthoul recognizes a psychological factor of war, although the *primum movens* of war is the demographic element. Apart from the demographic motivation, there is no doubt that in the eyes of many people the faith in a just idea legitimates every sacrifice. Even pacifists are reluctant to renounce violence when this is in defense of a just ideal. It seems that no one can help admiring the military virtues when these are put into the service of liberty. It will thus be necessary to probe the profound significance of ideology.

The spirit of sacrifice is usually mobilized in the young. It is the young who are easily moved by ideologies and who readily accept—much more so than adults—the prospect of dying for an idea. In this connection, Bouthoul calls our attention to an important trait of romanticism, namely, its glorification of adolescence.

In dealing with the problem of the emotional implications of the phenomenon of war, Bouthoul reaches the conclusion that it is sufficient to convince people that they are threatened in order to induce them to give up their rights. He consequently defines sovereignty as *"the right granted to one to intimidate others."*

It is essentially on the basis of mutual fear that two neighboring nations have the right to consider themselves in a state of legitimate defense.

Another psychological aspect of war is the importance assumed in it by *fanatical behavior*. The fanatic is not so much driven by the wish to save something as he is excited by the prospect of participating in a conflict, with the intention of receiving and inflicting martyrdom. Contrary to what might have been expected, with the advent of the scientific era in modern civilization we have had an increase in fanaticism. Nietzsche, Lawrence, Malraux (the courage to face death in order to give value to life—"I have thought much about death but since I have been fighting I no longer think about it"), Hemingway (the glorification of the bullfight), Jünger (what is important is not what we are fighting for, but the fact that we are fighting) are cited by Bouthoul as champions of the fanatical idealization of heroism according to which there is no need of a good cause to justify war, for "a good war halloweth every cause" (Nietzsche).

Describing *the psychological transformation in the aftermath of war*, Bouthoul states that the most important fact observable during the period immediately following the establishment of peace is a rapid decline of the bellicose spirit. Having insisted that their rivalry or disagreements were intolerable, nations suddenly find that they can come to terms with each other. The aggressiveness subsides, as if war were a sort of *orgasm followed by relaxation*. Mental states and actions, clearly understood by everyone concerned only a short time before, suddenly become incomprehensible. Bouthoul compares the euphoria of peace to the silent, secret joy that prevails, when someone dies, among his prospective heirs, and to the relaxation of tension experienced by students after examinations. The vanquished people often find a sort of satisfaction in the thought that war has freed them from their errors and show a distinct tendency to attend the school of the victor. The vanquished people's institutions are despised and their defeat rationalized as punishment for their crimes. In this manner defeat is a source of repudiations. The vanquished people deserved to be defeated on account of their errors: the vanquished are guilty. While sacrifice participates in war as a propitiatory procedure for future misdeeds, the expiatory attitudes following war are a reparation for past misdeeds. The sacrificing of scapegoats seems to be a part of the rites of atonement. Another phenomenon of the postwar period is an increase in criminality which is antithetical to the aggressiveness projected into the vanquished and condemned.

Referring to the research conducted on the relation between *aggression and frustration*, Bouthoul discusses the mechanism of *displacement of the aggression* generated by frustration which is particularly evident in a rigid hierarchy. Especially in the army, anger and frustration may resolve themselves in a downpour of bad temper from top to bottom of the hierarchic scale.

An increase in the projection of bad objects, as a reaction to frustration, is particularly evident in collective psychology. Surveys made in the American Middle West have shown that the party in power during a period of drought is never re-elected. In the American South, the persecution of blacks varied with collective frustration; thus a correlation was noted between the price of cotton and the number of lynchings.

In addition to the paranoid reactions, depressive reactions have been underlined as an answer to frustration.[5]

[5] John Dollard, *Frustration and Aggression* (New Haven, 1940); Evan Durbin and John Bowlby, *Personal Aggressiveness and War* (New York, 1940).

In the individual, frustration likewise gives rise to both paranoid and depressive reactions, but these reactions are usually concomitant and counterbalance each other. On the collective level, these reactions appear to be more uniform, with one or the other type occurring in pure culture, as it were. A characteristic of the noted ease with which a crowd can be roused to sudden aggressive action would seem to be the fact that it requires the instigation of a leader. The content of the reactions may vary; it is equally easy to move mobs to aggression as to mysticism.

One of the essential differences between individual aggressiveness and the warlike impulse, according to Bouthoul, is that while individual aggressiveness is momentary, transient, felt specifically as such and usually limited to one individual, the warlike impulse is *a generalized, profound emotional state. Often it is a general state of acceptance and approval of future violence rather than a manifestation of violence itself.* The warlike state corresponds, that is, to a sense of the need for a period of violence and destruction rather than to genuine aggressive excitation. Before it is an action, it is a conviction; sometimes it is merely a resignation to a calamity considered inevitable. The apparent absence of aggressive excitation in war as a festival destructive of humanity is certainly a peculiar problem and one to which we shall return.

In connection with the problem of frustration, Bouthoul notes that the causes of group frustration are various. A nation may consider itself frustrated because it does not possess a Holy Grail or because it wishes to occupy the Holy Places. It can equally well convince itself that it cannot endure being without an oil well or a port on a particular seacoast. It may also be unable to tolerate its neighbors having different institutions or beliefs from its own.

Depending on which of the above is the cause of a specific frustration, the war will be called religious, economic, ideological, etc. What is essential, however, is that after a motivation has been found, the warlike impulse stimulates the reactivation of a whole series of psychological processes which we must clarify and define.

One of the most typical effects of the warlike impulse is that it dulls the critical sense of the people, paralyzing above all their ability to evaluate the destruction rationally. Bouthoul observes that if we compare the difficulties a nation is trying to eliminate through war with the destruction and suffering brought about by the same war, we generally find that the *latter exceed the former.* Thus one receives the impression that the warlike impulse which precedes armed conflicts provokes a sort of distortion in reality testing. It is also interesting to note that combatants usually believe that they will go through war unharmed.

An interesting hypothesis advanced by Bouthoul is that war arouses unconscious psychic elements. According to him, the events of history are incorporated into our unconscious. He seems to think that changes in social structure, by modifying the general psychological tone, provoke complexes in individuals. These complexes prepare the unconscious foundations of the collective spirit and of the collective reactions which in turn generate new events. Although from a psychoanalytic point of view the hypothesis that complexes originate in historical events appears rather unorthodox, it could nevertheless constitute a point of reference for a more thorough investigation of the generally accepted fact that history modifies the psychopathological picture, in the sense that some mental disorders tend to disappear or to adopt a different phenomenology at different times in history.

The psychoanalytic reflection on the psychological aspects of war, as described by Bouthoul, permits us to trace them for the most part to the fact that *the group ideal becomes a love object* which takes the place of the original, individual love object represented—for the child —by the mother.

Surely one of the least edifying and at the same time most ambiguous and disquieting observations that may, from a psychoanalytic point of view, be derived from the examination of many of the psychological aspects of armed conflicts, as they are described by Bouthoul, is that relating to the ethical or rather ethico-religious significance of war as sacrifice-destruction. On a general level the observation that war (as an organized massacre and now also as a probable catastrophe) is sensed by men as a particularly cogent duty seems to confirm one of Freud's most profound intuitions, described by himself as "the heresy of having made morality derive from the death instinct."

But an even more surprising fact is that war as sacrificial duty, though performing essentially destructive functions, has for men the significance of a destruction put into the service of the preservation of what they love. Fanatic behavior, the idealization of the leader, the need to sacrifice oneself in the name of an ideal, the giving and receiving of martyrdom, and the soldier's being both the sacrificer and the victim in the sacrificial rite (see the myth of the body in the car later on)—all these psychological aspects pose a series of very complex problems. Expressed in a simplified form, however, all these situations may be encompassed in the following question: What lies at the basis of this peculiar tendency of man to create certain values in the name of which he feels he must sacrifice himself?

Psychoanalysis has attempted to throw light on the sacrificial attitude in general, connecting it with the general problem of masochism.

In its most elementary expression, and understood as the deriving of pleasure from a painful experience, masochism is not a specifically human prerogative. By appropriate techniques it can be experimentally provoked in dogs, through experiences of conditioned reflexes. In Pavlov's laboratory a masochistic situation was produced experimentally in a dog through the association of a painful stimulus (a powerful electric shock) with the presentation of food. Faced with a situation of this sort the dog at first reacts by rebelling and attacking what he perceives as the painful stimulus. After an adequate number of shock-food associations, however, a paradoxical reaction is observed in the dog. Instead of rebelling and attacking it, the dog responds to the painful stimulus —now given by itself and no longer accompanied with food—with pleasure.

Sherrington, after having witnessed an experiment of this type in Pavlov's laboratory, is said to have exclaimed: "Finally I understand the psychology of saints!" One day I happened to quote this remark of Sherrington's to an assembly of laymen, thereby provoking general hilarity. But when immediately afterward I added that the Pavlovian experiment also explains the psychology of heroes, the assembly reacted with obvious disapproval.

In general, then, we are inclined to accept the diagnosis of masochism for sacrifices made in the name of the valueless ideals of others but are more reluctant to do so in the case of sacrifices made in the name of ideals that we ourselves believe in. In the latter case, what we should in other circumstances consider masochism becomes instead a sort of supervalue.

Thus it remains to clarify what lies at the basis of man's tendency to transform his need to sacrifice himself for an ideal, in which he believes, into a sort of supervalue. If we remain in the field of conditioned reflexes and limit ourselves to the above-mentioned experiment with the dog, the *primum movens* of the masochistic situation appears to be constituted by the need for food. The whole technique of conditioned reflexes is based on a tube applied to the salivary glands of the dog. For the dog, therefore, food is an unconditional value (a sort of absolute) on which depends the development of all conditional (that is, relative) values, including the masochistic experience described above. Thus we may say that the dog joyfully wags his tail in the face of a painful stimulus because the painful stimulus has become the presentation of food. If, however, following the establishment of the conditioned reflex, the painful stimulus-food association is not reiterated, the conditioned reflex is lost and the dog once again reacts to the painful stimulus as to an enemy.

What is our equivalent of what food is to the dog? What is this absolute and unconditional something that would somehow justify the establishment of a masochistic-sacrificial position, which would in turn become a sort of supervalue because it would be put into the service of that absolute and unconditional something?

The psychoanalytic answer to this question, or at least a certain type of psychoanalytic answer, leads us precisely and again back to food as the mother's original gift to the child. This is that absolute and unconditional something that man carries in the deepest part of himself as a love object transfigured and absolutized, as a sort of paradise enjoyed in the beginning but quickly lost. And so human life becomes a continuous attempt, more or less hopeful, or more or less desperate, to regain this precious object.[6] With one of these vicissitudes of regaining the original food, and the unity with the mother and her lost gift, seems to be connected the deepest origin of group formation.

Although food appears to be linked with the establishment of unconditional objects and with subsequent conditionings in both man and dog, what seems to distinguish man from dog is that the dog remains bound to food in its elemental biological form while in man food as a biological object expands enormously as a symbol and in the original vicissitudes of love associated with its presence and in the primary experiences of hate connected with its absence. In this manner the dog's experience is ultimately more realistic, while the enrichment and the fantasy expansion of his original affective vicissitudes lead the human child to the formation of an internal world peopled with fantasy objects which add to the illusory dimension of man's psychic life an extension that seems to be lacking in other animals. The proliferation of the illusory lies perhaps at the basis of the processes of verification and reality testing as processes that are particularly developed in man; it is however undeniable that the expansion of the illusory exposes man, more than any other animal, to the experience of psychosis. We shall have occasion to deal with this problematic situation in chapter 4.

In an article dedicated to the clarification of the problems relating to the origin of the law as a group ideal, and to the war crisis, I sought to show that both paranoid

6 Franco Fornari, *La Vita Affettiva Originaria del Bambino* (Milan, 1963).

and depressive mechanisms participate in the war phenomenon.[7]

The psychological aspects of war, namely, the crisis of the instinct of self-preservation, the idealization of the need for sacrifice as well as the idealization of the leader, all seem to be phenomena that occur on the basis of the fact that individuals form a group on the basis of the identification with a common love object. Since the group ideal (as an object of love and identification) is fantasied as that which gives life to the individuals within the group, the preservation of the common love object is felt as a primary function as compared with the preservation of the individual. A situation of this sort is specifically human and justifies in a manner the need for sacrifice. Nevertheless I believe I have succeeded in showing that the group ideal, translating into an illusory dimension the concrete and vital function of the primary love object—and in a way usurping it—causes the evolution of the original need for sacrifice (expressed by the primitive need for guilt) into an illusory and unauthentic dimension.

In war, in fact, sacrifice is not aimed at mastering the bad parts of the self, as a function of preservation of the original love object threatened by the self, as happens in the ethics of the individual. In war, sacrifice becomes sadistic through the projection onto the enemy of the destructive tendencies originally directed against one's love object.

The best example of the illusoriness and the unauthenticity which the need for sacrifice acquires in war is offered us by the kamikaze. In the kamikaze, self-sacrifice is employed to deny one's guilt needs connected

[7] Franco Fornari, "Condizione depressiva e condizione paranoidea nell' origine delle leggi e nella crisi della guerra," *Aut Aut*, 64 (Milan, July, 1961); and *Psicanalisi della Guerra Atomica* (Milan, 1964).

with the hostile impulses against one's love object: a process that is revealed to us by the charging of the enemy with guilt in the fetial rite present, in one form or another, in every war.

An illustrious example of the need for sacrifice as an authentic process of reparation is offered us by Socrates who felt that he must sacrifice himself in order that his love object (his ethical ideal) might live. Thus while Socrates' ideal seems to have been really rendered imperishable through the philosopher's sacrifice, the kamikaze was powerless to save the ideal of the Mikado. The illusory and unauthentic aspect of the reparation process which is carried out in war through sacrifice seems to reside in the fact that, though set in motion by a love need, self-sacrifice in war is in reality expressed through hetero-destructive activities.

In other words war—while it makes men relive the primary psychic situations pertaining to the primary love and guilt needs in relation to their object of love and identification, threatened by destruction—betrays the love and guilt needs, elaborating them in the paranoid way. We shall be able to understand this better after having studied the mechanism of paranoid elaboration of mourning, mainly in the wars of primitive peoples. The verdict of guilty pronounced against the vanquished enemy, which is a typical postwar phenomenon, demonstrates in an exemplary manner that the defense of what is just, by which men are carried away in the beginning of a conflict, is an illusory situation that ultimately shows war to be a process extraneous to every idea of justice to the extent in which war is fundamentally connected with the paranoid axiom of *mors tua vita mea*, by virtue of which the vanquished nation is always in the wrong.

Thus I think that it was possible for war to become

so deeply rooted in the hearts of men because they were always able to see it as a necessary evil, for it contains not only destructive functions but also love needs. However, one of the most important contributions of the psychoanalytic investigation in relation to the war phenomenon is the discovery that war is perhaps the most unauthentic experience of love.

# 2

# WAR
# IN PRIMITIVE
# SOCIETIES

The psychoanalytic investigation of war must include a study of the forms of expression that war takes among primitive peoples. The psychoanalyst in fact believes that war in primitive societies is much closer to the ways in which war is fantasied in the unconscious.

A systematic study of war in primitive societies was made by Maurice R. Davie.[1] There is evidence that war existed in prehistoric times. Some anthropologists, however, maintain that *Pithecanthropus* did not wage war as such. Concerning historical times, Burton observed that in Gabon and the lower Niger war was much less frequent than in East Africa.[2] In this connection it is important to note that the scarcity of warfare in Gabon and lower Niger seems to have been due to the fact that war was not decided upon by the chief but required a consensus of all that were concerned (of a council of elders and often of all male members of the tribe). In East Africa, on the other hand, where belligerence was rampant, the chief's power was absolute. Thus in Africa as well as in Polynesia, as a direct consequence of the absolute power of the chief or king, war was deprived of every trace of a juridical character.

[1] Maurice R. Davie, *The Evolution of War* (Port Washington, New York, 1968).
[2] Burton, *Voyage au Grand Lac*, p. 655, cited by Davie.

*Initiation rites and war among primitive peoples.*

A particularly important chapter in the study of war among primitive peoples is the relation between war and initiation rites. These may in fact be regarded not merely as puberty rites but also as typical rites of initiation into warfare, for war is the specific attribute of adult males. Following initiation rites, the youth is authorized to bear arms. This prerogative is intimately associated with the neophyte's definitive separation from his mother and with his being admitted to the society of adult males. If he sees his mother, the initiate must hide himself.

Theodor Reik[3] analyzed the significance of the brutality to which the young initiates are subjected. The ceremonies are held in secluded huts, and the ritual practices often involve considerable injuries symbolizing death and resurrection. The symbolic castration, common in initiation rites, is connected by Reik with the Oedipal situation.

In addition to marking a drastic separation from the mother, the initiation rites also mark a rigid division of the masculine and the feminine occupations, the specific occupation of the male being warfare.

According to several authors, the apex of the initiation rites is the total submission and obedience to the chiefs, both closely connected with the initiation into war. Reik has shown the intimate bond between initiation rites and the Oedipal situation; he did not, however, take into consideration the bond between initiation rites and war.[4] The fact that initiation rites (ritual brutalities inflicted

[3] Theodor Reik, *The Ritual: Four Psychoanalytic Studies* (New York, 1946).
[4] Maurice N. Walsh interprets even modern war as the reproduction of initiation rites in our society. (M. N. Walsh, "Psychoanalytic Studies of War," *Philadelphia Association of Psychoanalysis Bulletin*, 12, 3, 1962.)

on the sons by the fathers) coincide with the initiation into warfare (ritual killing of enemies) clearly indicates the relation between Oedipal aggressiveness and war as a ritual displacement of this aggressiveness.

In addition to indicating a symbolic perpetration of the murder of the sons by the fathers, the rites of death and resurrection seem to indicate another apical event, namely, the termination of the son's relationship with the mother, perceived as death—castration, in order that he may be reborn into the relationship with the group; the group therefore takes the place of the mother (Róheim).

The fact that the initiation rite, in addition to expressing the initiation into warfare, also expresses the transition from the relationship with the mother to the relationship with the group, underlines the original sacredness of war and of membership in the group. The struggle between fathers and sons which takes place in the initiation rites ends in the sons' unconditional surrender to the fathers: the sons stand before the fathers as if castrated in order to be admitted to the group.

The price of manhood for the young initiate, then, is *castration*. It is therefore understood that if the admission to the group arouses castration anxiety, the group itself must provide the initiate with a reassurance against it. Among primitive peoples, then, war is the defense offered by the group against the castration anxiety aroused by admission to the group. We are now able to understand why the initiate, after having for the first time killed an enemy in battle, runs back to his village shouting exultantly: "I am a man, I am a real man!" It seems that the admission to the group and the initiation rite do not *in se* and *per se* invest the initiate with real masculinity; on the contrary, since they involve castration and passive submission to the fathers, as well as the renouncing of the mother, they arouse in him intense homosexual anxieties which are, as it seems, controlled by participation in war.

Géza Róheim, following Simmel, has shown us that the group replaces the original "dual unity" that the child lives with the mother; the unity which the individual achieves in the plurality of the group, the sense of belonging to a unity which is in fact multiple (the collective), is thus based on an illusory relation to a maternal imago projected into the group. The anxieties of exclusion from the group are therefore a repetition of the anxieties of separation from the mother.

*War and sexuality.*

Concerning the relation between war and sexuality, the two most important findings in our study of primitive peoples are the following: 1) War is distinctly the business of the male; 2) the object of war is often the abduction of women.[5]

Wars are waged in order to secure women as wives, but also as workers and slaves. According to Bennett[6] the principal causes of wars among the Fang are disputes over women, which may go on for years. Such a situation may keep the women from working and result in grave shortages of food. Among the Ba-Huana of the Congo, women are the chief instigators of war; if the men are peaceably inclined, the women make fun of them.[7]

Davie connects the fact that war is man's business with the division of labor by sex and with the physical strength

[5] E. Westermarck, *History of Human Marriage* (London, 1921); cited by Davie.
[6] A. L. Bennett, "Ethnographical Notes on the Fang," *Journal of the Anthropological Institute of Great Britain and Ireland* (JAI), XXXVI, pp. 92–93; cited by Davie.
[7] E. Torday and T. A. Joyce, "The Ethnography of the Ba-Huana," *JAI*, p. 289; cited by Davie.

of the male, which suggests that the subjection of women is a natural law of the human race.[8] The male domination of women is found to be the more pronounced, the more warlike the group or tribe. The women's tasks are care of the children, general labor, and in particular agriculture. Accordingly, the cross-fertilization of cultures and the diffusion of agriculture has been promoted mainly through wife capture and the seizure of women in war.

We have reflected on initiation rites and war in relation to the Oedipus complex, as well as in relation to castration anxieties and defenses against such anxieties. This will help us to understand better both war as the business of the male and the capture of women in terms of unconscious Oedipal contents and in terms of the function of the group as a function of defense against the anxieties connected with the Oedipal situation. Furthermore, we are able to understand why, when deprived of war, primitive men say they no longer feel like men and why prisoners of war among primitive peoples feel that they are "made women" and are confined to pursuits appropriate to women.[9] In the few instances of women's participation in war, as in the case of the female corps (called the Amazons) in the standing army of the kingdom of Dahomey (West Africa), women are masculinized and asexualized; they cannot be touched without danger of death. The equating of the vanquished enemy's position with that of a woman seems to lie at the root of—and in turn to be conditioned by—the equivalence of weapons and penis which characterizes the universe of sadomasochistic sexuality in our unconscious.

The men of the upper Congo are armed on all occa-

[8] A. E. Crawley, "Sexual Taboo," *JAI*, XXIV, p. 116; cited by Davie.
[9] In the last few centuries of Western history, the value of work has grown side by side with the social status of women. Engels, in fact, equated the proletarian condition with the feminine condition.

sions. An unarmed man is treated with contempt and told to "go and rear children." When the Fang of the French Congo shoot someone down in an ambush, they return to their town in triumph, shouting: "We are real men, we are real men, we have been to town and have shot a man, we are men, real men."[10] Similarly, a Masai or a native of the Papuan Gulf is not supposed to marry until he has bloodied his spear.

The acceptance of work—considered a female task— seems to have a direct influence on the diminution of the warlike spirit. The agricultural tribes are preponderantly peaceable. Among the Sarasin, an agricultural tribe, fights never develop into real war, for after a certain number of people have been killed the affair stops. The result of the fight is never conquest but only the fixing of boundaries between hunting grounds.

Cattle raising among agricultural tribes plays an important role in creating an unwarlike culture. Roscoe reports that "the Bahima of Africa form warm attachments for the animals, treating them like children."[11] Cases are not unknown in which men have committed suicide on the loss of a favorite animal. But for the tribes who live by plunder, to be deprived of war is to be deprived of livelihood. The existence of peaceable peoples, such as the Bahima, in the midst of predatory tribes therefore forces the peaceable tribes to be continuously on the defensive. In this manner endless conflicts arise between pastoral and agricultural tribes. The former are invariably more warlike and predatory than the latter. Agricultural tribes are usually enslaved by pastoral nomads who become their masters.

The conquest of an agricultural, peaceable tribe by a

[10] A. L. Bennett, op. cit., p. 93.
[11] Rev. J. Roscoe, "The Bahima," *JAI*, XXXVII, p. 93; cited by Davie.

nomadic, warlike tribe leads to the formation of the state.[12] The state, then, owes its origin to war. In its primitive form, the state is a social institution forced by the conquerors on the conquered. The state thus has its origins in the subjugation of one group of men by another; the conquering group is equated, in the primitive mind, with the masculine position and the conquered group with the feminine position.

The above data relating to the equating of the warlike with the male and the unwarlike with the female-castrated may explain men's instinctive aversion to pacifist positions. Since, in men's unconscious, weapons are equated with the penis, disarmament is in general feared as castration. This would account for the general unpopularity of disarmament.

## War and the magico-religious world of primitive peoples.

An aspect of the war phenomenon that most readily lends itself to psychoanalytic investigation is the magico-religious aspect war assumes among primitive peoples. The magico-religious world against the background of which wars are waged among primitive peoples appears to be traceable to *man's primal reactions in the face of death.* The gods of primitive peoples, in fact, are barely distinguishable from the ghosts of their departed ancestors.

To primitive men the world is peopled with countless ghosts and spirits which constitute a sort of imaginary environment. As many of them are the spirits of the dead, *the entire imaginary environment in which the primitive lives may be considered an elaboration of mourning.* Most of the ghosts and spirits are conceived as malignant and hostile, ready to harm the living.

[12] A. G. Keller, *Homeric Society* (New York, 1906), p. 248; cited by Davie.

From these observations on primitive peoples, it appears that in the imaginary environment where their dead ancestors' spirits are felt to exist, men experience the most elementary forms of enemy territory and relationship to an enemy object.

Because of their invisibility, and the powers ascribed to them, ghosts are more terrifying than animals and living men. In the eyes of primitive men it is preferable to wage war on visible enemies who can be killed than to be at enmity with invisible spirits who are immortal and cannot be overcome.

Through their belief in *mana*, an impersonal magical power which often manifests itself through the spirits of the departed, primitive people regard the latter as omnipresent. Having no conception of causality, and natural laws being to them less real than their own externalized anxieties, they ascribe all phenomena which they cannot understand, especially the ills connected with the "aleatory element" in their life, to the agency of spirits. In order to escape misfortune, therefore, they must appease the spirits. Although the spirits are felt to be hostile, primitive men cannot, for the reasons described above, wage wars against them but must attempt to appease them by sacrificing to them, by providing them with the things they desire. If this is not done, the spirits become angry and show their displeasure by sending calamities of all kinds.

The spirits, in other words, are in possession of a sort of absolute weapon. The primitive religion therefore appears to be a defensive organization against an invisible, omnipotent enemy who can be appeased only at the cost of sacrifices.

Although this defensive need is organized into religion, it does not, through reparative propitiation, succeed in controlling the persecutory anxieties aroused by the spirits of the departed. The intensification of ethnocentrism determined by religion then leads to the negation of the persecutory object through its idealization as "the protector of the chosen people," simultaneously producing the need for projecting into the enemy group the bad parts of the self which are displeasing to the spirits. The idealization of a tribe's relation to its ancestors' spirits, expressed in the belief that they are the chosen—therefore particularly loved—people still does not succeed in defending the tribe against the fear of being punished by the spirits. As it seems, this fear cannot be controlled except by the paranoid mechanism of projective identification through which the bad parts that constitute the mysterious reasons for which the dead are filled with desires of revenge against the living, are projected into the enemy tribe. Following such a projection, the slaughter of enemies is equal to the destruction of the bad parts of the self that are displeasing to the spirits.

Thus the Tupinambas of Brazil believed that only the souls of men who had lived virtuously, that is to say, had well avenged themselves and eaten many of their enemies, would go to the place of the blessed.[13] "Upon his arrival in the other world, the double of a Fiji Islander should be able to boast with good reason of having killed many people and destroyed many villages: these were his good works."[14]

The religion of primitive peoples who regard crime as a virtue therefore seems to express a crude coincidence between the id and the superego (among the divinities populating the Fiji paradise we find, for example, the Adul-

[13] E. B. Tylor, *Primitive Culture*, II (New York, 1874), p. 86; cited by Davie.
[14] B. Thomson, "The Natives of Savage Island or Niué," *JAI*, XXXI, p. 139.

terer, the Nocturnal Ravisher of Rich Women, the Quarreler, the Bully, the Murderer, etc.).

While these ethnological data may shock us, we cannot help being struck by the similarity between the religion of the Fiji Islanders and military ethics in general. It is precisely this curious situation of coincidence between crime and virtue that appears to express, in a typical manner, the singularity of the war phenomenon and to reveal its significance in relation to the elaboration of mourning or rather in relation to what I shall call *paranoid elaboration of mourning.*

While the propitiatory rites and the idealization of the relation to the ancestors-gods may be understood as the elaboration of the depressive anxieties of mourning (since he who performs propitiatory rites as acts of reparation does so because he feels that he himself has offended his gods), war-virtue, understood as a propitiation of the ancestors-gods, is based on a process of projection owing to which a tribe becomes convinced that its gods have been offended by the enemy.

The slaughter of enemies, or any atrocity committed against them, acquires the character of virtue inasmuch as it is a battle against, and a punishment of, the projected bad parts of the self.

Since the injuries fathers inflict on boys during initiation rites—injuries which at times are so severe as to cause death—intensify the boys' wish to kill their fathers, the fact that initiation rites are the rites of initiation into warfare leads us to believe that war itself is intimately connected with the struggle against parricidal impulses projected into the enemy tribe.

Viewed from the outside, both the behavior of primitive peoples and military ethics in general reveal a peculiar coincidence of the id with the superego. Viewed from within, however, military ethics as well as the religion of primitive peoples as a religion of war appear to contain a peculiar type of morality that may be understood as *paranoid elaboration of mourning.* Considered rationally, this form of morality appears to be *a veritable moral alienation, based on the alienation of one's guilt feelings, which are projected into the enemy.* A primitive tribe at war with another primitive tribe makes the other the receptacle of its own guilt needs, for which reason the slaughter of the enemy, who is perceived as guilty of the death of one's relatives or fellow tribesmen, is sensed as blood revenge and serves to avoid the depressive pain of mourning.

The paranoid significance of a primitive tribe's relation to an enemy tribe, as a relation to the projected bad parts of the self, is also revealed by their belief that all whom they kill in this world will serve them as slaves in the next. The slaughter of the enemy (who has become the representative of one's own id) is thus a means of controlling one's own id.

As for the gods of war and bloodshed clamoring for human victims, they are the spirits of the dead who express the attacks of a sadistic superego, which as a rule causes the evolution of mourning into melancholia. In this manner war, viewed in the context of primitive magic and religion, appears to be *a peculiar sort of funeral rite and represents the displacement of the propitiatory sacrifice on to the enemy* who, through projection, is perceived as the cause of the death of the members of one's own tribe.

Deprived of war as a paranoid reaction to mourning, primitive peoples evolve depressive positions. The bellicose tribes of Oceania have been in a state of a particularly depressive confusion ever since the Europeans imposed peace on them. Deprived of their chief occupation, the men are bored, consider themselves useless, and have lost all self-respect; they have become lazy, debauched; they drink heavily, have lost all dignity; they no longer feel like men and have lost their *raison d'être*. It is to this state of enforced peace that some ethnologists attribute the decline in Polynesian population.

Elaine Metais studied death-anxiety in one of the Kanachi tribes, after its colonization by whites and the subsequent abolition of war.[15] In this tribe, according to Elaine Metais, the abolition of war aroused profound fears of destruction experienced not in reference to their enemies or to the white colonists, but in reference to their own sorcerers. In the case of this tribe the abolition of war determined *the reinternalization of the persecutory object into their own group.* The tribe's fear of being destroyed by their own magicians would appear to have all the characteristics of a sadistic superego as a bad object internalized in a melancholiac situation. In this manner the double legality of peace and war, usually felt as hypocrisy, would seem to reveal itself as a paradoxical psychological need for war, being as it is an alternative to the development of an endogenous melancholiac process. Accordingly, war as the paranoid elaboration of mourning, would appear to be a defense against the melancholiac elaboration of mourning. It is surprising to note, through these facts, that *the fear of annihilation* (which the idea of renouncing war arouses in man) *would appear to arise not so much from his being threatened by a real external danger* (i.e., from his being disarmed and therefore at the mercy of an external enemy), *as from the fact that he finds himself confronted by annihilation as a totally illusory danger connected with a psychotic anxiety.* In addition to throwing light on the psychotic motivations for war, what has been observed among primitive peoples de-

[15] E. Metais, "Les sorciers nous tuent," *Cahiers Internationales de Sociologie,* XXV, 1963.

prived of war seems to constitute *a decisive proof in favor of the Freudian theory of the death instinct, since it confronts us with the realm of destruction not as an exogenous situation, but as a purely endogenous emergence.*

In connection with the relation between the magico-religious world of primitive peoples and war, Davie maintains that the religion of primitive man fosters war. It seems to me more correct to say that both religion and war originate in the elaboration of psychotic anxieties connected with mourning and that each of them constitutes a socialized mode of defense against such anxieties. Thus the relation between war and the violation of taboos also seems to be connected with the psychological realities illustrated above. Captain Cook, for example, was killed by the natives of the Sandwich Islands because he had violated one of their taboos by trying to seize the king's person. In Captain Cook the natives were punishing their own hostile feelings against their chief.

The same explanation seems to apply to the fact that to speak ill of the deceased, or simply to utter his name during the period of mourning, is a cause of war among the natives of Polynesia. In addition to being connected with this specific elaboration of mourning, the paranoid attitude operates in motivations for war in general.

Lawves[16] reports that the Motu of southeast New Guinea have a superstitious fear of the neighboring Koitapu to whose magical power they attribute any calamity that befalls them. In 1876 they lost much of their sago in a storm at sea because their canoes were unable to withstand the rough water and carry the cargo. They accused the Koitapu of having caused the disaster by hostile magic and killed many of them in revenge. Again in

[16] W. G. Lawves, "Ethnological Notes on the Motu, Koitapu and Koiari Tribes of New Guinea," *JAI*, VIII, pp. 375, 383; cited by Davie.

1878, after a prolonged drought for which a Koitapu village was held responsible, they attacked the village and killed many of its inhabitants. In the rain which followed soon after this murder, the Motu saw the confirmation of their projection. We may condescendingly smile at such projections yet, as we have seen, the average American behaves in an analogous manner: the political party in office during a period of drought is not re-elected, and the lynchings of blacks once depended on the going price of cotton.

The intimate bond between war and the paranoid reaction to mourning becomes particularly evident if we consider the close connection between war and *the belief that death is caused by magic.* The majority of ethnologists agree that the belief that death is caused by the hostile magic of alien tribes is one of the most frequent and most serious causes of war.

Among many primitive tribes when a man dies, someone else is, as a rule, charged with having been the cause. The tribes of Assam, for instance, hold that sickness and death are caused by an evil spirit sent by some member of a hostile tribe. A belief of this kind is sufficient cause for war.

Kingsley states that "the belief in witchcraft is the cause of more African deaths than anything else. It has killed and still kills more men and women than the slave trade."[17] It is no uncommon thing in Africa for ten persons to be killed in retaliation for the sickness or death of one.

The knowledge of the unconscious reactions to mourning permits us to affirm that *the fear that one's hostile impulses are capable of provoking the death of a loved person is one of the normal components of mourning.*

[17] Mary H. Kingsley, *Travels in West Africa* (London, 1898), pp. 315–19; cited by Davie.

The belief that witchcraft causes the death of loved persons therefore represents the most direct form of alienation of the depressive anxiety that accompanies mourning. The need to accuse someone else of the death of a loved person is the most obvious proof of *man's incapacity to bear guilt in the occasion of mourning*. It is surprising to have to note that among primitive peoples this incapacity to elaborate mourning is intimately associated with the outbreak of war.

In the same manner the need to fight in order to propagate our religion seems to be based on the projection into the other of the unbelieving parts of the self in order to compel ourselves, projected into the other, to believe. Religious proselytism as well as ideological proselytism in general would therefore appear to be the result of our own unconscious unbelief. The wars which primitive peoples wage in order to propagate their respective religions would also seem to be based on an unauthentic elaboration of mourning. Not only do we want to prove to others that we are good and do not hate our religion (i.e., the dead toward whom we have ambivalent feelings) but since the bad parts of the self have been projected into the other, it is the other who must make amends.

In addition to being elaborated in the ways described above, primitive people's fear of ghosts and of the dead in general is also intimately connected with *blood revenge*. Blood revenge among primitive peoples is set in motion by murder. Since in the unconscious every death is murder, every death sets in motion blood revenge. Accordingly, war becomes a duty. The unconscious fantasy may be expressed as follows: "Everyone who dies is murdered by me; I am guilty of every death. Since this would drive me to suicide in the melancholiac elaboration of mourning, I must project my guilt into the other and punish him as the representative of my bad self." That depressive guilt is mobilized in relation to the duty of blood revenge that has been left unfulfilled is particularly evident in the total loss of self-esteem and in the feeling of personal worthlessness. "The duty of avenging the death of his nearest relative is the most sacred duty that primitive man is called upon to perform, and he never neglects or forgets it. Should he leave it unfulfilled, the old women would taunt him; if he were unmarried, no girl would speak to him; if he had wives, they would leave him; his mother would cry and lament that she had given birth to so degenerate a son; his father would treat him with contempt and he would be a mark of public scorn."[18]

Murder is an offense that stains the honor of the murdered man's blood relatives. In Albania the man whose honor has been blackened is obsessed with the idea of his own impurity. In this instance impurity equals guilt. The stain (i.e., guilt) must be cleansed with blood; the stain may be cleansed (that is, the repulsion may be avoided) by finding the culprit and killing him (that is to say, by externalizing both guilt and punishment).

This is a process of verification and attestation that is typical of the social situation: "By killing the murderer I shall be able to show everyone that I am not the murderer. My relative was not killed by my own unconscious hostile wishes; he was killed by someone else." As we shall see later, society and its function as a collective witness seem to refer—in these cases—to a whole series of processes of accusation and absolution pertaining to the phenomenology of mourning and of the relation between mourning and war.

In Albania blood revenge is in effect a tribal problem. It suffices to kill any member of the offender's tribe, even if he is absolutely innocent and ignorant of the cause of the offense; his blood cleanses the honor of the offended man. Durham reports that a member of a Christian tribe of Albania who was seeking blood revenge was exhorted to desist by a Franciscan monk who threatened him with the torments of hell. "I would rather clean my honour and go to hell," the man replied. When, having fulfilled the duty of blood revenge, the man himself was mortally wounded, the Franciscan hastened to his side and begged him to confess and repent while yet there was time. The dying man said, "I do not want your absolution or your heaven, for I have cleansed my honour."

As Durham observes, "we may regret that 'his honour rooted in dishonour stood,' but there is a tragic grandeur about the man who is ready to sacrifice all he has, all that he holds dear, and even life itself in order that he may do that which he believes to be right. It is not everyone that is prepared so to act up to his ideals."[19]

The "tragic grandeur" of which Durham speaks contains a difficult human problem which we shall attempt to clarify later on. It is worth noting at this point, however, that the fear of hell as the exclusion from the relationship with God and the fear of dishonor as the exclusion from the relationship with the tribe are at a certain point the same thing: they are two different elaborations of the same primal anxiety, the same primal fear of separation from or abandonment by one's love object, first experienced in infancy and later relived in a religious or social experience.

For the moment, it is enough for us to have established a relation between *blood revenge and the paranoid elaboration of mourning* and to have found that one of the functions of society among primitive peoples is to estab-

[19] M. Edith Durham, "High Albania and Its Customs in 1908," *JAI*, XL, pp. 165–66; cited by Davie.

lish certain customs, which are closely connected with the war phenomenon and which are actually paranoid elaborations of the depressive anxiety of mourning.

## War and human sacrifice.

Among the various types of human sacrifice, two of the most important are the offering of victims as food for the gods and the providing of the dead with slaves-servants.[20] Human sacrifice presents itself as a typical reparative tendency set in motion by the depressive situation of mourning. Here again, however, the offering of the sacrificial victim does not involve a sacrifice of the self (which is what happens in the melancholiac elaboration of mourning) on the contrary, reparation is made by killing the enemy; it is the enemy, or rather the killing of the enemy, that is made the instrument of reparation.

The beliefs which lie at the root of human sacrifice may be summarized as follows: The spirits of the departed have the same desires and needs as mortals. If their needs and desires are not satisfied, they suffer, become angry, and take revenge on the living. To propitiate the spirits, the living must provide them with the things they desire or need. This must be done especially because the dead are envious of the good fortune of the living; their envy must at all costs be prevented because it could result in all manner of bad luck and calamities.

Accordingly, the custom of sacrificing human victims on the graves of the dead would appear to be a typical response to mourning, in which the dead person is unconsciously fantasied as a "child weaned from life."

[20] Sir John Lubbock, *The Origin of Civilization and the Primitive Condition of Man* (London, 1870), pp. 240–43; Tylor, *Primitive Culture*, II (New York, 1874), pp. 271, 383, 389, 403; W. G. Sumner and A. G. Keller, *The Science of Society*, cf. XXXV, XXXVI (New Haven, 1927); cited by Davie.

Primitive people, as it seems, are loath to inherit anything from the dead. This would appear to constitute a defense against the predatory impulses involved in inheritance. When a chief or anyone of importance dies, presents of slaves are sent in by all the neighboring chiefs as an offering to the spirit of the departed. In Dahomey, the immediate attendants and favorite wives of the departed were sacrificed at his funeral, so that he might find himself surrounded by those he knew and loved. At the death of a king, many victims were required, and to secure the great number needed for these occasions, war was regularly waged. In this instance guilt feelings aroused by unconscious fantasies of appropriation of the paternal potency and other paternal attributes appear to be elaborated in a reparative sense through war which provides sacrificial victims. The enemy then becomes the receptacle of the subjects' predatory impulses toward their dead king, and the ritual sacrifice of the enemy would seem to represent the negation of such impulses. The singularity of this reparative process, then, consists in a basic alienation of the sense of guilt aroused by mourning and in the subsequent war as a reparation which is also alienated since it is made by the enemy. War, in relation to human sacrifice, would therefore appear to have as its psychic motivation a basic process of alienation whereby the predatory impulses, the guilt feelings aroused by them, as well as the reparation made for such guilt feelings are deflected onto an alien-enemy object in a wholly paranoid elaboration of mourning.

## War and head-hunting.

Among the tribes of Borneo, among the Papuans of (British) New Guinea, and among the Kiwai Papuans, the desire to obtain the heads of enemies is the commonest cause of war. They often expect and obtain no other advantage from war than the acquisition of heads.[21]

This custom is based on the religious belief that the soul is located somewhere in the human body—more exactly, in the head. Consequently, when an enemy is decapitated, the possessor of his head also has possession of his soul. The head is treated as if alive, as if still the seat of the slain man's soul, and is usually preserved with the same devotion with which a Catholic would preserve the relics of a saint. The wrath of the slain man is feared, especially since he is now a spirit with greater power to injure the living. The spirit residing in the head must therefore be propitiated by offerings of food and gifts. Following such propitiation the head becomes a sort of tutelar deity who is prayed to.[22] The Fang pray to the skulls and believe that their prayers are always answered.[23] It is the spirits, it must be remembered, who control all phenomena. It is a great advantage therefore to obtain possession of a spirit by holding the object in which it resides; this gives the possessor absolute and omnipotent control over inauspicious phenomena. It is truly surprising to find that a custom which appears so crude to our eyes is evidently based on *fantasies of transforming an enemy object into a friendly one.* Head-hunting, with its magico-religious contents, appears to be comprehensible in the terms in which Melanie Klein described the mechanism of omnipotent sadistic control as the manic defense against persecutory anxieties. Whereas in human sacrifice, as we have seen, the elaboration of mourning was expressed in a typically paranoid process through the alienation, into the enemy, of hostile impulses, guilt feelings, and defenses, in the custom of head-hunting we find

[21] Davie, *Evolution of War,* p. 137.
[22] Ibid., p. 138.
[23] Bennett, "The Fang," p. 87.

*a manic process,*[24] whereby the basic persecutory anxiety felt in relation to the dead is controlled through a mechanism of negation. Such a process of negation, associated with the fantasy of omnipotent sadistic control, leads to the transformation of the persecutory spirits of the dead into tutelar deities, as idealized good objects. It seems that the character of the triumph and vanity connected with the rite of head-hunting may be understood in this manic sense. The head is the trophy that is exhibited by the warrior as a proof of his invincibility and courage;[25] this theme is associated with the maniacality of the triumph and glory which is intimately joined to the psychology of war among primitive peoples as well as to the psychology of war in general.

When primitive man reacts to the death of a member of his own tribe as if it were the result of the hostile magic of another tribe against whom he decides to wage war, we know that he is **reacting, through** a paranoid mechanism, to guilt feelings aroused by the death of his fellow tribesman. Accordingly, we may affirm that the psychic factors determining war among primitive peoples, though intimately connected with the sense of guilt, represent its basic negation.

*More than to guilt feelings, then, war would appear to owe its origin to a basic process of moral alienation.* It would seem that it is not the sense of guilt that produces war, but the paranoid defense against guilt, that is, an unauthentic elaboration of mourning. This discovery seems to us to be very close to Freud's discovery of the deflection of the death instinct, and indeed it has all of its tragic implications.

[24] *Manic process:* from mania, euphoric excitement that is the opposite of depression. The manic process is based mainly on mechanisms of negation of guilt and negation of the loss of the love object.
[25] Davie, op. cit., p. 217.

We have seen that the abolition of war (war understood basically as the outward deflection of the death instinct, in the paranoid elaboration of mourning) exposes man to the risk of self-destruction. Contrary to what is commonly believed, the abolition of war does not at all seem to constitute a dramatic situation because it exposes him who renounces war to the risk of being destroyed by his enemies but, surprisingly, because it exposes him to the risk of self-destruction as an event associated with internal dangers. It is the reinternalization of the bad object, as the reinternalization into the self of the death instincts, that creates the danger of a melancholiac elaboration of mourning.[26]

It may seem surprising to speak of certain experiences of collective life in terms of psychosis or parapsychosis. Our purpose in doing so is mainly to make us aware of the possibility of our alienation in the group, of which we shall have occasion to speak later when we shall speak of the functions of the group as functions of defense against psychotic anxieties. In reference to this it is worth noting that among primitive peoples, an individual can conceal his own madness through the group.

Speaking of the difference between a paranoia in Europe and a paranoid fantasy among primitive peoples, Róheim comes to the conclusion that the latter can be evolved without necessarily breaking with reality.

When a member of an Australian tribe expresses his paranoid fantasy, his delusion may suffice to set in motion

[26] The cited study by Elaine Metais indicates that it is disastrous to abolish war among primitive peoples. However, it appears that this is so because war is the basic institution of primitive peoples; deprived of war, they find themselves deprived of their most important cultural institution. In our society the abolition of war could not have such disastrous effects, since we have at our disposal, independently of war, many cultural institutions which are unknown to primitive peoples.

a blood revenge. The group offers war against a neighboring tribe as a means of resolving his persecutory anxieties. It is as if in offering war, the group offered to the individual a paradoxical but convenient psychotherapy for his madness by translating it into reality.[27]

In its most primitive form, therefore, society is an organization that *resolves psychotic anxieties in terms of reality.* Accordingly, war among primitive peoples allows the individual to hide his private madness by socializing it.

For this reason Róheim strongly opposes Davie's thesis that war is the natural outcome of the struggle for existence, i.e., that it arises from the group's instinct of self-preservation. According to Róheim, the Australian evidence alone completely refutes the theory of primitive warfare as due to the struggle for life. To confirm this, Róheim cites several illustrious ethnologists, among them G. C. Wheeler: "Warfare proper only arises as a result of a blood feud due to the killing of a member of one local group by a member of another local group, nearly always by magical means."[28]

Strehlow—cited by Róheim—gives an explanation of war among the primitive tribes of Australia that is surprisingly close to our theory of war as a paranoid elaboration of mourning: *"The aim of the avenging expedition is to give the inhabitants of another camp the same reason for mourning that they have had."*[29]

On the basis of his own field work among cannibals,

[27] Géza Róheim, "War, Crime and the Covenant," *Journal of Criminal Psychopathology* (1943), p. 4; "Projection and the Blood Feud," ibid. (1943), p. 5; "War and the Blood Feud," ibid. (1943), p. 5; "Crime in Primitive Society," ibid. (1944), p. 5.
[28] G. C. Wheeler, *The Tribe and Intertribal Relations in Australia* (1910), pp. 148–49; cited by Róheim.
[29] C. Strehlow, *Die Aranda und Loritja–Stamme in Ztnadol Australien* (1910), p. 20; cited by Róheim.

Róheim objects to Davie's affirmation that primitive men hunt men as one hunts animals. Róheim says that it is easy to be misled by one's native informants in these matters; they may affirm complete indifference and say they would just as easily eat a man as a pig, yet further inquiry shows that this is mere bravado and that underlying this statement there are the usual complicated mechanisms of anxiety, conflict, and defense. Human beings, according to Róheim, feel remorse even when killing animals, and humans who were not resolving a conflict in themselves when practicing cannibalism would be so primitive that they could not be considered human at all.

An important affirmation of Róheim's—and one that we shall have to return to—is that there is more "inward-turned aggression" in humans than in animals, and that this human prerogative can be explained on the basis of the mother-child dual-unity situation as a specifically human situation.

Also in connection with the dual-unity situation, Róheim suggests that human nature maintains as a fiction what is no longer a reality. Hence the ideas of society as "one body" with individuals as its "members." Through such fictions man tries to re-create the past, that is, the dual-unity situation enjoyed in infancy.

Extending to the group Freud's analogy that whatever is good or pleasurable is the ego and whatever is bad or painful is the non-ego, Róheim sees the psychological motivation for nationalism ("we are good") and for war ("they are bad").

To interpret social facts, Róheim proposes that we first reckon with the mechanisms arising from our infantile experience, and then with the possible "social," i.e., object-related, situations arising out of these mechanisms.

According to Róheim, society weeds out manifestations of the original mechanisms and contents if they are incompatible with reality or reinforces them, if they are usable. War and international relationships, says Róheim, are specifically based on the Oedipal situation: "The father is the first stranger in the infant's life and the stranger is always the father."

## *Reparative tendencies toward the enemy among primitive peoples.*

A proof of the strongly rationalized character of Davie's interpretation of war as the expression of the struggle for existence is the fact that in his book we find no explicit reference to the expiatory rites that follow war, rites which show in a striking manner the sense of guilt that accompanies the phenomenon of war among primitive peoples. Freud was particularly struck by this problem and, as we know, discussed it at length in *Totem and Taboo,* connecting the expiatory and purifying ceremonies which follow the killing of an enemy with the general ambivalence of taboo.

We need not concern ourselves, at this point, with the problem of totemism, much less with the problematic character of the very concept of totemism in modern anthropology, which Lévi-Strauss refers to as "totemic illusion."[30]

The facts that interest us regard the problem of taboo rather than totemism. It is of interest to us to note that the killing of an enemy is followed by the imposition of a series of taboos that are analogous to those observed by a tribe in relation to their own chiefs and deceased members. Frazer discusses these phenomena in the chapter entitled "Taboo and the Perils of the Soul."[31]

Among the rites that follow war and represent an elaboration of the sense of guilt aroused by killing, we may list the above-discussed treatment which captured heads receive at the hands of head-hunters. The purpose of such

[30] Claude Lévi-Strauss, *Totemism* (Boston, 1963).
[31] J. G. Frazer, *The Golden Bough* (New York, 1959).

treatment is to bring about a reconciliation with the killed enemy and to transform the enemy into a friend or into a tutelar deity. To achieve this effect, dances are given, songs are sung in which the dead enemy is mourned, and his forgiveness is implored: "Be not angry because your head is here with us . . . we have offered the sacrifice to appease you. Why were you our enemy? Would it not have been better that we should remain friends?"

The transformation of the enemy into a friend through the rites dedicated to the severed heads brought home from a war expedition is performed with a sort of funerary maternage confirming the previously advanced hypothesis that the dead person is fantasied as a child weaned from mother-life. The heads are treated for months with the greatest kindness and courtesy and are addressed with the most endearing names. The best morsels from meals are put into their mouths and they are repeatedly entreated to hate their former friends and to bestow their love upon their new hosts. Several of the wild tribes of North America mourn for their killed and scalped enemies. Dorsay, cited by Frazer, mentions that the Osage Indians, after having mourned for their own dead, mourned for their foes as if they had been friends. Freud explains the primitive peoples' taboo customs for the treatment of enemies in the following manner: "We see in them manifestations of repentance, of regard for the enemy, and of a bad conscience for having slain him. It seems that the commandment, Thou shalt not slay, which could not be violated without punishment, existed also among these savages, long before any legislation was received from the hands of a god."[32]

[32] S. Freud, *Totem and Taboo*, The Standard Edition of the Complete Psychological Works of Sigmund Freud, translated from the German under the general editorship of James Strachey in collaboration with Anna Freud (London, 1953), Vol. XXI, p. 12.

It is necessary to note that the propitiatory rites and the elaboration of mourning in the cases cited refer mainly to those tribes that are accustomed to carrying home parts of the dead enemy's body in order to preserve them as trophies and amulets. These customs whereby a part of the bad object is preserved and introduced into one's private world must be recognized as a direct confirmation of what Melanie Klein termed the process of internalization of a bad part object for the purpose of controlling persecutory anxieties. It is undeniable, however, that the propitiatory and mourning processes show that among these primitive tribes the vanquished enemy is elaborated also as a love object, as if, the persecutory anxiety having diminished with the killing of the enemy primitively elaborated on the paranoid level, a proper elaboration of mourning became possible.

Through their propitiatory and expiatory rites, some primitive tribes seem to be able, on the psychological level, to master the paranoid position toward the enemy.

This observation is particularly striking if we remember that following both world wars Germany was compelled by the victors to bear the total burden of war guilt. The typically paranoid need to eject from oneself the guilt aroused by the destruction and killing and to project it into the vanquished enemy appears, from the viewpoint of psychological honesty, to be clearly regressive in comparison with the customs of the primitive peoples discussed above.

Indeed primitive peoples seem to be more honest in regard to the guilt needs which man carries in his unconscious and which make him feel war as criminal. In Timor, for instance, the leader of a military expedition cannot return to his house under any circumstances. A special hut is erected for him in which he spends two months engaged in the observance of various rules of purification. During this period, he may not see his wife or touch food with his hands, as though the destruction, which he carries within himself because he has killed a number of his enemies in war, might somehow contaminate his wife or his food.

Analogous customs are observed among the Dayak in Logea, an island off the southeastern extremity of New Guinea. Among the Monumbas in the German New Guinea, a man who has killed an enemy in combat becomes "unclean," the same word being used which is applied to women during menstruation. He must not touch anyone, not even his wife or children; if he did so, they would be afflicted with boils. Beyond its apparent oddity, this situation affords us a glimpse of profound psychological truths which civilized man seems to have forgotten and which Freud connects with the ambivalence toward the enemy.

This fact seems to us of particular importance to the discussion of the problems of war in general and in particular with regard to the problems of nuclear war, to which we shall have to return. The ambivalence toward the enemy thus brings us to a paradox revealed to us by psychoanalysis, namely, that in the unconscious we hate even our friends and love even our enemies.

We have traced the motivations that seem to lie at the basis of the psychological causes of war among primitive peoples to the paranoid elaboration of mourning. We are therefore struck by finding that the rites following the killing of an enemy contain instead an authentic elaboration of mourning carried out with regard to the enemy, as if such an elaboration of mourning which involves the treating of the enemy as a friend were the rite of peaceful life. In other words, some primitive peoples seem to found their peace on their assumption of the responsibility for the enemy's death, as though the death of the enemy aroused in them the same psychic processes and the same feelings of guilt that are usually mobilized by the death of a loved person.

As we shall see later on, the psychological truths contained in the propitiatory rites and in the mourning for the killed enemy could serve as guides for the construction of a pacifist system based on psychoanalytical discoveries.

Furthermore, we shall see that according to Money-Kyrle the splitting between the good and the bad object is less pronounced among primitive peoples than among the more civilized ones. The current nuclear situation leads to the observation that war unites the good and the bad objects in their simultaneous destruction and this gives rise to the need for treating our enemies as sharing the fate of our friends. The road to the realization of this unity is strewn with problems; all the same, such a unity has been achieved before this, in some of the war customs of primitive peoples.

*War myths as a revival of primitive fantasies in modern war.*

At the end of World War II, Marie Bonaparte published a book in which she collected war myths that flourished among various nations during that conflict.[33] Tackling first of all the problem of German mythology, she notes that to the Germans Hitler represented the reincarnation of Siegfried. A postcard, widely distributed in Germany at the time, in fact portrayed Hitler arrayed in Siegfried's shining armor.

In the same manner as Siegfried, from the pieces of his father's sword which had been shattered in the fight with Wotan, reforged Nothung, the invincible sword, Hitler created his army from the remnants of the German

[33] Marie Bonaparte, *Myths of War* (London, 1947).

army, fragmented by the defeat suffered in World War I. As Siegfried had to kill the Dragon that slept on the treasure, the Rhinegold, the Nibelung ring the possession of which confers world power, Hitler had to fight the Jews who were the possessors of gold, i.e., international capital. As Siegfried awakened the sleeping Valkyrie who cried "Hail," Hitler reawakened Germany (*Deutschland erwache!*) and was greeted with "Hail Hitler." As Siegfried broke the lance of Wotan, the father of the gods, so Hitler wanted to break the lance of the fathers-leaders of the world—Churchill, Stalin, Roosevelt. And as Siegfried was finally betrayed by Hagen, Hitler too was betrayed—in the eyes of the defeated Nazis.

This, according to Bonaparte, is the legend of Hitler the hero and savior, created within his own country. Outside of Germany, however, Hitler had become the evil genius, the accomplice of the Devil. Similarly, Napoleon had been idolized by the French but hated as the Corsican ogre by the nations against whom he fought. This is analogous to the belief encountered among primitive peoples that only the gods of their own tribe are good while those of the enemy tribe are bad.

In addition to the mythology connected with the legend of Hitler, Bonaparte studied other curious war myths characterized by the reappearance of mysterious archaic elements: the myth of the body in the car, the myth of the guessed money, the myth of the doctored wine, the myth of the powerless enemy, the myth of the mother's tears, the myths of Britain in peril.

The myth of the body in the car and the myth of the guessed money arise from the same basic magic theme. The myth of the body in the car existed in various versions in various countries during World War II. In its most typical form, this myth is a prediction of Hitler's death and of the end of war, connected with the death of a man who has been called to arms. A mysterious person asks to be given a lift in a car and predicts that before long a man will be found dead in that car, that Hitler will die and that the war will end. Subsequently a man is indeed found dead in the car and this death strengthens the belief in the prediction of Hitler's death and of the end of war. This myth clearly shows that the soldier is both the sacrificer and the victim in the sacrificial rite of war.

The myth of the guessed money, also differently elaborated in different countries, tells the story of a gypsy who is able to guess, usually on a train or a bus, how much money some of the passengers have in their wallets. She is then encouraged by the passengers to predict when Hitler will die and when the war will end. She is promised money (the amounts she was able to guess) should her predictions come true. With regard to both myths, Bonaparte was assured by her sources of the authenticity of the stories.

Bonaparte interprets the story of the body in the car as a sacrificial myth in which the car takes the place of the altar, against the background of the sexual symbolism of the journey in the car. The prophet of death is usually a woman, the body usually that of a man. The whole event is interpreted in the Oedipal key, the man who dies being seen as corresponding to a double of the man who is driving the car and considered to be both the sacrificer and the victim. Bonaparte therefore suggests that the body in the car represents a sort of human sacrifice offered in propitiation to fate; the death of Hitler and the end of war represent the death of the father, while the peace regained stands for the mother.

In the myth of the guessed money, the gypsy's clairvoyance—demonstrated through her having correctly guessed the amount of money carried by the passengers in their wallets—is utilized to predict Hitler's death and rewarded with a promise of money.

On the basis of these myths, peace would appear to be a mother symbol, continuously alienated from the enemy-father. It seems as though the achievement of peace invariably had to be paid for by the sacrifice of the son who would be killed by the enemy-father.

The myth of the doctored wine regards the soldiers' belief—existing in almost every army—that an anaphrodisiac substance is being administered to them in their food or drink in order to render them impotent. This myth was encountered in various armies during World War II and is connected with the fact that at the beginning of that war, many soldiers found themselves temporarily afflicted with impotence. Bonaparte associates this situation, elaborated through persecutory anxieties in relation to the doctored wine or food, with propitiatory continence.

The abstinence from sexual intercourse through impotence, which did in fact occur in soldiers at the outbreak of World War II, constitutes, according to Bonaparte, the revival in our times of the archaic rites of protection of primitive warriors who, before going on a warlike expedition, had to abstain from sexual intercourse. Many primitive peoples believed that if they indulged in sexual intercourse before going to war, they would become weak and suffer defeat at the hands of the enemy.

Bonaparte notes that what is an institutionalized rite among primitive peoples has, in our times, become a neurotic inhibition elaborated in a persecutory manner through the fantasy of being rendered impotent by one's superiors. The phenomenon of the soldiers' impotence is related, according to Bonaparte, to the attitude of sacrificial propitiation found in the previous two myths.

The basic theme of the myths of the powerless enemy is the denial of the dangerousness of the enemy and the belief in one's own omnipotence. A typical version of this myth is the story of the car and the tank. An Englishman (a German in the German version) is traveling in a Rolls-Royce (a Mercedes in the German version) through the Rhineland (England in the German version). Suddenly, at a sharp turn, he sees a column of German tanks (English in the German version) approaching. The car crashes into one of the tanks; the car remains intact while the tank is demolished. The idealization of one's own strength and the negation of the enemy's power become the best manic reassurance against the persecutory anxieties aroused by the dangers of war.

The myth of the mother's tears concerns the effigies of Virgin Mary which, according to certain rumors, shed tears during the last world war, both in real and in symbolic form (the Sainte Odile spring in Alsace and the Holy Virgin of Sartène in Corsica). Bonaparte sees this phenomenon as the shedding of a mother's tears of propitiation for the suffering of her children.

In the myths of the powerless enemy, and of one's own omnipotent army, we find all the distortions of reality that characterize the military vicissitudes of war and are expressed in the belligerent nations' widely divergent reports of their own losses and of the losses of the enemy. Comparing the various bulletins issued in the last world war, we find that each nation's own reported losses were minimal in comparison with the heavy losses ascribed to the enemy. Accordingly, at the outbreak of World War II, the French and English papers spoke of "Hitler's bluff," while the Germans believed that the Western Powers were bluffing.

According to Bonaparte, the castration complex had a part in the genesis of World War II. One of Hitler's capital grievances against the Poles, as reported in his talk with Sir Neville Henderson in August of 1939, was his claim that they had castrated a number of Germans. Bonaparte says she had always felt that the Treaty of Versailles contained four clauses that were particularly threatening to the peace of Europe. One of these, namely the stipulation that Germany alone should bear the total burden of war guilt, seems to fit into the schema of the paranoid elaboration of mourning. But the most serious of these clauses had seemed to Bonaparte to be the establishment of the Polish Corridor and the severance of East Prussia from the German body (the phallic part of Germany?). The Polish Corridor exacerbated the castration complex of a great and virile people, says Bonaparte, and it was because of Germans said to have been castrated by Poles that war broke out in 1939.

The Munich plot, with its attempt on Hitler's life, set in motion the most far-fetched interpretations. The Germans attributed it to the perfidy of Britain and to the British Intelligence Service, while the Allies saw it as staged by Hitler himself in order to revive his declining popularity.

Speaking of women's archaic terror of being violated by the enemy, Bonaparte interprets the women's flight from the enemy as a flight from their own unconscious desires.

In Bonaparte's book the reader will find the documentation of all the distortions of reality that accompanied the military events of the last world war. As it seems, the need to project atrocities onto the enemy is a constant and common characteristic of all wars and all peoples who wish to be able to hate without guilt.

The belief in such extravagant inventions as Petrol Pellets, the "secret weapon" (a mysterious gas with which the Germans would put the English to sleep), the death ray, etc., clearly indicates the reappearance in war myths of the belief in magic. The myth of the English setting the sea on fire (by spreading oil on the sea and setting it on fire), connected with the myth of Britain's ally the sea, of the German attacks repulsed by Britain, of the Germans burned and drowned in their attempt to invade Britain and of Britain's terrifying use of fire as a weapon, are teeming with Oedipal material and primary anxieties. The inaccessibility of Britain protected by the sea appears to have given rise to the myth of the mother who defends her favorite son with all her might and ingenuity against the threats of the bad father.

The myth of the Devil-Jew is connected with the entire, difficult problem of anti-Semitism, which in turn appears to fit into the schema of the internal enemy, and cannot be discussed here in detail. Nevertheless I would like to advance the hypothesis that the same elements that unconsciously participate in the phenomenon of war also participate in the hostility toward minority groups. It is worth noting that anti-Semitism strove to make the Jews bear the responsibility for the wars of 1870, 1914, and 1939, because anti-Semitism seems to contain the moral alienation in pure culture. But one cannot help being struck by reading, in the *Stürmer*, the weekly of Julius Streicher, the inspirator of racist laws, the following three maxims:

1) The Jews are the cause of war
2) To fight a Jew is to fight the Devil
3) The Jews are our calamity

These three maxims, in fact, contain the same basic accusations the world directed at Hitler: of having started the war; of being the devil incarnate; of being the calamity of Europe. The most obvious conclusion that may be drawn from this observation is that the Nazis projected their own badness, or let us say the negative parts of themselves, onto the Jews. That is to say, the projective character of Nazism's concept of the Jews is fully verifiable.

At this point, however, a disquieting question arises. Is this new way of considering Hitler a pure and simple statement of objective reality, or does it also contain projective elements? In other words, in addition to what he really was, may Hitler also be considered the projection of the bad parts of every man? Must we think that our tendency to eject the cause of World War II outside ourselves (that is, into Hitler only) is in fact one of the many modes of paranoid elaboration of mourning? Or must we think that such a radical generalization of the operation of projection mechanisms is absurd and does nothing but engender confusion?

It may be obvious to all of us that anti-Semitism is a projection. But can we say the same about our projections onto Hitler? Of course, Hitler really was the executioner of the Jews. But did not Hitler become Hitler precisely because "without justification" he projected onto the Jews the bad parts of himself just as we now, "with justification," project our own bad parts onto him?

In reference to these disquieting questions, Bonaparte reminds us—and I think with great courage—that "loans are made above all to the rich," meaning that the really evil character of Hitler cannot be used to deny the projective nature of some of our ways of looking at him.

# 3

# THE PSYCHOANALYTIC
# LITERATURE
# ON WAR

In his *Index of Psychoanalytic Writings*, Alexander Grin-stein lists several hundred psychoanalytic writings on war. The majority of these works are concerned with the problem of war neuroses and the study of various individual psychological reactions, both in adults and children, during the last two world wars.

Instead of reviewing a great number of works in a manner necessarily brief, I will limit myself to examining just a few contributions, mainly those dealing with the problem of the unconscious implications in war in general. Accordingly, I shall review rather extensively the contributions I have considered essential as points of reference for a discussion of the problem of war from the psychoanalytic point of view.

We are indebted to Simmel for an important contribution to the study of war neuroses. A military psychiatrist, he has shown us how the "peace ego" is transformed into the "war ego." According to Simmel, the soldier develops a war neurosis (or a serious psychosis) when his ego can no longer face real dangers. The soldier then regresses and directs his aggressiveness against himself or against his superiors.

In the beginning, hate is directed against the enemy, as the bad father; but later on it is the officer who becomes the bad father, who exposes the soldiers to dangers, and who can therefore no longer be considered an acceptable superego. Accordingly, the aggressive tendencies are displaced and from this derives an increase in the rigidity of the internal superego, which in turn leads to a paralyzing sense of guilt that ushers in the war neurosis.

As the atomic situation jeopardizes the functions of survival, it is on the point of making us perceive *the sovereign state as the bad father who no longer guarantees the survival of the citizens.* The danger exists, therefore, that while the citizens perceive the state as a nonacceptable superego, their hostility (unconsciously felt against the state as the bad father) may lead to a paralyzing sense of guilt, which would prevent them from facing realistically the need to alter the relationship between themselves and the state in reference to sovereignty.[1]

*Freud's position in relation to war.*

In addition to *Group Psychology and the Analysis of the Ego*, to which we shall refer in the next chapter dealing with group formation, we shall examine two of Freud's writings on war, namely his *Thoughts for the Times on War and Death* and *Why War?*

In the first of these two works Freud speaks of the disillusionment brought about by war. War forces men to become disillusioned about the value of their civilization, since it leads them to rediscover the barbarity they be-

---

[1] Franco Fornari, *Psicanalisi della Guerra Atomica* (Milan, 1964). We should also like to call attention to the important contributions of J. C. Flügel, *Population, Psychology and Peace* (London, 1947), and *The Moral Paradox of Peace and War* (London, 1943). A. M. Meerloo recalls that during the last world war, Flügel conducted a seminar at Anna Freud's house in London while bombers could be heard flying overhead (A. M. Meerloo, "La psychiatrie face à la guerre et la paix," *Médicine et Hygiène*, XX, p. 610, 1963).

lieved they had overcome. He notes ironically, however, that our impression of war making us fall very low, into barbarity, is in turn an illusion because in reality we have not risen as high as we think; in other words, barbarity is always present in our unconscious.

"In reality our fellow citizens have not sunk as low as we feared, because they had never risen so high as we believed. . . . The individual citizen can with horror convince himself in this war of what would occasionally cross his mind in peacetime—that the state has forbidden to the individual the practice of wrongdoing, not because it wishes to abolish it, but because it desires to monopolize it, like salt and tobacco. . . ."[2]

Freud distinguishes two moralities existing in time of peace. One is based on the supremacy of the erotic impulses over the underlying, ever-present aggressive impulses; the other, on the fear of punishment, of social disapproval, and on external control. Freud considers the latter morality artificial and ultimately hypocritical because it promptly gives way when the external control is removed. It is, however, much more widespread than the genuine morality. War not only removes the control but encourages those tendencies toward cruelty and dishonesty which in peacetime the individual tries to hold in restraint.

Jones relates that Abraham, having read this essay, called Freud's attention to the analogy between the war phenomenon and the totemic feast among primitive peoples; in both cases men join together and are able, collectively, to perform acts forbidden to the individual. The collective action is the necessary condition for the criminal orgy to be carried out with impunity. Freud fully

[2] S. Freud, *Thoughts for the Times on War and Death*, 1953, Standard Edition, Vol. XIV, pp. 279, 285.

agreed with Abraham's thesis and was surprised at not having thought of it himself.

Freud's basic reaction to war seems to originate in the individual reaction, or rather in individual ethics, according to which war is a crime. That Freud's position on war is based on individual ethics (rather than on an objectivistic view which would neutrally consider war a "multi-functional social institution" [Leeds], or *"comme une chose"* of the physical world, extraneous to the subjects experiencing it) is shown by the fact that his observations on war are followed by his now famous thoughts on our attitude toward death. These thoughts in turn end with the motto, *"si vis vitam para mortem,"* which appears to be taken from the meditations of one of the Fathers of the Church.

Freud's attitude toward war could, therefore, be suspected by some of being non-scientific. As far as I am concerned, however, Freud's radical, ethical position on war, together with his open denunciation of the state as the monopolizer of private violence, could constitute the starting point for a study tending to clarify the specific modes of the individual's alienation in the state, by rendering conscious what is unconscious within us.

But in order to gain an understanding of the basic unconscious mechanisms that drive man to war we should perhaps first look at Freud's thesis in *Beyond the Pleasure Principle*, the thesis of the outward deflection of the death instinct. The wars of primitive peoples, which we have fitted into the general schema of the paranoid elaboration of mourning, seem to present tangible evidence, at a collective level, of the process of the outward deflection of the death instinct, which many had relegated to the realm of pure speculation.

The ideas developed by Freud in his correspondence with Einstein in *Why War?* also seem to have been dictated by an ethical inspiration. A large part of this work is in fact dedicated to clarifying the significance of laws. Here explicit reference is made to the death instinct in the definition of the destructive tendencies which drive men to war. Freud then commits the heresy of deriving morality from the death instinct, connecting Nomos with Thanatos. In this manner both war and the moral laws that ought to prevent it are traced to the same source. This gives rise to a position regarding the problem of war and of the human condition in general that is dramatic as well as ambiguous. We know from Jones that Freud remained unsatisfied with his exchange with Einstein, considering it sterile and boring. Why?

Jones also discusses the adolescent Freud's brief, militaristic dreams, tracing them to Freud's relation to his father. He specifically traces them to one incident in which the father appeared cowardly to little Sigmund because he refused to fight an anti-Semite who had knocked his fur cap into the mud. The young Freud's identification with Hannibal (whose father, Hamilcar, forced him to swear an oath of revenge) and with the Napoleonic general Masséna (usually believed to have been a Jew) could open to us the way to the unconscious sources of Freud's attitude toward war, which is connected with his own Oedipal fantasies. During the first few months of World War I, Freud was enthusiastic about it. "He was quite carried away, could not think of any work, and spent his time discussing the events of the day with his brother Alexander." One of his statements, namely that "the fury of the Germans seems a guarantee of victory,"[3] even betrays a certain amount of fanaticism. However, his great euphoria lasted only a few weeks. From Jones's narrative we learn that Freud had

[3] Ernest Jones, *The Life and Work of Sigmund Freud* (New York, 1961), Vol. II, p. 171.

moments of depression during the war; these moments of depression were perhaps elaborated into his condemnation of war. But it is *Beyond the Pleasure Principle* that represents—at least according to those who deem it one of his greatest works—Freud's real, cultural, reparative answer to the profound anguish aroused in him by war.

### Glover's contribution.

Glover's reflections on war mainly concern the role of sadistic and masochistic impulses in armed conflicts.[4] According to him, war provides perhaps the most dramatic piece of evidence that destructive impulses can be *completely divorced from biological aims*. Accordingly, he considers the politico-economic theories of war that see it as the expression of a fight for self-preservation reactionary and obscurantist because, in fact, the real functions of war are destructive. He suggests, therefore, that the task of psychoanalysis with regard to the war phenomenon should be to take an exact measure of the sadomasochistic forces through which it is expressed, tracing them to their unconscious sources and infantile origin.

Glover particularly stresses the fundamental identity between the impulses promoting peace and the impulses giving rise to war, saying that the latter differ from the former only in their end products. Accordingly, Glover connects even pacifism (as a defense) with unconscious sadism.

To the extent in which an attack on a small and defenseless nation mobilizes unconscious fantasies, it easily re-evokes, he says, the infantile fantasies in which the good child and the good mother are victimized by the bad father.

[4] Edward Glover, *War, Sadism and Pacifism* (London, 1946).

Discussing the reason why men "join up" at the outbreak of war, Glover says that it would be easy to attribute their doing so to the herd instinct, but the fact is that if the individual psychic situation were not already well prepared and all the unconscious justifications for war established, the factor of leadership would not of itself prove decisive. The attempt on the part of the man in the street to foist sole responsibility for war on the ruling powers is a piece of unconscious hypocrisy. And the warlike influence of the rulers on their subjects is not due to the herd instinct but to the fact that the rulers are father and mother substitutes. Glover further maintains that the same basic mechanisms that are operative in the cannibalism of primitive tribes are also operative in war; both phenomena are traceable to the unconscious sadism of man.

In comparison with primitive peoples, however, the civilized nation is at a distinct disadvantage, according to Glover, because it has lost the ritualistic control of killing effected by the primitive. This is why our wars are so much more devastating than those of primitive peoples. Because civilized nations rationalize their wars through deceptively objective aims, the unconscious and irrational causes of their wars are more easily obscured. Primitive tribes do not hesitate to declare that they want to make war in order to give their enemies a reason for mourning, while civilized peoples strive to consider their wars justified by objective motives, such as economic interests or the defense of a politico-economic system.

As evidence of the survival in our culture of primitive war rites, Glover cites the case of a certain private—in peacetime a conventional solicitor—who seized every safe opportunity of slipping over the top in order to draw the teeth of dead enemies lying in no man's land. Glover sees a psychic identity between this man's atavistic impulses and the ceremonial war activities of the head-hunters of Borneo. I have personally discovered, in the analysis of a preadolescent girl who had suffered sexual violence that she had dreams in which she saw heads impaled on sticks in front of a house, that is, in the same position as head-hunters display their trophies. I was surprised to find in this case the same significance of a transformation of the enemy object (the sexual aggressor) into a friendly one, which we discussed earlier in reference to head-hunters.

Glover regards war as a manifestation of conflict between human impulses, an attempt to solve some difficulty, some problem, "a mass insanity, if you like, provided you remember that insanity is simply a dramatic attempt to deal with individual conflict, a *curative process* initiated in the hope of preventing disruption, but *ending in hopeless disintegration.*"⁵ A situation of war, says Glover, brings the external world into an internal conflict. This is why he considers the concentration of peace propaganda on ethical or economic arguments, to the neglect of unconscious motivations, a reactionary policy.

Glover notes that masochism contributes considerably to an unconscious readiness to tolerate or even welcome situations of war. And it does so because the acceptance of suffering, in addition to being a primary form of gratification, represents a primitive method of overcoming unconscious guilt.

Since war deeply involves the unconscious conflicts of men, Glover is skeptical about the value of peace propaganda and disarmament, considering the exaggeration of the importance of the latter to be an obstacle to under-

⁵ Glover, op. cit., p. 31.

standing and ultimately to attaining a stable peace organization. The first effective step toward abolishing war, he insists, must be the most complete investigation and understanding of the unconscious motivations in war which he sees as *an epidemic caused by an unknown virus.* One way to begin this investigation, he says, would be to find out how many rulers and diplomats suffer from impotence or are unconsciously afraid of it.[6]

Immediately after the Munich crisis, Glover sent a questionnaire to the practicing members and associates of the British Psycho-analytical Society, asking for information as to reactions to the crisis observed in patients during therapeutic and consulting practice. Despite some difference of opinion among the observers, it was possible to establish that whatever the nature of the ultimate reaction to the crisis, its form and (to a lesser degree) its intensity were due to infantile and for the most part unconscious patterns and conflicts. Nearly all the observers agreed that patients reacted to the countries concerned in the crisis and to the personalities who played a leading part in it (e.g., Chamberlain, Churchill, Hitler, Goebbels, etc.) by treating them as if they were parental imagos. After having considered the problem of the relation between real events and unconscious repercussions, Glover comes to the conclusion that, at present, all we can say with certainty is that "repressed infantile sexual impulses (unconscious fantasies), using the archaic modes of symbolic thinking, are responsible for an ordinarily ineradicable confusion between, on the one hand, adult fighting and its real dangers, and on the other, infantile loving and its dangers both real and unconsciously imagined."[7] According to Glover, it is par-

---

[6] Alex Comfort, *Authority and Delinquency in the Modern State* (London, 1950).
[7] Glover, op. cit., p. 111.

ticularly interesting to note that almost identical changes occur in both normal and pathological groups as the result of a threatening war situation.

Glover summarizes briefly the "trauma" theory and the "conflict" theory of war neuroses, elaborated by Bibring and Kris as a result of experience gained during World War I. The implication of homosexual impulses in war neuroses is traced by Glover to the fact that the original conflicts over unconscious homosexuality are due to conflicts over sadistic and masochistic urges, which are specifically operative in war.

The factors leading to war neuroses are moreover connected, according to Glover, with anything tending to reactivate the individual's unconscious belief that he is not adequately loved, i.e., with anything that reduces his own unconscious "love potential," or with anything that arouses a sense of neglect without, however, affording an outlet for the hostile feelings thereby engendered. These factors presumably play a part in increasing the unconscious war readiness of normal people. Glover's diagnosis of war neuroses as a breakdown closely related to one's feeling of not being loved agrees with Freud's statement regarding the defeat of the Germans in World War I and—in my opinion—could be one of the starting points for an investigation of the problems of the atomic situation with regard to the crisis of war both as defense and attack. The war crisis seems to prevent our confidence in authority (by which we expect to be protected) as well as the possibility of deflecting our aggressiveness onto the enemy. In this manner the war crisis would appear to have produced a kind of *collective war neurosis*, with all the incongruities attending such a situation.

To return to the implication of homosexual conflicts in war and in manifestations of sadomasochism, this introduces the more general topic of the sexual symbolism of weapons, which every psychoanalyst encounters in his day-to-day practice. The problem of the sexual symbolism of weapons seems to confirm the thesis that fantasies of war, closely interwoven with infantile sexual symbols, are to be considered a sort of pandemic phenomenon, an almost daily event, in the preconscious of every man, even in time of peace. Accordingly, we may affirm that the unconscious strata of the human mind in peacetime are no different from what they are in time of war; on the contrary, they seem to be continuously "at war."

Glover sees war neuroses as possibly containing measures of war prevention. For the patient, in fact, war neurosis is a means of bringing his participation in war to an end.

Reflecting on war in general, Glover describes the danger inherent in stressing the importance of concrete political motivations for war. He warns us that "*the more righteous, virtuous, and legitimate our immediate motives appear to us, the less objective we are likely to be about unconscious causes, since the former allow us to rationalize war as motivated by our instinct of self-preservation; we are then inclined to advance the extenuating plea of self-defense on our behalf and to attribute the deeper, unconscious motives to the peculiar mentality of the enemy.*" On the basis of this radical acknowledgment of the unconscious hypocrisy of war, Glover (in contrast, as we shall see, with Money-Kyrle) does not hesitate to affirm that his countrymen, by accepting the naive notion that they were fighting a war to end fascism—and that theirs was "a war to end war"—placed themselves in a reactionary and obscurantist position.

The thesis that war breaks out approximately every thirty years, as a result of conflict between two subsequent generations (boys must grow up before fathers

can send them into battle), is usually connected with
the Cronus complex. In addition, Glover connects the
periodicity of wars with the periodicity of manic-
depressive outbreaks.

War propaganda is interpreted by Glover as *a basic organization for preventing depression in one's own country and for inducing depression in the enemy.*[8] In this
connection I would like to point out that during World
War II, the propaganda of the democracies was psychologically more adequate than that of the Axis Powers
which was based on bringing out the sadistic impulses of
the soldiers rather than on attributing the blame to the
enemy.

Turning to group psychology, Glover sees a similarity
between the wartime behavior of the group and psychotic
experiences, particularly schizophrenia.

Individuals live the group experience through the group
mind which, according to Glover, is a part of the psychic
equipment of each individual. He notes that we may get
a clearer idea of certain regressive aspects of psychic life
by studying the different varieties of group specializa-
tion than by studying the individual because, in the
group, archaic and superstitious systems retain a vitality
which they have to a considerable extent lost in the individual. Accordingly, war is considered a typical archaic
institution that has become extraneous to the mentality
of the individual who can reappropriate it only through
the archaic nature of his group mind.

Glover sees war as *a mental disorder of the group mind.*
But since group mind is a part of the individual psychic
equipment, the treatment of war should involve the
treatment of individuals: "Since war is a mental disorder
of groups and the group-mind is a part of the individual

[8] This formulation of the significance of war propaganda coincides
with my thesis of war as a paranoid elaboration of mourning.

psyche, it seems likely that the principles of treatment applied to individual disorders will also be valid for group disorder."[9] Glover, then, in order to demonstrate the legitimacy of a psychoanalytic investigation of the war phenomenon, traces group psychology to the subject, since the group mind is a part of the individual ego.

Since war, according to Glover, originates in our sadistic impulses, the principal task of the psychoanalytic investigation of war must be to gain a complete understanding of the defense mechanisms whereby we succeed in remaining unaware of our sadistic urges. Although Glover often indicates that the same unconscious factors are operative both in the psychic organization giving rise to war and in that giving rise to peace (the two organizations differing only in their end products), he does not take a neutral stand in regard to the principles and practice of war prevention. His suggestion to organize in all sovereign states the political and social systems of administration existing in countries which have enjoyed long periods of peace and to establish a federal union of sovereign states are no more than good common sense. However, I should like to underline another of his suggestions which, from the psychoanalytic point of view, lends itself to close examination, namely, *"the application to sovereign states of legal measures similar to those employed by these same states to suppress killing amongst individuals."*[10] It is obvious that a proposition of this sort implies the abolition of the sovereignty of the state.

Glover's thoughts on the situation of defensive war may be considered a contribution to the possibility of escaping from "group paranoia." Conceiving the relations between groups at war as mutually sadomasochistic, Glover in effect puts the aggressors and the defenders on

[9] Glover, op. cit., p. 198.
[10] Ibid., p. 196.

the same level. He notes, in fact, that *"the 'attacked'
are sometimes even more determined to win their 'defensive' war than the 'attackers' their aggressive war."*[11]
If we remember Bouthoul's description of the psychotic
transformation brought about by fanaticism as a typical
situation of warlike sadism, we are struck by the realization that the fact that the defenders are justified in defending themselves does not render them any less psychotic than the aggressors; fanaticism is apt to be aroused
in the defenders and the aggressors alike. Money-Kyrle,
as we shall see, gives a different interpretation of the
problem of defense against aggression; however, Glover's
position seems to be scientifically maintainable.

The measures of war prevention proposed by Glover
on the basis of the individual dynamics of instinctual life
are as follows:

1) Reduction of instinctual tension (i.e., sadism); a particular type of humane upbringing of children could contribute toward achieving this goal.
I should like here to mention the question of whether
children should be allowed to play with toy weapons.
The prevalent opinion among psychologists is that such
play performs functions of reassurance against profound
anxieties. Instead what seems to be important in a humane upbringing of children is that parents maintain a
reassuring, humane attitude toward the child. In other
words, war prevention on the pedagogical level would
involve the elimination of the element of domination
from the parents' relation to the child.

2) Inhibition of aggressive tendencies. Human civilization
in its entirety is founded on the change of aim of the aggressive tendencies through inhibition, sublimation, dis-

[11] Glover, op. cit., p. 197.

placement, fusion with Eros, etc. Indeed we must not forget that while the great majority of men achieve, in one way or another, sexual orgasm, only a very small and exceptional minority of criminals or madmen turn to murder as the aggressive equivalent of genital orgasm. War, therefore, seen in terms of a very general dynamics of the dualism of instinctual life, would appear to constitute *a collective destructive orgasm*. (Gaston Bouthoul's conclusions to the effect that the real functions of war are destructive would seem to agree with this description of war.)

*Through war, then, society allows the individuals to experience the destructive orgasm which usually cannot be reached on the individual level.* In this sense war would seem to be closely connected with the individual vicissitudes of privation of the aggressive orgasm. As far as maturation, in the sense of inhibition and transformation of aggressive tendencies is concerned, the individual has in effect already achieved an integral pacifism, in the sense that the great majority of men renounce concrete murder as a normal means of satisfaction of their aggressive tendencies. Those who hope for the individual rejection of war thus fail to realize that the rejection of killing has already taken place on the individual level and that accordingly the entire problem of war is reduced to the individuals' modification of society in relation to the institutions connected with war rather than to the alteration of individuals as such.

On the collective level, therefore, the problem of *the lack of inhibition* of the aggressive impulses, owing to which war-killing is considered normal, seems to be more important than the reduction of instinctual tension. To the extent in which the individual superego is connected with society, which assumes its functions, the problem of war brings into the focal point of the psychoanalytic investigation the problem of the coincidence of the id with the superego, brought about by the war phenomenon through specifically social processes.

To return to the problem of war prevention, as seen by Glover, he maintains that the first step toward a psychoanalytical brand of pacifism must be to discover *"a way to concrete action, especially in the direction of inhibition, and then to concentrate on the nature of the psychic forces involved as well as on the psychic systems through which these forces operate."*[12]

Glover classifies the various measures of war prevention suggested by different schools of pacifism as modes of dealing with instinctual tension. The pacifist systems that mainly affirm the necessity of creating judicial organisms such as international courts of justice, or the necessity for an international federal union (as forcible measures of inhibiting aggression), are considered by Glover less likely to be effective than those pacifist systems which are concerned with techniques of reducing instinctual tension either through displacement of aggression from primary to secondary objects (the "football" cure for war, modeled on the technique of the outraged husband who, having been worsted in argument by his wife, goes out for a walk during which he now and then kicks unoffending stones from his path), or through direct intervention into the vicissitudes of instinctual excitation.

Glover regards the Communist position as having adopted the latter technique, and he accordingly sees Communism as tending to alter human instinctual behavior through modifications of the political structure of society; he sees it as a political system exclusively directed to the restraint of the acquisitive instincts. In the case of the individual, Communism simply inhibits these

[12] Glover, op. cit., p. 203.

instincts; group acquisitiveness, on the other hand, is dealt with by forcibly establishing an identity of social aim in all groups, in other words, by suppressing the classes and their antagonisms. However, Glover accuses the Communist position of *"being quite ignorant of the nature of unconscious love and hate"* and of concentrating exclusively on modifications of group structure, which is interpreted exclusively in terms of acquisitive instincts. From the psychoanalytic point of view, the acquisitive tendencies represent, as Glover points out, impulses that are unconsciously connected with anal modes of object relations.

In my opinion, the insistence of the Communist position on the necessity of producing changes in social structures, for the purpose of altering the modes of the individual's experience in the group, cannot be easily evaded by psychoanalysis. If it is true, as Glover asserts, that the power which the individual has lost, for all practical purposes, through his group relations, is regained through the destructive, or rather heterodestructive activities of the group, the psychoanalytical investigation cannot evade these group functions of taking and again giving back to the individual the power or the possibility to engage in certain aggressive activities. In reality, a capitalistic society offers the individual a greater possibility of expressing his aggressiveness than a socialist society; this in reference to the possibility—or lack of the possibility—of private ownership of the means of production. However, as far as the possibility of expressing one's aggressiveness through war is concerned, there seems to be no difference between capitalistic and socialist states. Moreover, it does not seem possible at the moment to establish a clear-cut difference between the two systems in regard to the domination of the citizens by the process

of industrialization which, whether private or belonging
to the state, is in danger of turning against the citizens
instead of serving them. Psychoanalysis, if able to accept the Marxist thesis of the necessity for change in
social institutions, nevertheless affirms that this necessity
goes far beyond the transformations effected by socialist
regimes. There seems to be a particularly urgent need
to modify the attributes of the sovereign state which, as
Freud put it, "monopolizes" and capitalizes the violence
saved by the individuals. A transformation of this type,
however, seems inconceivable except as a totally new
revolutionary process which would require the reappropriation by the individual of all the violence and guilt
expressed by the war phenomenon.

Examining the state, which in its sovereignty is now
the arbiter of peace and war, Glover explicitly states that
a foreign office can in no sense be considered a peace
organization. In general, the state is the most arid and
loveless of human institutions. This is true of any state;
dictatorships are simply a perversion of this state of
things. Glover recommends that we return to family civilization and give due importance to the professional and
cultural groups through which a nation breathes; he moreover hopes for "a fusion of techniques and organizations
of politics with the techniques and organizations of
science." In his battle against the state, Glover does not
hesitate to propose that we should look for the most
suitable means of curtailing its power as well as for means
of extending the cultural authority of the family, and of
preventing the exploitation of the superstitious reverence
of authority. In addition, he advances the opinion that
"if only one powerful nation could establish an effective
peace organization backed by sound scientific research,
the windfalls it would collect in the form of increased
happiness and health in the community would soon

tempt other countries to follow suit."[13] Examining the peace organizations in effect since the last world war, Glover does not hesitate radically to condemn the principles and practice of the Nuremberg trials. He calls our attention to the fact that the atomic bomb was first evolved and used by a country which had ostentatiously paraded its idealistic desire to put an end to Nazi methods of waging war.

Finally, in his discussion of the problems of the atomic era and its perplexities, Glover seems inclined to optimism: "Humanity cannot perish so long as the obscure phantasies of good and evil that dwell in the unconscious mind maintain their present balance."[14]

## The contribution of Money-Kyrle.

Money-Kyrle extended the theories of Melanie Klein, applying them to war and political life in general; he has written various articles and monographs on these problems.[15]

In his article, "The Development of War," after a brief review of the most common theories of war (which attribute war to the struggle for existence, overpopulation, ambition of rulers or of whole nations, desire for vengeance, fear, etc.), Money-Kyrle recognizes that each of them contains a partial truth, in the sense that each of these factors may serve to inflame the warlike disposition. In his discussion of the contribution of psycho-

[13] Glover, op. cit., p. 223.
[14] Ibid., p. 273.
[15] R. E. Money-Kyrle, "The Development of War," *British Journal of Medical Psychiatry*, 16 (1937); *Psychoanalysis and Politics* (London, 1951); "Some Aspects of Political Ethics from Psychoanalytical Point of View," *International Journal of Psychoanalysis*, 25 (1944); "The Psychology of Propaganda," *British Journal of Medical Psychology*, 19 (1941); "Social Conflict and the Challenge to Psychology," *British Journal of Medical Psychology*, II, 1948.

analysis to the study of war, Money-Kyrle describes three theories of war, the first of which is *the sexual theory* of war. The implication of sexuality in the phenomenon of war is mainly based on the evidence offered by the exploration of the unconscious where the appearance of weapons as phallic symbols is a more or less daily occurrence. The sexual theory applies to war the fundamental discoveries made by psychoanalysts in the area of infantile sexuality.

The second psychoanalytic theory of war is *the Oedipal theory*. The psychoanalytic knowledge of the Oedipus complex permits us to understand the origin of the ties that unite men into a social group. The male child wishes to monopolize his mother and tends, at least unconsciously, to hate and fear his father as his most important rival. Since, however, he also loves his father, his ambivalence toward his father generates an intolerable conflict. From this conflict the boy escapes by a partial inversion. That is, to some extent he exchanges his masculine attitude toward his mother for a feminine attitude toward his father. He becomes a good son.

The partial inversion leaves a permanent impression in the boy. He repeats it in his relation to older boys or teachers at school, and later to his chief, his commanding officer, or his king. It is therefore, among other things, the basis of that loyalty which cements the human group. It is also the basis of the loyalty and co-operation which characterizes human warfare.

The partial inversion, however, explains only the solidarity within the group. The bellicose instinct, as the aggressive impulse that has been directed against the enemy, originates in the fact that the repressed hostility against the father continues to exist in the unconscious, in spite of the partial inversion, and seeks a paternal symbol against which to direct itself. Thus two types of father symbol affect the boy throughout his life: one evokes his loyalty, the other his hate. As a man, his loyalty to his own chief, or to his own group as a personified ideal, will be balanced by his detestation of some other leader, or some other group. And for this reason he will be predisposed to war.

There seems even to be a positive correlation between the amount of veneration for one's own leader or country and the amount of hatred directed against one's enemies. Up to a point, this process of dichotomy seems to increase with civilization. A further result of the splitting of the father image into two figures is that the gods of one people are the devils of another. A Mussolini or a Hitler may be a god in his own country, but these same names have a diabolic ring in the ears of many of their neighbors. Where the dichotomy of the father image takes place within a nation, the result is a tendency to civil rather than foreign war. There is a certain inverse relation between war and revolution: an increase in the probability of one decreases the probability of the other—a fact well understood and exploited by dictators.

The third psychoanalytic theory of war is *the paranoiac theory*. This theory is related to the discoveries made by Melanie Klein in her study of the child's early development. The infant originally regards the mother as the depository of all good things but also, paradoxically, as the depository of all bad things. This happens because the infant does not start life with ready-made concepts of other people; at first his world consists of part objects—breasts, hands, faces, etc. that attract his attention because they are associated with the satisfaction or thwarting of his needs. Moreover, he attributes his own feelings to these objects. So far as he loves them, he feels that they are themselves benevolent; but so far as he is aggressive toward them, he feels them to be malignant. In this state of things the child tends to introject and to project the witches and fairies he has himself created through the autoplastic animation of pleasure and displeasure.

Since the fantasies arising from the vicissitudes of internalization and externalization of fairies and witches deal with illusory entities, the current usage is to define the content of these fantasies in psychotic terms. Accordingly, when at the fantasy level the child is haunted by externalized witches, we speak of persecutory anxieties, since the child feels threatened by an enemy he has himself created. When, again at the fantasy level, one of these enemies is internalized, the child may feel threatened by an internal enemy. Money-Kyrle calls the process through which the child identifies himself with the internalized bad object (the enemy) *the manic process*, since this identification gives the child a rather manic sense of strength. ("If I myself am the bad object of which I was so afraid, I do not have to be afraid of it any longer.") According to Money-Kyrle, this manic process in the child seems to be the prototype of war psychology in the adult.

As an example of the manic process in the child, Money-Kyrle describes the case of a two-year-old boy who developed a very real terror of an imaginary lion, which haunted a certain peculiarly shaped tree stump and appeared to be the embodiment of his own projected aggression. At first he was much too terrified to go near it; but after a time he began to say that he himself was a lion, and then felt quite brave enough to go and roar at the other lion in the tree stump. In other words, he reintrojected, and identified himself with, the frightfulness he had projected.

If we transport this infantile experience to the adult level, and particularly to the level of war psychology, we must observe that nations are not tree stumps incapable of attacking one another. Human groups can and do come into conflict with each other. According to the paranoiac theory of war, these conflicts are transformed into war because real differences are not dealt with by realistic procedures, but rather through distortions of reality and through the assumption of a radically destructive attitude toward the other.

Here I would like to stress that the establishment of a radically destructive relation to the other is one of the most typical aspects of hate and war as a persecutory paranoia. In the experience of love, the existence of the other is indispensable to the self to the point of becoming constitutive of the self. In the experience of hate, the existence of the other is felt as the negation of the existence of the self.

Accordingly, conflicts deteriorate into destructive wars because the threat represented by the other, i.e., by the opponent in a conflict, is perceived as an absolute threat. In this manner, the very fact that the other exists, and so limits our omnipotence, is transformed into a radical threat to our survival, to be countered by nothing short of the destruction of the other, perceived as the destroyer. The transformation of a conflict into a destructive war, then, is brought about not so much by the opponent as a real danger, as by the psychotic distortion of him.

The paranoiac theory of war therefore affirms that wars break out because real difficulties are dealt with in a psychotic manner. What drives man to war would consequently appear to be *not so much his innate aggressiveness, a peculiar wickedness of his, as a sort of innate madness through which he establishes his earliest relations to his environment, that is, to his mother.*

It is relatively easy for political leaders to reactivate

and intensify man's original psychotic disposition. In times of discontent, when collective depressive anxieties are being aroused, people may choose as a leader someone who will protect them from depressive suffering by paranoid maneuvers—an individual, that is, who, though no longer a child, still roars at tree stumps because they still contain imaginary lions.

Turning from the unconscious sources of war to war in primitive communities, Money-Kyrle finds that the primitive man is also haunted by the good and evil spirits into which his ambivalence has split his first concept of his parents. So far as he has introjected this concept, these good and evil presences are felt to be inside him. Primitive man, too, tends to project the good spirits into his own leader, whose power consequently becomes much greater, and to project his bad spirits into strangers who thereby become enemies full of evil magic who must be killed. The killing of enemies, Money-Kyrle believes, "is often an obsessional or ritual act, which, on account of its magical attack on his unconscious bogies, saves the savage from his neurotic fears."[16]

Wars among primitive peoples may have rational motives, such as the defense of or attack on land, pillage, slave raiding, etc., but according to Money-Kyrle there is always some admixture of the irrational motives connected with the unconscious need to negate the bad presences and to firmly establish the good ones.

Discussing the mechanisms underlying one of the commonest causes of primitive warfare, namely, the blood feud, Money-Kyrle quotes from Haddon's book on headhunters the story of Kwoiam, one of the cult heroes in the Torres Straits, who exacted blood vengeance for the death of his mother, whom he himself had killed. To

[16] R. E. Money-Kyrle, "The Development of War," *British Journal of Medical Psychology*, 1937, 16, p. 233.

escape self-reproaches and the vengeance of his deceased relation, the primitive man feels he must at all costs project the bad parts of the self outside himself. This gives rise to what I have called paranoid elaboration of mourning.

Among semicivilized or civilized peoples, according to Money-Kyrle, the motive for war is progressively desexualized, rationalized, and moralized. The conscious sexual motive seems to have completely disappeared; however, a faint echo of the more archaic cause of rivalry seems to linger in the idealism of the soldiers, who often feel they are fighting not only for their king but somehow also for their wives and daughters, and for their country, that is, to protect their motherland from an invasion, which is metaphorically described as rape. Moreover, the enemy is usually accused of committing atrocities on women. The whole symbolism of invading, attacking, or killing, says Money-Kyrle, has in the unconscious the meaning of rape; and each side accuses the other of acts which they have themselves repressed.

The rational motives for war among civilized peoples, as Money-Kyrle points out, are less rational than they seem. The civilized man's desire for power, prestige, and possessions far exceeds his reasonable desire for necessities and comforts. This, as Róheim—quoted by Money-Kyrle—says, is a real puzzle to the comparatively contented Duau Islanders. Money-Kyrle believes a paranoid anxiety to be again the underlying motive. To the Faustlike European, the world presents a perpetual challenge: he cannot stand still but must conquer perpetually, or sink into depression. This drive takes many forms; when it is imperialistic, the usual result is war.

According to Money-Kyrle, nations are paranoiac about each other, each seeing in the defensive measures of its neighbors a sure confirmation of its fears. I should like to stress here that the intricate confusion of psychotic anxieties and real defenses in the form of armaments causes the concrete military measures taken in defense against imaginary threats to acquire the significance of real threats which obscure the psychotic origin of the whole situation.

Money-Kyrle traces conscious dislike of war and pacifism in general to reparative mechanisms arising from infantile depressive anxieties connected with the fear of having destroyed our good objects, that is, from a fantasy of damage done to our private love objects which is confused with the damage done by war. Accordingly, pacifist tendencies arise from the individual's unconscious feeling of responsibility for the damage done by war; and the pacifist feels he must oppose war because he perceives in it the destructive attacks which he would like to launch against his own good maternal imago. But if internal conflicts or external events, or a combination of the two, convince the pacifist of the futility of his desire for peace, he is apt to defend himself against self-accusations by believing that his good objects are injured not by him but by certain bad objects onto which he has projected his aggression. These he is apt to attack in the persons of the real or supposed enemies of peace—armaments firms, capitalists, Communists, autocrats, or foreign nations. From this analysis of pacifism proposed by Money-Kyrle, it would appear that not only war but pacifism as well is open to the danger of a paranoid elaboration of mourning.

In his book *Psychoanalysis and Politics*, he raises the problem of whether an intellectually satisfying alternative can be found to ethical relativism.

At the end of World War II, Money-Kyrle was invited to work at the German Personnel Research Branch (a branch of the Allied Control Commission), the purpose of which was to conduct a social survey and select suitable Germans as leaders in the new democratic Germany. This survey revealed different attitudes to the atrocities of the concentration camps. Some of the Germans interviewed were deeply grieved and acutely conscious of a sense of personal responsibility and guilt; others, however, responded with an anxious denial and a demand that the guilty should be punished. While the former had a sense of guilt which they consciously elaborated into responsibility, the latter defended themselves against responsibility by denying their unconscious guilt and projecting it onto others. Yet these same people who reacted with denial and projection of guilt were at the same time obsessively loyal to whatever authority they served; they were, for this reason, classified by Money-Kyrle as "authoritarian," while those who had a conscious sense of guilt, which they had elaborated into responsibility, were classified as "humanistic."

The authoritarians were not necessarily brutal, but they were not conscious of any sense of moral obligation to resist the brutality of others or of distress at their inability to do so. People of this type did not cling to a particular type of moral code, but rather tended to accept any moral code imposed from above—whether by the Hohenzollerns, by the Weimar Republic, or by Hitler.

Discussing the problem of how unconscious processes influence our political desires, feelings and beliefs, Money-Kyrle raises the following questions:

1) What means are most likely to secure an agreed political end?

2) What is the best political end to pursue?

Proceeding from the premise that only those situations can be scientifically investigated which are susceptible to proof, Money-Kyrle maintains that while we may indeed succeed in scientifically settling the first argument because an opinion about what means is likely to secure a given end expresses a belief, and beliefs must be either true or false, the second problem is practically insoluble because an opinion about the choice of ends to be pursued expresses a desire—and desires can be neither disproved nor proved—the categories of truth and falsehood do not apply to them. The second problem, therefore, cannot be objectively investigated. He further maintains that individuals' political attitudes may be analyzed scientifically and assessed as rational or irrational according to the truth or falsehood of the beliefs that determine their formation.

In his discussion of disturbances of character formation, Money-Kyrle shows their political importance. All disturbances of character formation consist of what is manifest in the operation of defense mechanisms against persecutory and depressive anxieties. And when they also include a denial of depression and of depressive guilt, they involve a distortion in the normal functioning of conscience.

Money-Kyrle describes *three distinct types of disturbed morality.* The first is found in those authoritarians who become inhuman in the pursuit of whatever they feel to be their duty. The second is found in certain hypomanics, in whom the superego seems to have been mastered by the ego. If successful, they become "world historical personalities" and found new moral codes. The third is found in many hypoparanoids, whose sense of guilt is continually projected so that they are sustained by a sense of righteous indignation against the real or imaginary sins of others.

According to Money-Kyrle, Kant is representative of the first type; Napoleon, as described by Dostoevsky's Raskolnikov, of the second; and Hitler, conceived as a perverted Don Quixote, may serve to illustrate the third.

The first type, obsessively bound to authoritarian morality, is a product of an early fantasy of the good mother attacked by the bad father; this type feels himself to be faced by the challenge of St. George but to be in a far weaker position to defy the dragon. In this case, in order to control the persecutory anxiety, the individual tends to submit to the feared object whose bad qualities are henceforth denied. The authoritarian moreover denies the good qualities of the mother who is assaulted by the father, both to avoid the painful feeling of having betrayed her and out of fear of the persecutory father. Thus the authoritarian conscience is the outcome of an unconditional surrender to an inner persecutor.

The morality of the hypomanics, on the other hand, is the outcome of an identification with the persecutory object, by means of which the persecutory object seems to be controlled (as in the case of the child who was afraid of, and identified himself with, the lion). In the hypomanic we also find an unconscious survival of a persecutory concept of the world, uncorrected by testing processes. In addition to this, the hypomanic also denies love. Like Faust, these individuals receive the elation of omnipotence from the devil—persecutory object—but only so long as they desire what the devil—persecutor— wishes. If Faust once allows himself to grieve for Gretchen (that is, he no longer denies love), his demon slave becomes his fearful master. The character of the hypomanics is based on the denial of important truths about themselves. Somewhere in their unconscious the spontaneous feelings of love, pity, grief, and guilt have survived, but until the final collapse, which is equivalent to the manic-depressive swing into the depressive phase, the existence of all these real feelings is denied.

The hypoparanoid is like the authoritarian and the hypomanic in that he has to deal with large quantities of persecutory anxiety. But he defends himself more by projecting his inner persecutors than by surrendering to, or identifying himself with, them.

Turning to the problem of the group in its relation to other groups, Money-Kyrle observes that according to one view of this problem, the intergroup relations must always be ruthlessly competitive (the Darwinian theory applied to group selection), while the opposite view is that the natural state of man—and therefore of the group —is one of universal peace and brotherhood.

Both the optimistic and the pessimistic views of human nature are influenced by unconscious impulses. Those who exalt the aggressive nature of man, says Money-Kyrle, deny their sense of guilt; those who cling to the idealistic view deny the predatory aggression that threatens to disturb their relations with their fellows.

Therefore, when predatory impulses arouse unconscious feelings of guilt, men will tend to deny either the guilt or the impulses in order to defend themselves against unconscious guilt; this, according to Money-Kyrle, results in a prevalence of either egoistic or altruistic impulses. Both the egoistic and the altruistic impulses favor the survival of the species, the former indirectly and the latter directly. It is dangerous to deny either of these two instincts. According to Margaret Mead, both the Mundugumor and the Arapesh are in danger of extinction from the exclusive development, the one of an egoistic trend, the other of an altruistic trend. The first are too self-assertive, the second too inhibited in their egoism to assert themselves at all. The condition of survival of an altruistic group would be that all other groups be as indiscriminately altruistic as itself.

Money-Kyrle maintains that every human being can simultaneously provoke the extremes of love and hate;

and that the distribution, or splitting, of the objects of ambivalence is influenced by cultural factors. Cultural tradition does not create the ambivalence but it can increase it, and it can and does determine who are the neighbors to be loved and who are the strangers to be hated. In developing our capacity for fear, nature seems to have made use of our capacity to hate; we first learn to feel threatened by objects by projecting our hate into them. Cultural selection increases the solidarity of groups, adding the fear of killing neighbors to the other forces of cohesion. It also encourages the hate of enemies in war. Cultural selection does not, however, create the conflict between hate and fear which causes distortions of reality.

The normal individual, according to Money-Kyrle, only distorts his concepts of those parts of the world with which he is unfamiliar. Reality may be distorted either by imagining inexistent dangers or enemies or by denying real dangers. The neurotic person, on the other hand, treats obvious cheats and tricksters as friends in defense against distress aroused by too much suspicion.

Regarding the world of politics as abounding with *per sonified abstractions,* Money-Kyrle places it somewhere between the world of concrete sensory objects and the world of mysticism and religion. The ordinary individual who is realistic enough in his domestic world of concrete objects is very apt to think irrationally as soon as he moves into the political world of personified abstractions. Here his emotional response is often far more relevant to fantasy objects than to the real objects with which they are associated. Here Money-Kyrle cites Jones's observation that analyzed people, including psychoanalysts, differ surprisingly little from unanalyzed people in the use made of their intelligence in such matters as political controversy. Money-Kyrle comments that their political egos can remain, as it were, the seat of an encapsuled illness in otherwise sane and normal personalities. Perhaps the most fundamental source of political distortions is the mechanism of *splitting*,[17] which lies at the basis of the persistent exaggeration of the difference between our own and the other side in every conflict.

Unconscious anxieties tend to produce false identifications. The identification of some group with a bad internal object makes us unduly suspicious of it and makes us attack it unnecessarily in the supposed interests of self-defense. But sometimes the outcome is altogether different: unconscious persecutory anxiety may be evaded by a conscious denial of a real danger. The classical example of such "wishful thinking," according to Money-Kyrle, is the desperate tenacity with which so many people, up to the eve of World War II, and against all evidence, clung to the belief that Hitler would be satisfied with an "honorable" settlement.

A still more surprising outcome of extreme anxiety is *a sudden change of sides*. Our own group is betrayed and the enemy becomes idealized instead. This kind of idealization tends to be particularly exaggerated. The new loyalty has to be limitless because in the unconscious its object is still hated and feared. (The fanaticism of many Nazi converts, including Quisling, was of this type.)

Yet another defense against persecutory anxiety is a cynical or depressive apathy. In the first, we feel that what cannot be defended is not worth defending; in the second, that a hopeless defense is not worth attempting. (Both of these attitudes were common among the opponents of fascism.) Thus the persecutory anxieties

---

[17] *Splitting:* The mechanism of splitting is one of the principal mechanisms of the schizo-paranoid position described by Melanie Klein. The use of this mechanism leads to the formation of good or bad "part" objects, separated from each other in a Manichean manner.

aroused by the identification of other groups with bad objects can either increase aggressiveness against these other groups or diminish resistance against them when they are really hostile and dangerous. Both the excess and the reduction in conscious aggressiveness are irrational in the sense that they are attributable to false identification.

False identifications can also be induced by depressive anxieties. When, for example, an aggressive country launches an unprovoked and brutal war against inoffensive neighbors, our intervention in their defense seems wholly righteous. Indeed we should feel acutely guilty if we did not intervene. But so far as our hate of another group is determined not only by what it is and does, but by a false identification with a bad object which is a split-off aspect of a good one, an unconscious sense of guilt is inevitably aroused.

The defense against the sense of guilt consists in its denial and projection into the enemy, whom we seek to punish for our sins as well as for their own—a motive which is responsible for the change of wars of liberation into wars of vengeance, and in general for all political vindictiveness. Another defense against the sense of guilt is *the pacifist attitude:* our capacity to hate is paralyzed and we become incapable of defending what we love. In this manner the defense against the sense of guilt also plays its part in those sudden surrenders, or changes of sides, as in Nazi converts. Unconscious guilt feelings can be aroused by an actual attack from which we have to defend ourselves, but they are even more apt to be aroused when the actual motives are of little importance. In extreme cases the feelings of guilt are denied through the delusion that we have been attacked.

According to Money-Kyrle, the denial, projection, and sometimes the exaggeration of guilt play an enormous role in all class conflicts.[18] Rival classes thus form distorted pictures of each other through false identifications. Those classes which seem greedily determined either to withhold the good things we want (capitalists), or to take from us the good things we possess (socialists), symbolize the bad parents who "deny us what we most desperately need or demand back from us what we have got from them."[19] But these bad parents are originally split-off aspects of the good ones, and the good objects in dispute are originally parts of the body which cannot change hands without a destructive mutilation. The economic conflicts between capital and labor are liable to arouse great quantities of guilt feelings in both classes involved and can thus either paralyze aggression or enormously increase it. The paralysis of aggression may be seen not only in those periods of history when a dominated group makes no point against intolerable conditions but also when dominant groups become incapable of self-defense.

But perhaps we are more familiar with the second process, that in which the guilt is projected in order to justify and increase aggression. This process seems to lie at the basis both of the nineteenth-century concept of the poor who owe their poverty to sin, and therefore deserve to be left in their condition, and of the Marxist concept of the vampire capitalist.

If the various unconscious processes which produce these distortions were to become more generally understood, according to Money-Kyrle, the distortions themselves would tend to disappear, and group and class re-

[18] See Elliot Jacques's essay on this problem: "Social Systems as a Defense Against Persecutory and Depressive Anxiety," *New Directions in Psycho-Analysis*, edited by Melanie Klein (London, 1955).
[19] R. E. Money-Kyrle, *Psychoanalysis and Politics* (London, 1951), p. 110.

lations would become more rational. In my opinion there is little probability of this, considering Jones's observation mentioned above. In order to become operative, such an understanding of unconscious processes first needs to be fitted into an interhuman relationship. In the analysis of an individual, the insight into the distortions of the ego becomes operative in the transference relationship. But how does it become operative in the group situation? This is a problem to which we will return.

Discussing the group in its relation to the individual, Money-Kyrle asserts that the influence of the state results in the main from the fact that the state is nearly always personified as a parental figure. It is something into which we tend to project our superegos. One consequence of this is that we tend to think of the authority of the state in terms of the nature of our superegos. The state has the same influence on the character of its citizens as parents have on the character of their children.

The child's picture of his parents is partly determined by what he projects into them. An increased authoritarianism in the state produces an increased authoritarianism in the morality (superegos) of the individuals. Conversely, one would expect that an increased humanism in the state would result in an increase in the humanistic tendencies of the citizens. Money-Kyrle mentions the authoritarian movement in Germany and the humanist movement in England as typical examples of how a vicious or a benevolent social spiral can change the nature of a state toward the authoritarian or the humanist end of the scale.

In his analysis of political motives, Money-Kyrle describes the concept of normality as equivalent to rationality; and rationality, from the psychoanalytical point of view, is equivalent to self-knowledge, that is, to our understanding of our own unconscious mind, in order to prevent the distortion of our reality functions by undisclosed unconscious fantasies.

In Money-Kyrle's view, the aim of psychoanalysis is not to make the individual well adapted to the society he lives in. The result of a successful analysis is a rational individual, one who has become free of the influence of the unconscious fantasy world which he was falsely confusing with the world of his perceptions. The analyst need have no idea of what his patient will be like when well. In the same manner, a clear concept of a good state is not a necessary prerequisite to action designed to further its achievement.

Money-Kyrle also observes that the analyst who studies political motives and war must be prepared to become the target of hostilities. In his discussion of persecutory and depressive anxieties as basic factors in the psychopathology of politics, Money-Kyrle first asks himself what disturbances in political thought and feeling each is most likely to produce. Persecutory anxiety seems to begin with the sense of an indefinite and terrifying threat to the self from something inside the self. The most primitive known defense against the internal threat is its projection into the outer world.

We are all familiar with the political paranoia of Hitler, but we are less familiar with the part played by psychotic anxieties in disturbances of political thought in general. When the personified abstractions of parties or ideologies other than our own arouse in us persecutory anxieties, we unconsciously attack them and expect and fear the same treatment in retaliation. Such fears do not create imaginary dangers, but they do exaggerate the dangers that are there. The victory of another party may be justly feared if it is likely to reduce our wages or increase our taxes or put us more in the power of officials we have reason to distrust. Our real fear, however, is in-

creased by paranoid anxieties, owing to which our unconscious sadism is projected into the outer world; thus an
increase in anxiety determines an increase in hate.

This tendency to exaggerate real dangers is not, however, the only defense at our disposal. As we have seen
previously, there is a secondary defense against anxiety:
to avoid the recognition of a replica of our disowned malignity in others, we may deny it in them when it is really
there. Because of these two opposite mechanisms, one
tending to overestimate, the other tending to under-
estimate concrete dangers, it is not easy to preserve a
balanced judgment. Thus the danger of certain political
situations tends to be exaggerated into a veritable nightmare or dismissed as entirely groundless. The underes-
timation of a real danger, which consists in a denial of
the real malignity of a terrifying object, can be complicated by the idealization of the feared object.

The relative indifference to the atomic danger and, at
the same time, the naive belief that nuclear bombs can
put an end to war derive, in my opinion, from a combination of these two mechanisms.

Following his examination of the political effects of the
defense mechanisms against persecutory anxieties, Money-
Kyrle considers the political effects of the defense mechanisms against depressive anxieties. Depressive guilt begins when the child first realizes that he has hated, and
in fantasy destroyed, the object he loves. In this primary
form it is thus a direct result of his ambivalence. But
depressive guilt soon appears in a different situation—
that in which the child feels he has deserted or betrayed
a good object because of his terror of a bad one. If what
we consciously hate is to our unconscious a "mixed"
(i.e., an object perceived as both good and bad) rather
than a wholly evil object, unconscious guilt is aroused if
we destroy it. Conversely, if from fear of it, we refrain

from defying it at all, we shall feel unconscious guilt at having betrayed the good object. But since such feelings are painful to admit, we shall be likely to defend ourselves against admitting them.

Perhaps the most primitive defense against the sense of having destroyed a "mixed" object is to regress to the mechanism of splitting, which splits the mixed object into two: a good and a bad one. Money-Kyrle notes that the mechanism of splitting operates, sometimes for generations, after a successful revolution. Charles I, Louis XVI, Nicholas II may have been both obstinate and weak, but none of them was in himself cruel or evil, and each had qualities that would have made a private citizen liked rather than detested. The killing of them must have aroused a great deal of unconscious guilt; as a defense against it, the mechanism of splitting was reinforced. The dead kings and the regimes associated with them were painted blacker even than they seemed at the time, while the benefits derived from the revolution and the virtues of its leaders were exaggerated. In Money-Kyrle's opinion, even now the historians who value the freedoms won in the French or English revolutions are apt to overstress the benefits of these revolutions as if they were identifying themselves with the successful regicides and had to defend themselves against their sense of guilt.

When we hate another class or nation, in unconscious fantasy we may have already destroyed a parent, a brother, or a sister who is more favored than ourselves. If so, we shall be likely to defend ourselves against unconscious guilt by denying that the class or nation we hate has any good qualities at all and by seeing in them only their predatoriness and greed while we are convinced that we ourselves and our supporters are inspired only by altruistic motives.

Another defense against guilt is to project it. This in part accounts for the excesses that so often characterize the later stages of a successful revolution, when the revolutionaries begin to execute each other. But in fact no revolution is wholly a success. This partial failure brings guilt feelings nearer to the surface and creates a need for scapegoats. The same defense operates after wars in general, when all blame is attributed to the vanquished enemy. This, incidentally, also explains the excesses of a counterrevolution. The loyalists have not been free from unconscious feelings of revolt so that they too have an unconscious load of guilt to project; they vent their rage on the revolutionaries also because they represent the bad aspects of themselves.

The defense by projection of guilt is by no means an occasional phenomenon which follows wars or revolutions: it is institutionalized in our law courts. The criminal has done what good citizens have unconsciously desired to do. The projection of guilt presupposes its denial. Man is by nature a predatory animal, and as he preys for the most part on his own species whom he loves and hates, he is often in situations that inevitably arouse great quantities of guilt.

Again and again nations have chosen that leader who promised best to satisfy their greed and arrogance. But when overtaken by calamity or hardship, they claim that they had always wished to live at peace and treat all nations as brothers. In order to support this myth, the real conditions of our world are denied. In reality, there has never been enough for all, and we must live by competition. If we have enough to eat, it is because someone else has too little; and what luxuries we have could be enjoyed by someone else only if we are deprived of them. Our own desires cannot be met without depriving other people. Because this conclusion is likely to arouse feelings of guilt, it is usually denied, and such a denial is comforting especially for those individuals who have great possessions. This mechanism, according to Money-Kyrle, was used to deny the existence of any real basis for Germany's anxious obsession with the need for *Lebensraum*. Throughout the whole field of economics, civilized man's competitiveness arouses so much unconscious guilt that he has to deny, not only that he is selfish, but also that without some selfishness he could not live comfortably and perhaps could not live at all. What makes the sense of guilt so hard to bear is probably that it is excessive. A patient in analysis behaves as if the money he takes from others, or is taken from him, is a part of the body, the loss of which is a physical mutilation. Because the guilt felt at depriving others of commodities is excessive, there is a stronger need to deny that they have been deprived of anything.

Yet another defense against the guilt feelings aroused at depriving others is to exaggerate their failings, which serves the purpose of denying that any sympathy need be felt for them. In the nineteenth century, the distress produced by the industrial revolution, and the fact that little could be done to lessen it, did disturb the consciences of the prosperous. But because of their impotence in the face of so great a mass poverty, they had to deny their concern, together with their sense of guilt, and persuade themselves that the deprived had brought their sufferings on themselves and were being justly punished for their sins. Consequently, the prosperous vigorously opposed the more rational explanations offered by Malthus (pressure of population) and by Keynes (periodic shortage of purchasing power due to excess of savings over investment).

An element of the same defense appeared, according to Money-Kyrle, in the indignant argument, often heard after World War II, that we should not deprive ourselves to feed the starving Germans because they deserved their fate. In all such cases, the real faults, whether great or small, of other people are exaggerated to justify their deprivation and deny the unconscious guilt aroused in those who rightly or wrongly feel responsible for it. These are all examples of guilt that has its source in the conflict between love and hate.

The same kind of depressive guilt is also aroused by conflicts between love and fear. An example of a situation of this kind was the Munich agreement. At that time, as Money-Kyrle observes, most Englishmen felt a moral obligation to challenge the aggressor, and the failure to do so aroused a great deal of unconscious guilt. As this was very painful, all the familiar defenses were mobilized against it. Some denied that there was any obligation while others admitted it but put all the blame for the desertion on the French allies; others asserted that Czechoslovakia had brought her troubles on herself.

There can also be a direct conflict within the self between two kinds of conscience: one demanding loyalty to something loved and the other, obedience to something feared. Many Germans, under the Third Reich, experienced this conflict in its acutest form. Some, whose superegos were closely identified with the state, felt "morally" compelled to surrender to it but remained conscious of having betrayed another morality. In such cases, a common solution was to apply for a transfer to the front in the hope of getting killed; they felt compelled both to serve the state and to punish themselves for doing so. We may well ask ourselves to what extent such a situation could be considered a common mechanism of war. Others, however, were able to erect defenses against this depressive guilt and became executioners in concentration camps. They provide typical examples of how normal humanist morality can be submerged in any people who surrender their consciences to a church, a party, or a state.

Money-Kyrle observes that it may seem absurd and embarrassingly reminiscent of revivalism to stress so much the importance of an unconscious sense of guilt. Many people believe that guilt was manufactured by religion and that both will disappear together. It would be truer to say that religion was created to relieve a sense of guilt which was already there and which people have always been trying to get rid of. Not only Christianity but also the political philosophy which tends to take its place begins with a myth about guilt. And both myths, while admitting guilt, express the impulse to project it. The myth of the original sin attributes the blame to our first parents. Similarly, Rousseau's myth of primal innocence, which has had and still has an enormous political significance, admits the badness of man as he is but puts the blame on the social environment that nurtured him. It is true that if we had a better society, we should all be better off and have much less cause to feel conscious or unconscious guilt; but it is a fact that the myth serves merely to deny, without diminishing it, the guilt that people, as they are, do feel unconsciously.

Proceeding to investigate the significance of ideologies, Money-Kyrle begins by mentioning certain clinical experiences in which a patient tends to belittle, rather than to conceal, certain beliefs of religious or philosophical nature. The patient has always been aware of these beliefs, but they have seemed to him quite irrelevant to his analysis. His unwillingness to discuss them derives from his fear of their being undermined by analysis. Finally he will admit that they are the mainspring of his life which would be meaningless without them.

Money-Kyrle feels that these beliefs, whether true or

false in themselves, are being used only to deny some truth which is felt to be intolerable. Perhaps the most painful truth anyone is ever called upon to face is that some loved person is dead beyond recall; and it can become intolerable if this loved person was also an object of hostile death wishes. The patient as a child may have been faced with such a situation, for example, by the death of his father. At the time, he may have accepted the event with insensitivity—but only because unconsciously he had succeeded in denying its occurrence. Often, a kind of private myth is built on the foundations of this initial denial of an intolerable truth. It may begin by regressing in unconscious fantasy to the period before the disaster, to a time when it could still have been prevented. Then, instead of feeling responsible for it, the patient will feel responsible for preventing its occurrence. Even his sense of triumph of having ousted and become his father, which is the source of his sense of guilt, is used in the service of an omnipotent fantasy of reparation. For, if he is his father, his father is still alive inside him, and what is more, he has also absorbed the magic power to defeat death by creating life in the external world. All this, when combined with a strong creative impulse, may be expressed in the sense of a vitally important mission.

In Money-Kyrle's opinion, the rise of an ideology is closely associated with the elaboration of mourning, by a private myth of reparation which consists in our identification with the dead person, rendered alive through introjection of his magic qualities. In place of a sense of loss, we then experience an elated certainty of being able to achieve some enormous purpose. In this manner we are able not only to deny the death of the loved person, but actually to feel that it is possible to prevent his destruction by denying the evil impulses to which we at-

tribute his death. Because hate has to be confronted in
its projected rather than its original form, it is to be eliminated not so much from our own heart, where we deny
its presence, as from the entire external world. From
here we may go on to evolve a new system, or to adapt
an old one from religion or philosophy, for the salvation
of mankind.

It can be no accident, says Money-Kyrle, that a decline
in religion has been accompanied by a recrudescence of
political ideologies, each promising a better world. The
sociological theories behind these great expectations may
or may not be true. But those who hold them often feel
that, if they were not true, there would be nothing left
to live for. It is this which makes ideologies potentially
so dangerous. If they were believed with the same degree
of conviction usually accorded to scientific theories, no
great harm could result from trying them out in practice,
and thus ascertaining whether or not they corresponded
to reality. But since they are believed as articles of faith,
they can never be disproved because this would create the
same sort of depressive situation which the ideology is
trying to cure. The result of trying an ideology out in
practice may be a decline, instead of the expected increase,
in general prosperity and happiness, and indeed a whole
series of calamities each more grievous than the last. The
dogmatist will then find ways of explaining away the negative effects of his beliefs: he will argue that these unfor-
tunate effects are due not to defects in his theory or to
the fact that what works in theory does not always work
in practice, but to the malice of his opponents. So all
the hate the dogmatist is trying to eliminate from the
world will well up within him against his opponents.

As the prospect of war in our times is greatly interfered
with by rationalizations and ideological conflicts, Money-
Kyrle's thesis on the origin and function of ideologies

can be useful to us in analyzing the significance of ideological conflicts in relation to the prospect of nuclear war.

One of the probable results of a nuclear war would be the destruction of the very ideologies in the name of which, and for the preservation of which, such a war would be launched; in other words, in the nuclear era war ceases to be an instrument of defense and affirmation of one's ideologies. Since, as we have seen, ideologies take the place of a lost love object, denying its loss, the fact that war can no longer fulfill its traditional functions may give rise to serious depressive anxieties, in the sense that the prospect of being unable to defend our ideologies would bring to the surface those very experiences of mourning which it is the specific task of ideologies to deny.

Thus while the paranoid elaboration of mourning seeks to defend against the destructive tendencies and feelings of guilt for the death of one's love object, by projecting them into another, into the enemy, the elaboration of mourning through ideology makes use above all of the mechanism of denial, that is, the loss of the love object is denied through a manic elaboration of mourning. The dogmatized ideology becomes an omnipresent object, a god on earth, in a manner. The mechanism of negation, as a typical manic defense, leads to specific distortions of reality which may be found to be particularly operative in the assumption contained in the axiom of ideological fanaticism: *Fiat justitia pereat mundus.*

The fact that one's ideological love object (in this case, justice) is imagined as existing, even though the whole world may be destroyed, seems comprehensible only on the basis of the intervention of a strong mechanism of denial of destruction and loss, that is, denial of mourning whereby—in extreme cases—existence is confused with non-existence, and the most forceful affirmation coincides with the most forceful denial.

A further proof is available of the fact that the relation to an ideology (especially if it is an ideology organized into a political movement which represents its concrete expression and has, in a way, the significance of a god on earth) constitutes an experience connected with mourning in the sense of being its denial. This further proof may be had when the interruption of the relation to an ideology, or the relation with the group representing that ideology, arouses anxieties of mourning. In this connection I should like to quote Ignazio Silone's deeply felt words on his leaving the Communist Party: "My leaving the Communist Party was for me a very sad event, an occasion of grave mourning, the mourning for my youth. And I come from a place where mourning is observed longer than elsewhere."[20]

*Some general thoughts on the psychoanalytic literature on war.*

If after this exposition of the thought of Freud, Glover, and Money-Kyrle on war we attempt to grasp the directive that inspires their investigation, we may understand it as a tendency to trace the war phenomenon to the content of the impulses, anxieties, and defenses which psychoanalysis has been discovering in its clinical practice with neurotics, psychotics, and so-called normal people. We may, therefore, understand the significance of the psychoanalytic investigation on war by seeing it in its entirety as an attempt to trace the war phenomenon to the subject, to each subject as such. Thus when Freud speaks of the process of monopolization of violence by the

[20] I. Silone, *Uscita di Sicurezza* (Vallechi, 1965).

state, he opens his discussion with the words: "The *indi-vidual citizen* can with horror convince himself. . . ."[21] In this case it is the contrasting of the morality of the individual citizen and the morality-immorality of war that permits us to see the monopolization of violence by the state as a collective process. Without such an antithesis, war could be—and in fact often has been—calmly described as "a form of communication between nations, evolving from prior political communication and conducive to a different but continuing communication" (Clausewitz). Now it is obvious that for the individual citizen, war will have one meaning if it is presented to him as a form of communication between nations and another if it is explained to him as "a process of alienation of private violence and monopolization of such violence by the state." The road traveled by Freud in order to arrive at this formulation therefore leads through the acknowledgment of one's own private desire for war, as a disposition to experience destructive impulses, which are in turn connected with one's individual infantile history implicated in unconscious parental conflicts.

When war is understood as "a form of communication between nations" it is instead viewed from above and from the outside, without traveling the uneasy road that leads through the subject, or perhaps even through the subject's unconscious with all of its private forces of violence, love, guilt, anxieties, and defenses.

Those who seek to grasp the significance of war without traveling this disquieting road would like to have us believe that their method is scientific since it avoids our personal involvement. Their attitude toward war is supposedly that of impartial observers who can see war as it really is, without distortions due to personal involve-

21 The italics are mine.

ment. Accordingly, they condemn psychoanalysis as non-scientific because its method of investigation is based precisely on personal involvement in the transference and countertransference, and because it claims to derive the significance of group life and war from what it finds in the unconscious of individuals, from the individual's unconscious sadism and masochism (Glover), or from his psychotic distortion of reality (Money-Kyrle).

A good example of how the fear of being non-scientific may affect psychoanalysts themselves is offered us by a symposium on violence and war published in the sixth volume of *Science and Psychoanalysis*, edited by Jules H. Masserman.[22] In his final comments on the symposium, Masserman criticizes the psychoanalytical concepts of aggression, superego, libido, etc., as personified abstractions and says that Anthony Leeds has completely demolished "various ramshackle and labyrinthine slums in our thinking about war." Leeds's paper, entitled "The Functions of War," states in fact that war should be studied in the same manner as any other phenomenon. Leeds strictly avoids any value judgments, which he considers useless in an analysis (except, of course, for implicitly attributing value to his own type of analysis). He regards war as a social institution with specific sociocultural functions which he purports to delineate. Values are seen as culturally important, but their expression is merely *an individual subjective affair* without significance for the study of war. To bring the world of values into the investigation of war, he says, would be to risk straying into a world of psychic visions without relevance to the real events of war. Accordingly, he criticizes the psychological conceptions which see in war the interference of psychotic—therefore dereal—

[22] *Violence and War, with Clinical Studies*, Jules H. Masserman, ed. (New York, 1963).

mechanisms and maintains that war should be recognized on the basis of its specific social functions which have autonomous validity.

Peace alone or war alone would ultimately deprive society of certain functional prerequisites (a thesis which seems to confuse the necessity for the integration of peace and war with the necessity for the integration of Eros and aggression which, however, are—or may be— integrated in peace as well as in war). Leeds sees an orderly continuity in the alternation of the laws of peace with the laws of war, instead of the reversal noted by the majority of the authors.

He defines war as a self-regulating system, with its own feed-back processes, which may be understood without recourse to such psychological notions as conscience, will, etc. War is a system based on adaptations to its own specific requirements.

*The internal adaptive functions of war* are the consolidation of central power, the coalescence of tendencies which are already present in society prior to the outbreak of war, the increased control and co-ordination of the community with a weakening of the opposition, destruction of antiquated functions, revitalization of existing norms and values, technological innovations, and either solution or intensification of old social conflicts. Since these functions of war may produce irreversible social changes, war is regarded as a form of evolution which creates new forms of adaptation.

*The external adaptive functions of war* are intensification of relations between systems, a redefinition in new terms of laws which had been crystallized by peace, tendencies toward the development of a supersystem of government, the creation of no man's lands and of neutral zones, fragmentation of supercommunities, increase in available resources, cultivation of marginal zones, destruction of resources (seen as functionally limiting the continuation of war), reorganization in the distribution of rewards in society, redistribution of values in armies, cultural diffusion, greater mobility of population, genetic redistribution, and greater genetic variety of the human race. The destructiveness of war is considered a part of the self-regulating forces which establishes the limits of change and creates the need for a new equilibrium.

All functions listed above are essentially social, and assertions relating to the motivational states of the individuals are rejected as not only hazardous but in many cases erroneous. The emotional states, as phenomena pertaining to individuals, are without importance for the sociocultural questions and answers expressed in the above-mentioned internal and external functions of war.

Since war is a multifunctional institution, Leeds believes that it would be extremely difficult to find a substitute that would perform all of its functions. Both the sublimation of aggressiveness and a different education of children are regarded as irrelevant. Considering the effect of the nuclear era on the future of war, Leeds feels that the only possibility is *to remain always on the brink of war* without ever actually waging it. By acting as if war were imminent without ever being engaged in war, we would avoid the destructive effects of war, while benefiting from its positive effects. As we can see, Leeds contradicts himself in the end by admitting the destructive functions of war.

As a purely technical reply to the list of the functions of war compiled by Leeds, and remaining in the sociological sphere, we could offer the conclusions of another sociologist about whose contribution we spoke at length in the first chapter: Gaston Bouthoul. Bouthoul's book on war contains all of the facts to which Leeds refers in order to establish the functions of war. In Bouthoul's view, however, these facts, rather than indicating the real functions of war, are merely its concomitant aspects and often superstructures which mask the real destructive functions of war. In order to understand the latter it is often necessary —according to Bouthoul—to have recourse to those psychological or even psychopathological concepts which Leeds calls "distortions."

In reality, when one discusses war avoiding the uneasy road that leads through the subject, he ends by speaking of war as of a fact extraneous to men, while they are its true subjects. I believe that to trace the war phenomenon to the subject through psychoanalysis is, though disquieting, the way to prevent a scientific investigation of war from turning into an abstraction of the type proposed by Leeds. In his attempt to present war as an extrahuman feed-back operation—rather than as an operation of concrete human motivations containing a meaning that is apparent in the evidence of our instinctual drives, our anxieties and defenses—Leeds gives us an exemplary demonstration of how man can use science to defend himself against the uneasiness which each of us is apt to experience when the emotions aroused in us by the thought that we are personally involved in the war phenomenon are not precluded.

Since Leeds speaks of war as a process of evolution that prevents the "ossification" of old social structures, I should like to point out that if in the investigation of war one does not avoid the uncomfortable road through the subject, then war may truly appear to him, *in its current historical conditions, as a gigantic ossified institution which prevents the new human historical prospects from taking the new form sensed as necessary by the individuals as such.* So we may say that Leeds, precisely because he wished to avoid the psychologistic distortions connected (in his opinion), with having recourse to the motivations of individuals in order to explain the phenomenon of war, was induced to describe as an instrument of evolution the most antiquated and ossified institution of human society in our times. This institution, far from being a guarantee of evolution, now threatens to put an end to all forms of it.

# 4

# FORMATION
# AND FUNCTIONS
# OF THE GROUP

The study of the formation and functions of the group is aimed at clarifying the significance of the behavior of the individual as a member of the group, i.e., as a part of a collective unity. Ever since the apologue of Menenius Agrippa, the formation of a group has been described as the formation of a unity consisting of multiple individuals, through the metaphor of *the members uniting to form the body*.

Nevertheless, the coincidence of plurality with unity constitutes the enigma of the group; and this enigma was traced by Freud, in *Group Psychology and the Analysis of the Ego*, to the process of identification.

The comparison with hypnosis, however, which Freud used to explain the suggestive influence of the leader on the group, already affords us a glimpse, beyond the process of introjective identification, of the process of projective identification which the Kleinian school regards as the mechanism of group formation. For the subject, the hypnotist is a sort of sorcerer in possession of *mana*. Thus a relationship would appear to be realized in hypnosis with an externalized inner object by which the subject allows himself to be dominated and reduced in a typical alienating relationship.

The processes of group formation may also be clarified

through the study of initiation rites. Theodor Reik's investigation of initiation rites, referred to in chapter 2, permits us to regard symbolic castration as a rite of group formation. The fact that initiation rites, in addition to being associated with castration, are also directly connected with the interruption of the relationship with the mother, and with the vicissitudes of death and resurrection, induces us to advance the hypothesis that *membership in the group implies a mutilation of a part of the self.*

Róheim's thesis that the social relation takes the place of the relation to the mother (in the sense that man tends to maintain as a fiction that which he cannot preserve as a reality) allows us to say that the individual's experience in the group has a significancé that tends to be illusory. Since it is aimed at denying her loss, the illusory recovery of the lost mother in the group is related to what we have called manic elaboration of mourning. The participation of individuals in a collective experience would seem to rest on a relation to a fantasy presence which constitutes the invisible presence, within the group, of the maternal imago as the illusory body of the group which unites the individuals as its real members.

While in interindividual relations the body of the other forms a concrete basis for our mental representation of him, in the group, the individuals relate to a "mystical body" as a mental presence that is not traceable to the concrete individuals who physically form the group. A fictive body, then, but one that is experienced, in the vicissitudes of belonging to or being excluded from it, through the mobilization of the feelings and anxieties which were originally experienced by the individual in his concrete relation to his mother.

In other words, the fact that the group cannot be traced to the individuals forming it—in addition to deriving

from a *Gestalt* situation (Kurt Lewin)—would appear
to derive from specific fantasy presences.

In the Church, examined by Freud as a typical organized group, the fiction of the body as mystical body
becomes particularly significant, and the initiation rites
of the Church seem to be comprehensible in terms of
ceremonies that translate into ritual form the processes
of *introjective identification*. Baptism, communion, confirmation, extreme unction, and the anointing of the
priests all imply the putting onto, or into, the body of
each individual, a charismatic entity. Through this charismatic entity each member of the group introjects a sacred
entity that appears to be indispensable for the sanctioning of membership in the group and for the continuity,
within the individuals, of the invisible presence of the
common love object which, in the Freudian formulation,
is implied in the constitution of the ego ideal.

The participation of the mechanism of projective identification in group formation becomes particularly evident in the myths of the founding of certain primitive
tribes.

In this connection I should like to cite the myth of
the founding of the Ashanti tribe, connected with the
story of the golden footstool. The establishment of the
golden footstool as the object of identification which uni-
fies the Ashanti tribe goes back to the seventeenth century. The king and queen and all the chiefs were gathered together when the grand priest raised his arms to
the sky in order to invoke the god Onyame. Following
this invocation, Onyame sent his response via a white
cloud, which dispersed to reveal a golden footstool. The
priest announced that the footstool was sent from above
and represented the spirit of the nation. Each of the
chiefs, as well as the king and queen, then cut off a
fingernail and some of their hair, from which the priest

made an ointment for anointing the footstool. After this ritual, the footstool became the object of identification, the common love object from which emanated the life of the Ashanti tribe. In 1900, when the English tried to take this object from the Ashanti, the latter felt that to be deprived of the golden footstool would signify the destruction of the tribe, and they fought desperately to keep their object of identification.[1]

The cited examples of the initiation rites of primitive peoples, and of the Church, and the myth of the founding of the Ashanti tribe show that group formation can be effected through processes of introjective identification (whereby parts of the love object, the charismatic element, are put into each member of the group) or through processes of projective identification (whereby parts of each member of the group are put into the common love object).

These realities of the group concretely and directly reveal those psychic processes that psychoanalysis has gradually and with effort discovered to be the mental processes operative in the formation of the ego and of the primitive object relations, i.e., in the formation of the internal and the external world through the processes of internalization and externalization.

However, if we examine more closely the operations of projective and introjective identification as they are expressed in interindividual relations and in collective relations, we find that there are basic differences. In the child's interindividual relation to the mother, these processes operate in a mutual intercorporal exchange, the concrete reality of which continuously participates and is integrated into the processes of verification of the fantasy emergences in the external world. In the case of

[1] See Encyclopaedia Britannica.

group formation, on the other hand, the processes of introjective and projective identification do not operate on concrete realities, but on reified fictions.

It seems, then, that group formation is brought about through such a mode of declination from the processes of introjective and projective identification that, were a single individual to employ it exclusively, we should have to diagnose a psychotic situation.

It follows that the mode of formation of reality, on the part of the individual as a member of the group, differs from the mode of formation of reality by the subject as such in relation to other subjects and in relation to the world in general as relations subject to reality testing.

However, since the examples we have selected from which to derive the dereal mode of the reality group formation are extreme examples—for both in the Church and among primitive peoples we find a marked interference of magic factors—I think it appropriate, in order to discuss objectively the formation of reality in the group experience, to refer to a typical and universal social phenomenon, namely, the ritual of mourning.

Our investigation of the psychological significance of war among primitive peoples, mainly through a psychoanalytic interpretation of its magico-religious aspects, led us to understand the war phenomenon as fitting into the context of human reactions to mourning and in general as related to human attitudes toward death.

Linguists, as we know, derive the word *homo* from *humus*, and, accordingly, the symbolic name of the human species seems to derive from the funeral rite, the rite of inhumation, as that which distinguishes man from other animal species.

Unamuno tells us that "what distinguishes man from other animals is that man, in one way or another, watches over his dead." Seen in the light of the death instinct and its sadomasochistic meaning, then, human civilization in its entirety appears to be acting as a reaction to death. Thus the Freudian intuitions of *Totem and Taboo* could be remeditated in terms of reaction to mourning. We know that at the basis of mourning, as well as of taboo, lies the fundamental ambivalence of human affective relations. Freud himself noted, in *Totem and Taboo*, that the interpretations proposed by him, which were based on the hypothesis of a real murder of the father of the primal horde by his sons, could have been elaborated starting from the hypothesis of a fantasy of murder only and, therefore, starting from mourning as a purely unconscious event. In other words, we know that for the depressive elaboration of mourning, man need not have really killed the loved person: it is sufficient for him to have experienced hostile fantasies against this person.

The relation established by Freud between mourning and melancholia would thus ultimately appear to contain, both in its significance as an empirical, clinical finding and in its general, theoretical interpretations, the same abundance of psychological meanings as the Oedipus complex.

It is not surprising, therefore, that Kleinism has accorded the empirical and theoretical content of the depressive position the same meaning of a nuclear situation which Freud reserved for the Oedipus complex.

Since war is the industry of death, we deem it particularly useful here to examine the significance of mourning, for mourning, in addition to its private aspects, has a typical social dimension, even among so-called civilized peoples.

Whereas love has a certain character of reserve, with the lovers forming a unity of two which is separate from the relation to society (for it is only in privacy that the real meaning of love can find its full expression), mourning is an eminently social ritual, performed in order to be witnessed by society. The ostentation of mourning in our civilization, though less clamorous than among certain primitive peoples, remains nevertheless an essential social custom.

Alix Strachey[2] has examined the funeral rite as practiced in our culture and considers it a typical example of how our unconscious attitudes find freer and fuller expression through our behavior in social life than in our private behavior. The solemn cortege of mourners, who slowly accompany the body to its last resting place, the coffin under its black pall, and the wearing of black clothes express, according to Strachey, our identification with the dead person.

While love and sexuality have no need for public display (but on the contrary shun the testimony of society), the pain of mourning, as pain for the loss of the loved person, must manifest itself. The mourner must submit to a public funeral rite, and if he does not, guilt feelings usually arise.

According to Strachey, the necessity of showing one's grief to others is due to the fact that death, before it is known as a natural event verified in the external world, is fantasied in the internal world as the result of our hostile impulses against the deceased.

Thus when we find that the primitive seems incapable of experiencing death as an inevitable natural event, this is not due so much to his inability to test reality as to the strivings of his internal world prevailing over the tests of reality made in the external world.

Although civilized man knows death to be a fact of nature, at the time of mourning his whole behavior seems to be conditioned by the belief that death is pro-

[2] Alix Strachey, *The Unconscious Motives of War* (London, 1957).

duced by unconscious destructive fantasies. The ritual of mourning, then, inasmuch as it is aimed at showing to others our love for, or our identification with, the dead person, would appear to have the significance of calling others to bear witness to our innocence in regard to his death. The showing to others of our identification with the deceased thus has the significance of engaging them as witnesses and absolvers: "My being crushed by sorrow, my being dressed in black like the dead person, show to you that I am not the killer, but the killed." Thus to have others verify our innocence becomes more pressing than the purely objective verification of the loved person's death. The socialization of mourning assumes the definite meaning of a control of the depressive and persecutory anxieties which the death of the loved person arouses in the unconscious. The belief in the immortality of the deceased likewise seems to derive from the need for reassurance against such anxieties, since it implies an obvious mechanism of denial of his death and constitutes the best guarantee against the anxieties aroused by the whole destructive reality. "If the loved person is not dead, I have not killed him" (manic elaboration of mourning). However, this mechanism of negation fails to achieve its purpose precisely because of the belief in the survival of the dead in the form of spirits. In reality this belief is intimately connected with the fantasy that the dead person, if he is still alive in the form of a spirit, will be able to return and harm the living. Thus the belief in the immortality of the dead, obtained through the mechanism of negation, fails as a method of reassurance and determines the reappearance of the dead person as a persecutory agent. The reaction to this anxiety is connected on the one hand to tumulation (the placing of a stone upon the dead person so as to prevent his return from the tomb), and on the other, to propitiation of the dead by offerings (food and all other things that serve to promote earthly well-being, among primitive peoples; and in our civilization, prayers and masses serving to promote eternal salvation).

The phenomenology of mourning, therefore, may be regarded as paradigmatic for showing us that dereal contents may enter into the social phenomenon without disturbing the value of the social experience itself.

The significance of social processes as shown by the reassurance functions of mourning thus brings us to the conclusion that the social phenomenon does not make use of reality testing. What seems to constitute the specific aspect of the social experience, therefore, is the use, on the part of the subject, of other subjects as copresent in the collective experience, for purposes of defense against unconscious anxieties. Accordingly, the criterion of validity of social experiences seems to reside in the fact that they are verified by the process of coparticipation rather than by reality testing. It follows that the social phenomenon is often nearly devoid of rational validity, but this does not mean that it has no validity. The social phenomenon disregards the reality problem associated with the verification of the hypotheses of the internal world in the external reality. It seems typical of the social phenomenon to place itself in a mode of experience whose value and validity arise from its being shared by the individuals belonging to a group, i.e., whose criterion of truth is sharing.

If, for example, we face death as a fact of nature; if, that is, we verify the reality of a dead body, that body as a part of the physical world offers us evidences of its existence that we can compare with the evidences gathered by other individuals who also verify that dead body as a part of the external world. In this case, too (as in the social experience), our relation to others participates in our establishment of the objective physical reality, understood as the mere ascertaining of whether someone is dead or alive. But the process of verification here makes use of evidences found in the external world as data which we perceive as realities separate from us and which we verify to be such. In other words, it is a matter of one truth for all men where the perceptual evidences of the external world are concerned, evidences that are neutral and separate from the men experiencing them.

The reality of mourning, however, does not find justification in the external world, but in the internal world. Mourning does not resolve a reality problem, but an internal problem of guilt.

Understood in this sense, the social reality as revealed by the investigation of mourning is to a certain extent analogous to dreams in which we commonly see the residues of the day's waking life (realities of the external world) used to express an internal reality. As in the dream, in mourning as a social experience the problem of whether or not it corresponds to an objective reality does not arise. The dreamer, when dreaming, is usually not concerned about ascertaining whether or not his dream corresponds to reality. It is only when we are awake that the dream appears as an illusory reality. In the same manner it is only when the individual removes himself from the concrete group experience that he can recognize its differential features in comparison with the individual experiences subject to reality testing in an objective sense.

What we call objective reality seems to take shape in an experience of single subjects who place themselves in relation to something separate from themselves as a third element (the world) which must be verified as such, through what is commonly called reality testing.

However, the formation of objects ultimately regards

the subject's private relation to the world. What we call the social experience, on the other hand, acquires its character of truth in the very fact of being shared by the subjects belonging to a group, without the subjects' being able to refer to a third neutral element presenting itself as external reality. That is, the external reality, though it may be shared with other subjects, can be validated in the subjects' private relation to the world: it is then established in a relation to the world of reality as separate and independent from the relations between the subjects. In the same manner as placing itself beyond reality testing is a part of the dream experience, it seems to be a part of the social experience to place itself in a psychic dimension which is beyond reality testing.

But on the other hand, the fact that in the social experience we are not required to carry out reality testing, but only to express our internal human needs, does not mean that the experience is valueless. On the contrary, the social experience seems to be of fundamental importance to man, so much so we may safely assume that to deprive man of it would expose him to the same primary frustrations aroused by the deprivation of dreams.

In contrast with the dream experience, of course, the social experience takes place in waking life. In order to explain the paradox whereby men in waking life undergo an experience which seems to have certain functions analogous to those of the dream activity, it is necessary to presuppose, as Freud did, a particular alteration of the ego, or more accurately, of the functions of the ego delegated to reality testing.

This modification of the individual in the social experience seems to consist in the fact that reality testing (as a system, separate from, and independent of, the interhuman experience, of validating the world) *is replaced by a particularly vigorous validation system gov-*

erned *exclusively by the interhuman relation.* What is shared by a group of men contains an autonomous source of validity which is independent of reality testing in the world of reality. Accordingly, what is called "Group Mind" would appear to function as the validating agency of a certain mode of being human. This mode of being human implies an alteration of the individual ego in the sense that the functions delegated to reality testing are put, as it were, in parentheses (instead of being inhibited, as during sleep). Whereas during sleep the inhibition of the reality functions occurs in a subject who has interrupted all relations with other subjects, the suspension of reality testing which takes place in the social experience occurs in individuals who are awake and whose mutual relations, aimed at sharing the same experience, become the very source of its validity, with no need for other verification.

This seems to be the reason why the social experience, though containing obviously illusory elements, gives a strong and stable impression of reality in comparison with dreams. Not only this, but while the dreamer, on awakening, separates himself from the dream and finds before him a real world where he can concretely satisfy his desires, an individual, wishing to separate himself from the social experience and, so to speak, awake from the strongly cathected social experience, would find himself assailed by an anxiety of exclusion that would have all the characteristics of the child's original fear of separation from the mother.

Accordingly, we might juxtapose the social experience with *the transitional experience* (described by Winnicott), *in which reality is never examined or questioned.* According to Winnicott, the transitional experience is a continuation of the relation to the mother and serves to control the child's feelings of loss and mourning and therefore to avoid depressive anxiety. To deprive man of the social experience would thus have the same anxiety-arousing significance as to deprive the child of the transitional object.

The reference to the transitional experience as a primary infantile experience, with its intimate connection with the fantasy implications of the child's psychic life in the primitive relation to the mother, thus brings us to a reconsideration of the relation between the original dual unity and the pluralistic unity of the group experience: a relation enunciated by Freud himself and investigated, in the frame of ethnological research on primitive peoples, by Géza Róheim.

Mainly on the basis of the oral symbolism encountered in the primitive world of magic, Róheim formulated a theory that "society is a repetition of the original society, of the dual unity of mother and child. Milk, symbolized by blood, is the bond, and oral aggression is the prototype of crime."[3] Parin and Morganthaler also found, in their study of the Dogon, that the group is a mother surrogate.

The fact—which we have emphasized—that the initiation rites constitute the definitive severance of the relationship with the mother, and at the same time the admission to the society of adult males, supports Róheim's opinion that group formation is a mystical attempt to restore the dual unity of mother and child, in a peculiar coincidence of multiplicity with unity, brought about by the group. The group, then, or at least the group as we see it formed in primitive human societies, would appear to arise acting as a sort of symbiotico-narcissistic bond[4]

[3] Géza Róheim, *The Riddle of the Sphinx* (London, 1934).
[4] *Symbiotico-narcissistic:* This expression indicates a particular type of relation in which the other does not exist as an individuated and autonomous object, but only within the limits of a dual unity, a plural unity, or as a mirrored image of the self.

whereby that which is meaningful acquires its meaning in being shared with the other, or others, in a narcissistic pluralism, rather than acquiring it in a relation to something different and separate from the self. In the group experience, the separate from the self tends to be felt as incompatible with the group system of validation and seems to be elaborated in the following sequence: separate therefore different, therefore extraneous, therefore alien, therefore enemy. Through this sequence, the different from the self which in the formation of the ego is inseparable from the awareness of the self becomes in group formation the same thing as a situation of abandonment experienced as an alien persecutory entity.

The fact that the social experience is controlled by a plural unity through a solidarity of the symbiotico-narcissistic type causes the social experience to coincide with itself as a criterion of its own validity, in the sense that it not only does not apply to itself criteria of validation other than itself, but in fact cannot tolerate their application. This kind of autistic[5] situation is connected with the problem of the dimension which—for lack of a better word—may be called psychotic dimension of group life, and which would appear to find its most clamorous realization in the war phenomenon. As the awakening destroys the dream, so the impossibility of the social reality becoming such except by coinciding with itself causes anything that presents itself as "other" to be perceived as a threat to the symbiotico-narcissistic unity.

Since the group's grand illusion is that it re-creates the dual unity of mother and child as an experience of perfect love, the group itself, though assuming many of

---

[5] *Autistic:* from autism, which may be defined as the total incapacity to conceive or establish a relation to another or to identify with another.

its members' realistic functions, ultimately directs them toward illusory ends.

Although illusory at the reality level, it is undeniable that the tasks performed by the group are of formidable importance. Among these tasks, the necessity of controlling depressive and persecutory anxieties, mobilized by the experience of mourning (in turn connected with man's ambivalence toward his original love objects), seems to be one of the fundamental functions of the group, with which the war phenomenon also appears to be connected.

Group epistemology, understood as the formation of reality through a symbiotico-narcissistic validation system—the strange epistemology whereby primitive man feels that he becomes a "real" man when he kills another —seems to find its logical coherence in the war phenomenon.

In fact, to the extent that a symbiotico-narcissistic logical system can avail itself of reality only because it coincides with itself as a criterion of its own validity, that is, only because it contains a sort of autistic truth, any situation that presents itself as "other than the self" is perceived as a threat to, or destruction of, the reality of the self. Thus the killing of the "other than the self" coincides with the affirmation of the reality of the self. Two groups starting a war, even today when war is no longer thought of as the judgment of God, entrust *the process of killing* with the function of deciding which of the two groups is "right," precisely as if the process of rational verification were replaced *by killing as a criterion of truth*, in a massive sadistic transformation of the validation processes. This sadistic transformation would in turn appear to be sustained by a tendency of the ego, the id, and the superego to fuse, which is why the juxtaposition of certain aspects of the social experience with psychotic experiences seems to be justified.

The thesis that psychotic processes interfere with the formation and functions of the group has been advanced in particular by authors of the Kleinian school. Even Glover, however, who certainly cannot be suspected of Kleinism, affirmed, as we have seen, that group life expresses itself through psychotic processes.

A statement of this sort requires qualification. If we refer to ourselves as subjects participating in a group event, it is easy for us to discover that in the same group situation we have integrated and perfectly realistic experiences. Each of us is familiar with his professional group, his political group, etc. The realistic function of the professional group is expressed in its concrete task of communicating technical information, and in our society, as we know, initiation rites have been replaced by schools whose essential purpose is to prepare people for admission to these groups as work groups.

However, apart from what we know about the unconscious examination phobia, even the group life of the professional psychoanalytic group could lend itself as an object of study for the individuation of mechanisms that are not completely realistic.

The problem of the realistic as well as of the dereal functions of the group has been tackled by W. R. Bion in his work on group dynamics.[6]

According to Bion, the psychotherapeutic experience of group psychoanalysis, which today constitutes perhaps the best instrument for the study of group psychology in general, shows that in his contact with the complexities of life in group, the adult resorts, in what may be a massive regression, to mechanisms described by Melanie Klein as typical of the earliest phases of mental life. Bion

[6] W. R. Bion, "Group Dynamics—A Review," in *New Directions in Psycho-Analysis*, edited by Melanie Klein, R. E. Money-Kyrle, and Paula Heimann (London, 1955).

interprets this regression as the result of the difficulties encountered by the adult in establishing contact with the emotional life of the group in which he lives; Bion compares these difficulties to those met by the infant in establishing the relationship with the breast. The belief that a group exists, as distinct from an aggregate of individuals, is itself considered by Bion to be an essential part of this regression.

The conclusion at which Bion arrives, by applying in groups the intuitions developed by present-day psychoanalytic training, is that the group gives evidence of realistic functions, which he calls *work* group functions, together with behavior, often strongly emotionally colored, which suggests that groups are reacting emotionally to one of three basic assumptions. He believes that such basic assumptions are made involuntarily, automatically, and inevitably. The basic assumptions, which are expressed by the individual's experience in the group, are of an essentially dereal character and have the function of cementing the group together.

The first basic assumption is that the group is met in order to be sustained by a leader on whom it depends for nourishment—material and spiritual. Bion calls this state of mind *the dependent group*. The second basic assumption also concerns the purpose for which the group has met. It is the assumption that pairing is taking place; the group in which this assumption is active is therefore called *the pairing group*. It is characterized by an air of hopeful expectation that the pairing of members will result in the production of a Messiah, be it a person, idea, or Utopia. The third basic assumption is that the group has met to fight something or to run away from something. It is prepared to do either indifferently. Bion calls this state of mind the *fight-flight* group. The cementing force of the group is *guilt and depression* in the dependent group, *Messianic hope* in the pairing group, and *fear and hate* in the fight-flight group.

To the work-group functions, Bion attributes organization and structure, i.e., the concrete and realistic aspect of social structures in general, while the basic assumptions offer, according to him, the cementing valency —a term he borrowed from the physicists to express a capacity for instantaneous, involuntary combination of one individual with another for sharing and acting on a basic assumption. The basic assumptions, because of their regressive character, often obstruct or divert work-group functions.

The army and the church examined by Freud in *Group Psychology and the Analysis of the Ego* are seen by Bion as specialized work groups. According to him, the church and the army give concrete expression to, respectively, the dependent group assumption and the fight-flight group assumption. The concrete institutionalization of these assumptions into specialized work groups, budded off the main group of which they form a part, serves the purpose of neutralizing the basic assumptions and of preventing their obstruction of the work-group functions of the main group. Bion recognizes libidinal ties in the pairing group, but maintains that the bonds in the dependent group and the fight-flight group are of a different type and are more aptly described by the term "valency."

To return to the problem of the psychotic nature of certain aspects of the social experience, particularly in reference to the group experience of war, I should like to quote Money-Kyrle's description of a rally Hitler and Goebbels addressed in Nazi Germany.[7] Although both

[7] R. E. Money-Kyrle, "The Psychology of Propaganda," *British Journal of Medical Psychology*, 19 (1941).

speakers repeated the same clichés, the audience did not seem at all annoyed by the repetition. As in Ravel's *Bolero*, the repetition of the theme augmented the emotional effect. Money-Kyrle, an eyewitness to this event, does not hide the fact that it was difficult for him to maintain his own equilibrium. He succeeded, however, in disassociating himself from the crowd and was then able to see the mob audience as a terrifying superindividual:

> The people seemed gradually to lose their individuality and to become fused into a not very intelligent but immensely powerful monster, which was not quite sane and therefore capable of anything. Moreover, it was an elementary monster . . . , with no judgment and only a few, but very violent, passions. Yet there was something mechanical about it too; for it was under the complete control of the figure in the rostrum. He evoked or changed its passions as easily as if they had been notes of some gigantic organ. The tune was very loud, but very simple. As far as I could make out, there were only three, or perhaps four, notes; and both speakers or organists played them in the same order. For ten minutes we heard of the sufferings of Germany in the thirteen or fourteen years since the war. The monster seemed to indulge in an orgy of self-pity. Then for the next ten minutes came the most terrific fulminations against Jews and Social Democrats as the sole authors of these sufferings. Self-pity gave place to hate; and the monster seemed on the point of becoming homicidal. But the note was changed once more; and this time we heard for ten minutes about the growth of the Nazi Party, and how from small beginnings it had now become an overpowering force. The monster became self-conscious of its size and intoxicated by the belief in its own omnipotence.

So far, there was no essential difference between

Goebbels and Hitler. . . . But Hitler ended on a peroration which was absent in Goebbels' speech. This was a passionate appeal to all Germans to unite. The monster became sentimental and far more human than it had been before. But this sentimentality ceased; and in deathly silence, the Commander of the serried ranks of uniformed Nazis cried out a single sentence as a sort of Amen: "Germany must live; even if we must die for her. . . ." The monster was ready, indeed anxious to immolate itself.[8]

According to Money-Kyrle, the success of Hitler's propaganda implies the existence of preformed unconscious fantasies. Nazi propaganda was effective because it had the ability to arouse the fundamental psychotic processes of the group. First, they initiated a typical melancholiac reaction through a description of the sufferings of the German people and mourning their losses. Then, the group was indoctrinated to the paranoid position by the casting of blame upon the Jews and the Social Democrats (paranoid elaboration of mourning). Subsequently, the audience was moved to a position of paranoid megalomania, with boasts of the invincible power of the Nazi Party, in which every member of the group could share. The internal persecutory agent was transformed into an ally who was dangerous only to a common enemy. The devil became the phallic Teutonic god of war, and every listener could feel his force within himself. In such manner a manic response was elicited: a paradise where every wrong would be righted was close at hand—a paradise, of course, which was open only to the faithful Nazi group member.

[8] Money-Kyrle, op. cit., pp. 86–87.

# 5

# PSYCHOANALYTIC
# REFLECTIONS
# ON THE NUCLEAR ERA

*The paradoxes of the nuclear era.*

In *Civilization and Its Discontents* Freud concludes his thoughts on human civilization with the following statement:

> The fateful question for the human species seems to me to be whether and to what extent their cultural development will succeed in mastering the disturbance of their communal life by the human instinct of aggression and self-destruction. It may be that in this respect precisely the present time deserves a special interest. Men have gained control over the forces of nature to such an extent that with their help they would have no difficulty in exterminating one another to the last man. They know this, and hence comes a large part of their current unrest, their unhappiness and their mood of anxiety. And now it is to be expected that the other of the two "Heavenly Powers," eternal Eros, will make an effort to assert himself in the struggle with his equally immortal adversary.[1]

It is undeniable that the conclusion of this work appears to contradict the thesis put forward earlier. The en-

[1] S. Freud, *Civilization and Its Discontents*, The Standard Edition of the Complete Psychological Works of Sigmund Freud, translated from the German under the general editorship of James Strachey in collaboration with Anna Freud (London, 1953), Vol. XXI, p. 145.

tire work, in fact, seems to accuse civilization of having grown at the expense of the instincts and attributes to the sacrifice of the instincts produced in men by civilization. In the concluding observations, however, the origin of the discontent, the restlessness, the unhappiness, and the anxiety is traced to the existence of aggressive and self-destructive instincts which, with the new technical instruments of destruction, could bring us to the extermination of man. Eros now appears mainly as a reparative, rescuing force. All human conflicts and strife are thus traced to the destructive impulse and to its enigmatic and typically human transformation into the sense of guilt.

Freud lucidly considered the possibility of the self-annihilation of mankind long before the discovery of atomic energy, and his thoughts on the subject have for us, in this day and age, a prophetic significance.

In his book *War, Sadism and Pacifism,* Glover concludes his reflections on war with these considerations:

> There has been no change in fighting methods since Cain threw the first stone with intent to kill. Nevertheless, the actual and potential destructiveness of the atomic bomb plays straight into the hands of Unconscious. The most cursory study of dream life and of the phantasies of the insane shows that ideas of world-destruction (more accurately, destruction of what the world symbolizes) are latent in the unconscious mind. And since the atomic bomb is less a weapon of war than a weapon of extermination, it is well adapted to the more bloodthirsty phantasies with which man is secretly preoccupied during phases of acute frustration. Nagasaki destroyed by the magic of science is the nearest man has yet approached to the realization of dreams that even during the safe immobility of sleep are accustomed to develop into

nightmares of anxiety. The first promise of the atomic age is that it can make some of our nightmares come true. The capacity so painfully acquired by normal men to distinguish between sleep, delusion, hallucination and the objective reality of waking life has for the first time in human history been seriously weakened.[2]

In the present catastrophic age, then, we seem to be experiencing as a reality what until now we have always experienced as a nightmare. But since what until now we have experienced as a nightmare was always felt to be "unreal," to face the problems of the nuclear era may involve a crisis of our very capacities adequately to witness the reality in which we live.

We are able to verify as illusory the "absolute" of destruction experienced in a nightmare because, on awakening, we are able to confront the absolute destruction in the nightmare with the relativity of every real destruction. However, from the moment that the real destruction which is contained in the actual and potential destructiveness of nuclear weapons tends to approach an absolute of real destruction, the process of verification tends to become impossible. Not only that, but since in our minds the idea of the destruction of humanity "to the last man" as a possible event coincides with the idea of the suppression of man as a subject capable of witnessing and verifying the destruction, the very fact of thinking of the extermination of man coincides with the impossibility of regarding it as a really verifiable event. In this connection I was told by someone that the idea of a possible nuclear catastrophe where there would be no survivors did not upset him but that the thought of even one man surviving the catastrophe

[2] E. Glover, *War, Sadism and Pacifism* (London, 1946), p. 274.

filled him with anxiety; as though, paradoxically, in order for it to be verified in its drama, the catastrophic situation had to be denied as an absolute situation and relativized through the idea of someone not involved in it.

In order to clarify the logico-emotional implications of this situation, which is the greatest paradox of them all, I shall relate an extract from clinical history. Some years ago I had under psychiatric observation a melancholiac woman who suffered because she felt guilty: She believed that through her fault no more children would be born and that spring would never again arrive. Naturally, this was more than sufficient for a diagnosis of mental illness.

But we can no longer be sure that in the next fifty years spring will follow winter or that children will continue to be born. It was certainly a delusion of guilt for the patient to believe that through her fault no more children would be born and spring would never again arrive. Yet we can no longer be sure of being perfectly sane if, at the thought of a possible catastrophe, we do not somehow feel a certain sense of guilt.

We found the case of the American Major Eatherly, who, as a reconnoiterer, participated in the first atomic bombardment, and the content of his correspondence with Gunther Anders somehow disquieting; a district judge may ask a psychiatrist whether in his opinion a person who feels guilty for having participated in an atomic bombardment is mentally sane or not, while the cited affirmations of Glover induce us to believe that psychiatry is no longer able to resolve these problems with a diagnostic label.[3] Can psychoanalysis accomplish anything more than psychiatry in the face of these problems?

[3] Franco Fornari, *Psicanalisi della Guerra Atomica* (*Psychoanalysis of Nuclear War*), ed. di Comunità, Milan, 1964.

Is it reasonable to involve psychoanalysis in these problems? Do not these problems fall within the natural competence of politicians, as Freud said in a letter to Einstein? It would certainly seem so. But if we reflect for a moment, we cannot but agree with Gunther Anders that it is absurd to speak of natural competence in relation to the problem of the destruction of humanity.

Nevertheless, let us return to problems within our competence, namely, the melancholiac patient. Psychoanalysis, as we have seen, traces the war phenomenon to the subject and, specifically, to the subject's unconscious. In tracing my patient's melancholia to unconscious evidence, I was able to trace the contents of her delusion to unconscious fantasies of destructive attacks against her mother; the spring that would never again arrive pointed to the symbol of the mother (earth) robbed of all her children, in a series of sadistic fantasies of jealousy which were experienced by the patient when she was three and her mother was expecting another child. The patient's catastrophic delusion of guilt was thus traceable to real destructive attacks which aroused a strong sense of guilt, attacks implying the patient's wish that her mother have no more children.

The catastrophic situation expressed by the delusion of guilt and ruin (in which we could perceive something that could be juxtaposed with the real pantoclastic prospect connected with a possible nuclear catastrophe) was not, then, at all derived from the historical situation in which we live. Our patient derived the occurrence of a planetary catastrophe not from history but from unconscious fantasies of sadistic attacks against her mother which aroused intense guilt feelings.

Thus we find ourselves confronted with an unforeseen situation, leading to the following hypothesis: *In order to*

*be able to perceive the catastrophic situation as a real
historical situation, each of us must somehow associate
himself with an illusory catastrophic situation relating to
our sadistic attacks against our love object.* Does it, then,
become possible to feel guilty for the possible destruction
of mankind only inasmuch as each of us sees the destruction of humanity as symbolizing the destruction which in
our unconscious fantasies we have wrought on our love
object? This is exactly the situation that Melanie Klein
has shown to be central to the fantasy elaboration of the
infantile depressive position. However, since the infantile
depression has a purely fantastic and therefore dereal
character, it would appear to follow that the possibility of
facing realistically the problems of the catastrophic age
involves *treating as an instrument of verifying reality
something which we are accustomed to consider a psychotic process.*

What we are accustomed to call madness may, then,
become an instrument of verifying reality. So the possibility exists that the melancholiac patient, though in-
sane, was in effect closer to the catastrophic reality of
our times than we who, while apparently undisturbed
(as if such a prospect did not exist), could be the un-
suspecting victims of a collective delusion of negation of
reality.

Paradoxical as it may seem, the conscious elaboration
into a sense of guilt and responsibility of the fantasy contents of the infantile depressive position served to Money-
Kyrle as the basis for judgment in assessing the normality or abnormality of the Germans' reactions to the
atrocities committed in concentration camps. It was a
question of whether or not they felt guilty and personally
responsible for a collective crime. In the case of the pantoclastic prospect, to feel guilty and personally responsible

for the possible destruction of humanity would thus seem to correspond to the humanistic type of reaction that Money-Kyrle defined as normal.

## *The original emergence of the enemy in the infant and in the group. War and guilt.*

Taking as my starting point the conclusions we have reached in our investigation of war among primitive peoples and in our review of the psychoanalytic literature on war, particularly with regard to the Kleinian theory of war, I should now like to develop some thoughts on the significance of the anxieties and defenses aroused by nuclear war, in relation to the schizo-paranoid[4] and depressive anxieties and defenses discovered by Melanie Klein in her study of early psychic development.

The stranger anxiety of the infant in its eighth month of life, described by Spitz,[5] may be regarded as the original emergence of the other as enemy. Spitz, as we know, interpreted the eighth-month stranger anxiety as a result of the infant's ability to recognize that the stranger is not the mother. Spitz sees the stranger anxiety as connected with the realization that the mother is absent. Although this interpretation of the eighth-month stranger anxiety appears to be valid, the fact that the child attempts optically to avoid the stranger is an indication that the stranger is sensed as a bad presence which the child tries to eliminate as such. Because the enemy first emerges in the child's stranger anxiety, without the child's ever having experienced an attack from the part of the stranger, the original establishment of the other as enemy is comprehensible only in terms of ex-

[4] *Schizo-paranoid anxiety:* The principal content of this anxiety is a relation to a bad persecutory object which we fear may annihilate us and from which we try to defend ourselves.
[5] R. Spitz, *The First Year of Life* (New York, 1965).

ternalization onto the stranger of a bad internal object, that is to say, in terms of a psychotic process.

If we now compare the infant's eighth-month stranger anxiety with the way in which an alien tribe becomes an enemy tribe among primitive peoples, we may say that in the two cases the enemy emerges illusorily in analogous circumstances. The death of a member of one's own tribe, as the loss of an ambivalently loved object, activates the projection of a bad presence onto the alien tribe, in the same manner as the mother's absence, as a loss and a mourning, activates in the child the projection of a bad presence onto the stranger. That is to say, both situations may be understood as paranoid elaborations of mourning. The lion-tree-stump phobia, cited by Money-Kyrle, also fits into the same schema of the originally illusory emergence of the enemy (the father) at a more advanced level of fantasy interaction with the external world. The child's subsequent identification with the lion-father offers us the schema of the manic elaboration of mourning, which participates in the development of war as an attack against the enemy as a persecutory, previously externalized object.

The central schema of war seems to be constituted by a particular fantasy elaboration of the world of absence, in the context of the experiences relating to the loss of the loved object, a loss that is perceived as brought about by the bad self (depressive position). However, instead of being elaborated into a reparative restoration of the loved object on the part of the subject who destroyed it (more accurately, destroyed it in fantasy), the depressive position becomes paranoid and manic through what we have called paranoid elaboration and manic elaboration of mourning. War, especially among primitive peoples, would seem to break out not so much because one feels threatened by the enemy as a force persecutory of the self as because of the fact that the enemy is experienced as the force that destroys our love object. *This is why men see war as a duty and why it is considered one of the basic human values.* Those who make war are not driven by a hate need, but by a love need. Moreover, they feel they must accept the need for self-sacrifice so that their love objects might live.

The fact that men see war as a duty toward their love object has been, I think, neglected even in Kleinian literature. The problem (if there is one) is to disclose the ambiguous character of war as an experience of love, for it is based on the alienation of the bad parts of the self which are projected onto the enemy, who is consequently experienced as the destroyer of one's love object.

The paradox on the basis of which the instinct of self-preservation becomes inoperative in war—so that men no longer seem to care about death but, on the contrary, accept it as an essential part of the game—seems to find its explanation in the fact that in war the instinct of self-preservation does not function on the individual level but rather on the level of the collective love object. Thus the essential function of war is the preservation of the common love object, and the reason why men see war not as a collective armed aggression but as a duty to risk death and to kill, to become simultaneously hunters and prey, sacrificers and victims, is that what is at stake in war is not so much the safety of the individual as the safety of the collective love object.

The story of the Ashanti, referred to in chapter 4, can be particularly demonstrative in this case. As long as they maintained possession of the golden footstool, the Ashanti were able to accept colonization by the British, inasmuch as, at the reality level, their primitive arms could accomplish little or nothing against the superior military power of the whites. In psychoanalytic terms, it can be supposed that in the unconscious this inequality of weapons could be symbolically fantasied as the inequality of power between father and child. But when the Ashanti saw themselves deprived of the golden footstool (the love object—soul of the group), they threw themselves into a hopeless war because they felt that they could not survive the loss of their love object.

Although the sophisticated Westerner may smile at the behavior of the Ashanti, we psychoanalysts know how to understand the psychological and human truth of the golden footstool, regarding it as the occurrence on the group level of what is, on the individual level, a formative and specifically human event, namely, that the availability of a primary love object as constitutive of the ego through the process of identification is necessary for the formation of the human ego.

If we now compare these considerations on the significance of love in the wars of primitive peoples with the psychological aspects of war among the so-called civilized nations, we note that in the latter case the illusory functions of war are not at all as readily discernible as in the former. Perhaps this is because our golden footstools have become less concrete, less tangible; they are more rationalized and obscured by the concrete organizations assumed by our civilized life.

However, if we remember Hitler's and Goebbels' speeches and Money-Kyrle's analysis thereof, we must admit that it is not too difficult to discern in them, as a sort of watermark, fantasies of mourning for Mother Germany, derived from the economic crisis and the suffering which this crisis brought upon the German people; fantasies pertaining to the paranoid elaboration of mourning, derived from the fact that a few Jews or Social Democrats had turned the economic crisis to their advantage; fantasies of manic omnipotence, derived from the actual swelling of the ranks of the Nazi Party; with all of this transposed into the fantasy of the sacredness of sacrifice through the acceptance of war as the essential and only instrument for preserving the love object destroyed by the enemy: "Germany must live even if we must die for her."

Although traceable through psychoanalytic investigation, however, the human themes lying at the root of war, among primitive peoples as well as among civilized nations, can no longer be found in pure culture among the latter; they appear to be closely intermingled with elements of the economic and political realities. On the basis of these realities we may institute differential investigations and compare, for example, a war of liberation with Hitler's war. In the case of a colonial war of liberation, the paranoid elaboration of mourning, ever present, matches the observation of reality, for colonists in reality destroy the colonized people's cultural values which constitute their love objects. In other words, the colonists create a concrete historical reality which coincides with the fantasy event of paranoid elaboration of mourning. In Hitler's case, however, reality testing indicates that the economic crisis, as a real occurrence, was not necessarily conducive to paranoid elaborations.

On the other hand, however, the fact that the Treaty of Versailles forced the Germans to bear the whole burden of war guilt (as was again the case at the Nuremberg trials after World War II) reveals a paranoid elaboration of mourning on the part of the victorious allies and is, according to our interpretation of it, equivalent to a declaration of war made by the victorious allies to the vanquished enemy.

Since the sacrifices of a nation at war also have the function of constituting a defense-reparation with regard to guilt feelings, the fact that the vanquished nation is accused by the victors of being the sole guilty party signifies that the victors wish to arouse in the vanquished enemy the authentic process of mourning (whereby one feels guilty of the destruction of his love object) which the victors themselves are incapable of elaborating; as though, paradoxically, the vanquished ought to be morally superior to the victors. On the ethical level, or at least on the level of individual ethics, the demand that the vanquished nation bear the whole burden of war guilt is morally more ambiguous than war itself. The Nuremberg trials have, on the psychological level, the same significance of cruelty toward the weak (the vanquished) which lies at the root of the sadism in concentration camps. It is easy to understand, therefore, why Glover so strongly disapproved of the Nuremberg trials. I would only add that to attribute war guilt exclusively to the vanquished people implies a form of moral sadism, while in concentration camps we find sadism *tout court*.

We might feel here that the part of us which approved of the Nuremberg trials as just does not find it easy to live with the part of us which discovers them as also unjust. We can make a negative statement about the Nuremberg trials, taking as our starting point the individual's modes of dealing with the problems of guilt and responsibility. Thus our analysis leads us to see certain meanings of group life as valid on the individual level but not valid on the collective level. We become aware within ourselves of a sort of conflict between individual ethics and group ethics; a conflict which Freud intuited as central to war neuroses. The position which we have been taking would thus appear to reveal an unresolved conflict that awaits solution.

As a psychoanalyst, I am convinced that any investigation of a collective experience that does not take the road through the subject is misleading. On the other hand, to investigate collective phenomena from outside of themselves may be equally misleading. The difficulties arising from these two opposite requirements appear to be insurmountable.

## The war crisis.

Seen as a system of maneuvers concerning the preservation of the love object through the concrete projection of the cause of its destruction into the enemy, war appears to be—if we overlook its dishonesty—an admirable institution from the psychological point of view. War permits one, especially in the case of victory, to face and resolve at one stroke both of the basic psychotic anxieties: the depressive anxiety and the paranoid anxiety, with which are connected the most intensely painful emotions man can feel with regard to self-preservation and with regard to the preservation of his love object. Although a maneuver of this sort entails an enormous amount of sacrifice, it seems that men have always accepted these sacrifices cheerfully: a sign that the game is worth the candle. In our day, however, war as nuclear war is on the verge of losing the capacity to perform its functions; this is a new and unexpected fact of which we are becoming increasingly aware. In the nuclear era, war no longer allows one to live the paranoid delusion that by killing the enemy into whom one has projected the cause of the love object's destruction, one is preserving the love object. War, then, has entered a state of crisis, as has been affirmed by, among others, Toynbee, an authority on history. This new fact, in my opinion, merits special investigation because, in addition to involving the paradoxes of the atomic era which we have discussed, it is the specific crossroad of individual psychology and group psychology.

If we accept the thesis that war is in a state of crisis with regard to its function of resolving the basic problems of individuals in group life, the individuals themselves, at the moment they become aware of the fact that a basic function of the group has entered a state of crisis, simultaneously become aware of themselves as individuals abandoned by the group. We may assume that if so fundamental an institution of group life as war is in crisis, group life itself is radically involved in this crisis, for group life, deprived of one of its basic institutions, might no longer be able to fulfill its basic functions. In the concrete event of war, when the leader dies, that is, when the group's common object of identification is beyond preservation, panic arises. Freud's discovery that the group disintegrates, when the common object of love or identification is lost, indirectly proves that group life is unthinkable without a love object as the object of common identification. This would appear to correspond to what Durkheim called *the anomie*[6] *of the group.* Freud's discovery further authorizes us to think that from the moment that the war institution—as nuclear war—has lost its function of guaranteeing to the individuals in a group the preservation of their love object, it places the individuals in the group into a situation where each man must fend for himself. The war crisis therefore seems to imply a reversion to the individual of the functions of survival, as a relative desocialization at the moment when the process of socialization, or more accurately, the process of warlike socialization, reveals itself as the very cause of the destruction of the group's common object of love and identification.

The first result of the war crisis seems to be a thrust toward desocialization. Desocialization means that the

[6] *Anomie:* a condition of society characterized by the relative absence of laws or moral standards.

subject withdraws the contract and reappropriates his sovereignty alienated in the sovereignty of the state. The latter is closely connected with the militarized organization of the group.

Before we discuss this process of relative desocialization which, as we have seen, Glover proposed as desirable in the form of a weakening of the ties between the individual and the state through the return to private love objects, that is to say, through the rebirth of familial culture, I think it is necessary for me to explain what I mean by the phrase "the war crisis" in psychological terms.

I should define the war crisis as that situation in which it is no longer possible to destroy the enemy object without involving the love object in the destruction. Through the force of man's destructive anxiety, then, the enemy object and the love object, brought together by an identical fate of destruction, tend to become fused with each other. That is, in the place of two distinct, antithetical objects (the enemy, the friend), a situation tends to emerge which is comparable to a "mixed object."

Historically, this condition has been brought about through a technical process, namely, through the discovery of nuclear weapons. We know that nuclear war devices could be constructed so that even if the enemy were totally annihilated by a surprise attack, the increased radioactivity in the atmosphere could serve to trigger automatically (without human intervention) the launching of nuclear weapons in the attacked country, which would, in turn, destroy the aggressor country. If this possibility were to become a fact, primitive man's belief that the dead are to be feared because they wish to take revenge on the living would cease to be a purely magic belief and would become a concrete reality that would, however, no longer be magically propitiable through war as a paranoid reaction to mourning. This is another confirmation of Glover's intuition that the nuclear age threatens seriously to weaken—or even destroy—man's capacity to distinguish clearly between delusion and reality.

If, from this historical and politico-military reality of human groups in the nuclear age, we pass on to the individual, or rather, to the individual's inner world, we are struck by the realization that the war crisis (i.e., the fact *that it is no longer possible to destroy the enemy object without simultaneously involving the love object in the destruction*) is something that the individual as such carries within himself as a fact constitutive of man as such.

I am referring here to the psychic events described by Melanie Klein in connection with the transition from the part-object stage to the whole-object stage,[7] a transition intimately connected with the emergence of the infantile depressive position. As we know, the increased internal integration of the original good and bad fantasy presences, associated with the maturation of the child's capacity for perceptual integration of the mother into one real object, leads the child to the formation of the whole object. The child is thus exposed to the anxiety of feeling that his attacks against the mother-witch now also involve the mother-good fairy. The child's depressive anxiety arises from the fact that he now experiences the mother as a "mixed object," for the two fantasy images of the mother, one good and the other bad, are perceived as incorporated in the same mother as a whole object. Accordingly, the experiences of the depressive position in their entirety may ultimately be traced to the simultaneity of love and hate toward the same object and to the intimate feeling that it is no longer possible to destroy the mother as a

---

[7] *Part object: see* splitting.
*Whole object:* a synonym for "mixed object" which contains integrated good and bad parts.

bad fantasy entity without simultaneously involving the love object in the destruction.

The war crisis in the nuclear age would thus appear to correspond to a historical depressive position whose significance, though new to group life, contains a dramatic reality that man, on the individual level, carries within himself. We could say that the war crisis contains the premises on the basis of which the history of group relations, which has always realized itself through relations of the part-object type, finds itself propelled to elaborate the same anxieties that the subject experiences in the transition from part-object relations to whole-object relations.

Is it possible, then, in this state of things, for the group to evolve toward an authentic coexistence, to the point of being able to perceive the other than the self as constitutive of the self, as is required of the individual as such?

My answer is that a transition of this kind seems impossible in the framework of the present group structures, which have become ossified through the attributes of the sovereign state as the indispensable basis for the functioning of the war institution. It does seem possible, on the other hand, that the tracing of the war phenomenon to the subject as such would create through a process of relative desocialization the conditions and premises indispensable for a new socialization that would rest on new social institutions. Thus, it can be meaningful to speak of tracing the war phenomenon in its entirety to the sadism and masochism of each man, to his primary need for love and violence and to his primary need for guilt and reparation with regard to his love object, only inasmuch as to trace the war phenomenon to the subject would prepare the ground for the formation of new social institutions.

I believe that to prove scientifically that it is possible to trace the war phenomenon to the subject—a task which would be impossible without a scientific knowledge of the human unconscious—should be the specific task of psychoanalysis in the nuclear era. However, in order that this specifically psychoanalytic task may also prove historically useful, it seems indispensable that the data discovered in the human unconscious, which permit us to trace the war phenomenon to the subject, do not remain a private problem, but become a collective love object in a new socialization, and that this new socialization constitute, as our love object, a new *nomos* based on individual responsibility for war. Having pronounced the group incapable of evolving toward an authentic coexistence with another group and having therefore postulated the necessity for a return to the subject, we now find ourselves compelled to reaffirm the essential function of the group in rendering valid, with its mysterious validation processes, what might become truly irrelevant were it to remain on the individual level.

*Possibility of love between individuals and the necessity of hate between groups.*

I should now like to discuss the reasons for my belief that a return to the subject is indispensable for opening the way to a new socialization which would allow individuals to escape from the anomie created by the war crisis and concurrently to resolve, on new bases, the problem of the preservation of their private and collective love objects. Each one of us is familiar with the concept that every experience of love is connected with the existence of a body. All human vicissitudes of love in particular are based on the bodily intimacy between mother and child. The instinctual vicissitudes of man derive their human significance not so much from their physiological reality as from their fantasy animation which leads to the externalization and internalization of illusory psychic entities (imagos). But it is undoubtedly true that no love object could be created without the concrete instinctual gratification offered to the infant by the real body of the mother. While destructive fantasies originally arise autoplastically in a child who, left to himself, fantasies his frustration as a bad presence, libidinal fantasies are directly related to the real gratification provided by a real mother. Once adult, human bodies become mutual love objects, for they are necessary to one another in the exchange of love.

In group life we likewise speak of love objects as basic and constitutive of the group experience as objects of common identification. These love objects, however, are fictive bodies that seem to derive their vital significance from the fact that they preserve as a fiction what was at one time a real and concrete bodily presence.

Accordingly, the group would appear to originate in the general phenomena of transference. But while the transference occurring in interindividual relationships has at its disposal, in the body of the other, a real presence in which to realize itself in a concrete manner, in the group things seem to happen differently. The very impression that the group exists as something separate from the individuals who form it is a result of a regressive situation (Bion).

In spite of the illusoriness of its love object, however, the group can and does enjoy experiences of love in its internal relations, and the outward deflection of the aggressive drives, as a typical group function (in Bion's theory associated with the fight-flight group), facilitates the concrete experiences of love between the individual members of the group.

Turning to investigate the relations between groups (in reference to the fact that war crisis makes it necessary for groups to find between themselves a possibility of love relations of the type occurring between individuals), we realize that, in contrast with individuals who possess concrete bodies, groups lack the instruments of love, while they do have—and have always had—at their disposal, instruments for mutual destruction. If it is true that the function creates the organ, then weapons which are the specific instruments of aggressive intergroup communication are the best proof of the fact that the intergroup functions of the groups are exclusively those of aggression. *Whereas, as we have seen, in interindividual relations the experience of love is less illusory than the destructive experience, in intergroup relations the destructive experience is less illusory than the experience of love.*

I have often used the story of Romeo and Juliet as a paradigm of groups' great capacity to hate, and their fundamental incapacity to love, one another. Members of different groups can love each other, but only through a return to the subject as such. The Montagues and the Capulets, ruled by the strictest kind of familial group orthodoxy, must hate each other. The possibility of love, therefore, is associated with Romeo and Juliet as individuals. However, this relationship of love which is formed outside, and in opposition to, the rivalry of the two groups, has for the latter all the aspects of a violation of a group taboo; for this reason it becomes a dramatic event that will end in tragedy. The same situation is exemplified still more clearly in *West Side Story* where the groups are not of the familial, but of the socioethnic type. The love of a member of one group for a member of another group thus seems to be perceived as a breach of the group's morality, while hate toward the other group is approved of as rightful and just. Thus we find ourselves face to face again with that *conflict between group morality and individual morality* which seemed to us to present insurmountable difficulties.

In Sartre's *The Devil and the Good Lord*, the theme of the need for violence as an intergroup-relations need and the theme of the need for guilt as an individual need are dramatically confronted and, in the end, Goetz triumphantly rejects guilt (expressed by the priest friend of the poor) and accepts war. In order to justify the rejection of guilt, however, Sartre is forced to deny love. He affirms, through the lips of his hero, that love is two people's hate of a common enemy. In his introduction to Fanon's book, *The Wretched of the Earth*, Sartre again insists on the rejection of guilt and shows a certain tendency toward the idealization of violence. In my opinion, positions of this sort clearly express the difficulty, and I should say the impossibility, of groups' experiencing love except in the form of hate of a common enemy. As for guilt, it constitutes a psychological reality even though it may be denied. And I believe that it is precisely the problem of war with its current pantoclastic prospect that compels us to re-evaluate the significance of guilt.

Although it is undoubtedly true that hate toward a common enemy is the groups' form of love, a paradox of this sort seems to find its explanation precisely in the projection of guilt which is the essential process sustaining the paranoid elaboration of mourning. Since the guilt for the destruction of the love object is projected into the enemy, hate toward the enemy appears virtuous and assumes the semblance of love, precisely because the hate toward the enemy is ultimately directed against the bad parts of the self projected into the other. Even though in an alienated form, the hate toward the enemy gives the illusion of love, for it is a projective elaboration of the sense of guilt. Now the unexpected fact is that the war crisis no longer permits us to have recourse to the paranoid elaboration of mourning as an operation destined to alienate from ourselves the world of guilt. In this manner the fact that war itself, as nuclear war, destroys our love object at the same time it destroys our enemy seems to have as its inevitable consequence a reactivation in man's inner world of the original sense of guilt for the destruction of his love object. The war crisis will compel us to mobilize within us a depressive anxiety which the group experience seems to be constitutionally incapable of elaborating. However, it is precisely the incapability of groups to elaborate authentically a depressive situation that can constitute the premise for an urgent necessity of returning to the subject. Only the individual as such, inasmuch as he has mastered within himself the dramatic situation implicit in the primary experience of love, contained in the depressive position, will find within himself that capacity for love which the obligation (created by the war crisis) of finding a new mode of coexistence between groups seems to have rendered indispensable.

*The re-evaluation of the human meanings of guilt.*

Freud has shown us that in our unconscious we are far more criminal, and at the same time far more moral, than we consciously believe ourselves to be. He saw in war the expression of the unconscious barbarity of man. However, on the basis of his study of the expiatory practices of the primitive warrior returning from battle, Freud called our attention to the fact that primitive peoples, who are closer to the unconscious than ourselves, oddly show a moral sensibility superior to ours in the face of war. In our unconscious, murder—any murder including the purely illusory murder committed in fantasy—mobilizes guilt feelings. The phenomenology of mourning is the most impressive testimony that we feel guilty for our unconscious affective ambivalence toward the persons we love, even though our destructive impulses toward them may be experienced only in fantasy.

*In se* and *per se*, therefore, guilt as experienced in the unconscious concerns illusory crimes. Thus we might think that both our unconscious criminality and our unconscious morality are illusory entities and that it is the task of psychoanalysis to reveal them to us as such. In reality, however, even though there is an element of truth in this affirmation, psychoanalysis causes us to take seriously our unconscious as a situation that is dynamically and continuously operative in our conscious life. To regard our unconscious criminality and our unconscious morality as purely illusory entities would correspond to a mechanism of negation of our internal world, which would in turn result in our loss of the sense of the external world. In other words, the denial of the fantasy world would expose us to the impossibility of verifying our inner presences in the external world.

In analysis, we encounter this type of problem precisely in connection with the experience of mourning. In our clinical experience, we meet with cases where the denial of mourning (indifference to the loved one's death) lies at the root of grave disturbances in affective relations. In such cases we find, moreover, that when in the transference relationship the patient relives the experience of mourning (or, more accurately, lives for the first time, perhaps after a lapse of several years, the previously denied experience of mourning), the analytic elaboration of the suffering and of the guilt feelings inherent in it allows the affective life of the patient to turn toward new possibilities of integration. In these cases it seems that to live the unconscious guilt feelings is an indispensable experience for acquiring the capacity for love, as if the elaboration of the world of guilt, by reason of man's ambivalence, were in general a prerequisite for his capacity to love.

A formulation of this sort seems to contradict what clinical experience has repeatedly confirmed, namely, that it is the sense of sexual guilt that lies at the basis of emotional disturbances, and that consequently the sense of guilt precludes love.

Freud resolved this contradiction himself when he traced the problem of the sense of guilt not to Eros but to the aggression mobilized by the frustration of Eros; that is to say, frustration determines aggression, which is in turn transformed into a sense of guilt.

However, since a love object that would not be in some way frustrating is inconceivable, the problem of the sense of guilt is intimately connected with the aggressiveness felt toward the love object. At this point we discover that the sense of guilt, because it preserves our love object from destruction, seems to be put into the service of the preservation of the experience of love. Ultimately, guilt would appear to be an indelible result of man's affective ambivalence toward his love object; it is this ambivalence that is the intimate source of the drama of every experience of love.

Seen in this perspective, war would seem to arise from a series of psychic maneuvers which are closely connected with the individuals' life in the group, and the final result of which would appear to be to allow man to free himself from the load of ambivalence through the alienation of guilt, in turn connected with the paranoid elaboration of mourning. But if the alienation of guilt is one of the fundamental psychological processes of the war phenomenon, and if war has become the concrete destruction of every love object, then it seems inevitable that the discussion of war lead to a re-evaluation of the problems of guilt.

In his correspondence with Einstein, Freud noted that we are forced to confess that the destructive tendencies which lead us into war are closer to nature than the feelings of guilt with which we try to resist them. Freud considered the great development of the world of guilt in man an enigmatic problem to which an explanation must yet be found.

The reason why Freud considered the problems of guilt enigmatic is that, placing himself in a biological rather than a psychological perspective, he thought them to be further from nature than man's instinctual life. Thus when he uses the phrase "closer to nature," he lets us understand that he means nature in general and not human nature. In fact there is no doubt that the problem of guilt represents a novelty brought into the world of nature by man as an animal who is in conflict with his instinctual life. As the elaboration of guilt themes is a general human phenomenon, common to all known human cultures, we are induced to believe that the rise of the peculiarity of guilt is due to a condition of primary "mutation" (used here in the same sense that this term is accorded in biology).

In biology, mutations are generally understood as the permanent assumption of new modes of existence which are hereditarily transmissible and which tend to occur in direct proportion to the creation of a threat to survival; thus biological mutations are usually traced back to radical alterations in the environment which separate the various geological eras.

The new and unforeseeable fact, which we are historically witnessing, is that the instruments of destruction in our age have the capacity to determine (by increasing the level of radioactivity) an alteration in our terrestrial environment which would have all the aspects of a threat to our survival analogous to that created by the modifications that mark the end of one and the beginning of another geological era.

Surprisingly, while all this is happening (or at least looming on our historical horizon), we experience it all without being aware of any significant guilt feelings within ourselves. We, the private citizens, feel no guilt because we have the impression that it is no affair of ours; the politico-military leaders (we ourselves unconsciously identified with them) likewise feel no guilt because they believe that it is an evil necessary for the preservation of their love object. My thesis is that a humanly responsible elaboration of a situation of this sort is impossible except through the uncovering of our individual guilt needs, which each of us has experienced as an individual in feeling that he himself was the cause of the deterioration of the original life-giving environment (the mother). It seems to us that only from the recovery of the primary guilt needs would it be possible to derive the reparative force necessary for the restoration of the deteriorated environment-mother.

Having traced the current catastrophical situation to the infantile fantasy depressive catastrophe, we again note with astonishment that in our internal world the historical situation which we are currently experiencing at the reality level is not an entirely new situation. On the contrary, it reveals itself as an ancient crisis which is intimately bound to man's primary depressive conflict in his relation to the love object—a conflict that has driven man to that primary human mutation which is expressed by the world of guilt.

The reason why Freud and psychoanalysis in general assumed a negative attitude toward the world of guilt is connected, as we know, with the fact that the sense of guilt is particularly implicated in psychopathology. For those who are familiar with the world of psychopathology, it is certainly not permissible to speak in terms of moralistic idealization of guilt. Precisely because psychoanalysis has shown that guilt is an internalization of Thanatos, we can understand that, for man, the guilt need contains the drama of self-destruction; this is so, even though the process of the development of the sense of guilt may be considered an attempt to preserve the love object by directing the aggressiveness toward the self. The saving significance of guilt lends itself to idealization—this is especially evident in the realm of religion—but we must not forget that —in the form of idealization of sacrifice—guilt was also an integral part of Hitler's propaganda: "Germany must live, even if we must die for her."

The sense of guilt seeks to prevent the destruction of the love object, creating, however, a threat to the survival of the self. Ultimately, therefore, it leads again to *the destruction of the love relationship as such, since it sacrifices one of the two partners.* The sense of guilt seeks to transform the paranoid position of *mors tua vita mea* into the depressive position of *mors mea vita tua.* The love relationship, however, requires something other than the antithetical reciprocity which is implicit in both the paranoid and the depressive positions. The love relationship finds its authentic expression in the symmetrical reciprocity of *vita tua vita mea, mors tua mors mea.*

In the primary infantile situation, the problem of guilt can be overcome because the child has at his disposal a "concrete" relationship with the mother who reacts to the child's experience of guilt through love as a concrete offering, as a gift of forgiveness; this is a situation which seems to contain in the form of a concrete relationship that which is fantasied in the myths of redemption. Since the mother is bound to the child by a relation of love which implies *vita tua vita mea,* she will be compelled by this intimate necessity of the love relationship to preserve the child from the destruction to which the unmitigated process of the development of the sense of guilt would expose him. Subsequently the mother's gift of forgiveness will permit the child to identify with a reparatory subject and so the real solution of the anxiety produced by the sense of guilt will consist in the intimate feeling of being able completely to restore the love object through concrete reparative processes. In this manner *guilt is subtracted from the insoluble dilemma of the deflection and introflection of aggressiveness* and put into the service of Eros who resolves it into reparative responsibility.

The insolubility of the dilemma of violence and guilt as a pure interplay of the deflection and introflection of aggressiveness is presented and resolved in the myth of Orestes. When Orestes, persecuted by the Erinyes (guilt) because he had killed (violence) his mother, presents himself before the judges in Athens, they are divided: half of them acquit him, the other half condemn him. The dilemma, therefore, is insoluble. But the vote of Athena (the symbol of maternal forgiveness) will transform the Erinyes into Eumenides: thus the forgiving vote of Athena transforms the sense of guilt into reparative forces, subtracting the whole problem of violence and guilt from the purely aggressive dialectic toward the object or toward the self, to cause it to evolve into love needs which are in turn mysteriously connected with wisdom. (Athena, in addition to being the mother goddess of Athens, is also the goddess of wisdom.)

Now the fact that the psychoanalytic treatment is essentially based on a diminution of guilt feelings, for the purpose of permitting an elaboration of responsibility, does not signify a denial of guilt, but an attaching of value to its human meanings aimed at the preservation of our love object while we feel that we are personally responsible for being capable of destroying it, or for having destroyed it, *in a continuous integration and verification of the fantasy destructive evidence of our internal world and of the concrete destructive evidence which we may or may not find in the external world.*

The dangers which the universe of guilt creates in our internal world, therefore, cannot be minimized in any way. Freud's discovery of the transformation of Thanatos into Nomos retains all of its value. However, I believe that, even though dramatic, the human mutation connected with the guilt need must be considered central to the constitution of man.

While all other animal species are locked in a rigid determination fixed by instinctual schemata, man appears as a species open to continuous necessities and possibilities of change. It is precisely because guilt contains a threat to the survival of the self that the world of guilt represents the immanence within man of a continuous mutative force, determined by a continuous threat to the survival of the self. In contrast with other species which mutate through external causes, through alterations which occur in the external environment as exogenous threats to their survival, *man would appear to represent the singularity of a species that mutates through internal causes because he carries within himself the world of guilt as an immanent threat to his survival. This threat continuously compels man to new adaptations.*

Thus we certainly cannot minimize this dramatic condition, but neither must we idealize it. It seems to be a specifically human condition, connected with the formation of the ego through the identification with the love object threatened by the ambivalence. The human ego is necessitated to preserve his love objects, through guilt, inasmuch as the human ego is constituted by the other. (See Freud's formulation of the ego as a "precipitate of objects".)

The mutative function Leeds attributes to war (as a multifunctional institution destined to renew ossified human institutions) is in our investigation assigned instead to *guilt-reparation, as a pre-eminently individual force which group life, and war in particular, seem to lack, or more accurately, to avoid through paranoid processes.*

In our castastrophic age, it is actually war itself that has become an ossified structure unable to meet the new demands of our era. And since in addition to becoming ossified, war has also become nuclear, the war institution now promises to put an end to every mutation by destroying the subjects of mutation; or, in the best of the hypotheses, promises to give origin to the monstrous mutation described by Huxley in his novel *Ape and Essence,* where, following a nuclear catastrophe, men worship the devil who may be regarded precisely as the personification of the negation of guilt and of the impossible reparation.

The true and authentic mutative force, which man has always carried within himself, would accordingly appear to reside in his feeling personally responsible for the destruction of his love objects, since they are constitutive of his ego, and in his feeling, for this reason, compelled to restore or preserve them. Seen from this angle, human civilization no longer appears to be an enigmatic and sterile sacrifice on the part of men of their instinctual life, but rather a gigantic reparative feedback. Human civilization may thus be understood as a reparative response to the sense of guilt, as a continuous need to restore the destroyed objects in the form of objects of value, that is, love objects.

However, since this significance of human civilization is derivable from the specific formation of the ego through the identification with the love object and from each individual's internal and private need for violence, guilt, and love, integrated into individual responsibility, any social investigation which would separate, in the name of a supposed objectivity, the social facts from the concrete individuals who form the society must be regarded as reactionary and obscurantist in the present historical period.

To the extent in which it separates social life from the deep individual human needs of which the social phenomenon is but a function, such an investigation ends by giving a pseudoscientific pretext for the process of renouncing responsibility which is offered to the individuals by group life. Tracing group life to the subjects, psychoanalysis can become a valuable instrument with which to fight the individuals' alienation in the group. Psychoanalysis, as we know, has made men responsible for their slips of the tongue, their dreams, their neuroses, and even their death, thus opening to human ethics an area that had always been considered extraneous to it. In this manner psychoanalysis has taught man that he must, when in trouble, come to terms with the stranger that he carries within himself—the unconscious—if he is to resolve the problems that beset him.

Thus it was not by chance that Freud used military terms in his description of the human personality: "conflicts," "defenses," etc. According to the Freudian description, the primal war is within ourselves, and each of us must settle his conflicts if he is to achieve "spiritual peace." If we take a look at dreams, we note that war is endemic in our unconscious. Every one of us carries within himself silent, secret murders. Every one of us, as Glover has shown, in moments of acute frustration experiences the fantasy of omnipotent sadistic control over the frustrating-enemy object. Now the technico-cultural progress has translated the fantasies of omnipotent sadistic control into nuclear weapons as concrete destructive omnipotence. Nuclear weapons have always existed in the unconscious of human individuals in the form of concrete destructive intent, that is, in the form of wishes for absolute sadistic control over the persecutory objects of our fantasy world. The extreme alienation, described by Gunther Anders—whereby the apex of man's culturo-scientific evolution has gotten out of his hand and it now faces him as an extraneous and hostile entity in the form of nuclear weapons—ultimately seems to represent nothing other than the translation into a concrete historical reality of the psychological experiences associated with the process of externalization of the bad parts of the self which are then experienced as external persecutory entities, in the primitive paranoid elaboration of primary sadism.

In this manner, the tracing of nuclear weapons to the unconscious allows us to escape from the alienation described by Gunther Anders. The process of reappropriation, even though paradoxical at first sight, leads us to understand nuclear weapons as created by the same ancient and primary process of alienation which lies at the basis of the establishment of the other as enemy.

As this process of reappropriation leads to a depressive position, we come to the conclusion that the only possibility of escaping from the condition of total alienation, to which we find ourselves exposed because we live in the nuclear, catastrophic age, is offered us by the need to feel personally responsible for this alienation, that is, the need to personally reappropriate the destructive intent of nuclear weapons as our original wish, concealed in a paranoid position, to destroy our love object.

War is endemic in the unconscious, both in the destructive fantasies and in the process of omnipotent sadistic control over the bad object. Since the tracing of war to the unconscious brings us to the discovery that the establishment of a group as enemy of another group involves individual operations of externalization onto the other of the bad parts of the self, we are induced to define war psychoanalytically as *a criminal act, fantasied individually and consummated collectively for the purpose—which has proven to be historically and definitively illusory—of preserving the love object through a paranoid process.*

*The alienation in the sovereign state and the individual responsibility for war.*

If, on the basis of the instinctual contents and defenses which psychoanalysis has derived from its study of the unconscious, war may be defined as an individual crime, fantasied individually and consummated collectively, the responsibility for war seems to be traceable to man as an individual as well as to men as members of the group.

If we consider the evidence offered us by history in regard to concrete wars between sovereign states, we find ourselves face to face with the paradox that *apparently the discussion of group responsibility can only be based on individual morality.*

The sovereignty of the state, in fact, as *legibus solutum potestas*, stands outside the law and therefore outside responsibility. The sovereign state represents the strict coincidence between the id and the superego. The origins of the state, as we have seen, are traced to war; according to ethologists, the state in its original form was based on the domination of an agricultural tribe by a nomadic warrior tribe. To those of us who have witnessed World War II, it is obvious that the responsibility for that conflict is attributable to Nazism and Fascism. However, to speak about responsibility in relations between sovereign states is absurd if no reference is made to the ways in which the individual as such judges interindividual aggressive relations which are governed by laws.

The need to justify war, which Bouthoul defined as juridical illusionism, is the most evident testimony of the sense of guilt men feel and which they must deny in order to make war. Affirming the individual responsibility of the Nazi criminals, the Nuremberg trials and the more recent Eichmann trial appear to be sustained by a fundamental ambiguity whereby the sovereign states who place themselves outside the law demand that the law be applied to their vanquished enemies.

Grunberger noted the absurdity of Eichmann's behavior during his trial. Eichmann, who had listened to all the accusations made against him as the executioner of the Jews as if they had been senseless phrases, reddened and became extremely embarrassed when it was pointed out to him that he was violating a banal rule of etiquette by remaining seated while speaking with the president. This absurdity which Grunberger traces to a pregenital superego appears obvious to us when confronted with the ethics of individual responsibility. But we must admit that from the viewpoint of the ethics of the sovereign state, Eichmann had all the advantages on his side. This realization allows us to convince ourselves, in the middle of the nuclear era, of an appalling fact, namely, that the sovereign state is a specific instrument of moral alienation of the individuals.

Freud intuited this reality when he affirmed the state to be the monopolizer of the citizens' private violence. The process of monopolization and capitalization of the citizens' private violence by the state makes it so that in war, as the industry of death, the sovereign state truly becomes the industrialist of the private violence saved by the citizens.

This realization permits us to affirm that the alienation of which Gunther Anders speaks in reference to nuclear weapons is in reality based on the alienation of private violence on the part of the state. It is our moral alienation, then, that makes our savings of violence rise against us, inflated by the state into a persecutory agency.

Once again, therefore, in order that we may escape from this process of alienation, it seems inevitable that each of us personally reappropriate the defensive intent of the sovereign state, an intent which now reveals itself as purely destructive. The process of reappropriation cannot consist in anything but our realization that the sovereign state, which we now experience as a sort of alien persecutory entity, was after all established on the basis of our having put into it our own violence.

Thus we find ourselves in a situation which appears to be close to Rousseau's pessimistic view of the state, for we realize that the social contract has brought us to the state-industrialist of destruction. However, it seems that the state did not bring us to this point by trampling on a primal innocence of ours, as Rousseau would have it, but *by employing our private capital of violence and by simultaneously trampling on our individual guilt needs*, that is to say, the state has monopolized our id, alienating us from our superego. But after all, if the state was able to carry out an operation of this sort, this happened because we had been experiencing deep anxieties against which we were able to defend ourselves by precisely this type of maneuver: this function of the state, however, has now disclosed itself to be definitively illusory. We realize that the war crisis has brought with it the crisis of the sovereign state as a force that controls our depressive and persecutory anxieties. If the state, as a state-beast, founded on the principles of "the lion and the fox," is dead, we feel, in an authentic elaboration of mourning, that we ourselves have destroyed it, and that we ourselves must restore it as a state-man, that is to say, as a state that would no longer be the instrument of our moral alienation but would obey the same laws which govern men as individuals. If war is based on a paranoid elaboration of mourning, the antiwar process seems to be closely associated with the authentic elaboration of mourning, which is traceable to the feeling that we ourselves are the cause of the destruction of our love object. Only inasmuch as we re-establish, through an apparently illusory process of assuming responsibility, a link with the guilt needs associated with the original infantile depression, do we seem to be offered the possibility of escaping from the total alienation and of making our unconscious guilt feelings evolve into the recognition of the possible nuclear catastrophe as the concrete destruction of every one of our love objects.

The mobilization of the unconscious primary guilt need in regard to the destruction of the original love object seems indispensable for giving a non-alienated sense to the possible destruction of humanity and thus for making it possible for reparative mechanisms to be set in motion for the restoration of the love object destroyed in fantasy.

The return to the subject, and to his unconscious need for violence, guilt, and love, seems to be the indispensable condition for bringing group structure to the whole-object level, at the moment when group structure, remaining on the part-object level, exposes humanity to the destruction of all of its love objects. The purpose of the return to the individual is to rouse us from our alienation in the group because of which, faced with the prospect of the destruction of mankind, we feel neither violent nor guilty, as though we were all involved in a gigantic delusion of negation of the external as well as of our internal reality.

At the end of the first millennium, as we know, men were seized with a kind of collective hysterical anxiety regarding an imaginary catastrophe. But at the end of the second millennium, now that the pantoclastic prospect is truly beginning to appear on our historical horizon, we are struck by observing that, faced with this situation, men behave as if it were not real. This confirms Glover's statement that the first and perhaps most dangerous consequence of the nuclear age is that it has seriously weakened man's capacity for reality testing.

*The responsibility of our unconscious for war as a thesis introductory to holocracy.*[8]

The tracing of the war phenomenon to each human subject rests on the original basic human needs, such as the need for violence, guilt, and love, which psychoanalysis has shown to be the fundamental needs of our internal world. Our investigation, which seeks to verify these needs on the level of group functions, does in no way mean to deny the concrete historical evidence into which group life translates itself. On the contrary, it wishes to investigate the new significance acquired by group life at the moment when the pantoclastic prospect of our catastrophic age seems to have caused the crisis of war as an antiquated social institution that is unable to fulfill the new demands of history.

The results to which our investigation has led us seem to justify the general thesis that when a society enters a state of crisis through the crisis of one of its basic institutions, the solution of such a crisis implies the reversion of responsibility to the subject, to all subjects as such, as the concrete foundations of the group. The return to the subject as such becomes particularly indispensable at the moment when the historical situation, imposing peaceful coexistence on the groups, seems to require the rise of new functions which we have been so far unable to elaborate in intergroup relations. This inability derives from the fact that intergroup relations are molded by paranoid needs, which are in turn conditioned by a fundamental and essential impossibility of love between groups, understood as autistic or symbiotico-narcissistic entities.

The last two great revolutions, the French and the Russian, were preceded by ample culturo-theoretical prepara-

[8] *Holocracy:* In his *Psychoanalysis of Nuclear War,* Dr. Fornari defines holocracy as government by all. (Translator's note.)

tion made by individual researchers who had become aware of the new historical realities. This appears to confirm the need for the return to the subject as such, as a condition for the elaboration of schemata in which society will be able to express new social institutions when the old ones have failed. In the revolution itself, as outlined by Freud in a letter to Einstein, is implicit a moment of transitional desocialization (the anomic moment of a revolution), which corresponds to the reversion of the responsibility for the laws to the individuals as such.

In the present period of history, however, the necessity for the reversion of the sovereignty to the individual assumes a more important and different meaning. Whereas every revolution in the past could benefit from the fact that it was able to grow through a paranoid process within the group, in the sense that it was able to find an enemy to fight (feudalism in the French, capitalism in the Russian, Revolution), the revolution which now appears necessary must, as it seems, be an essentially depressive revolution which would involve, on the part of each man, feelings of guilt and responsibility for war, understood as group paranoia.

It would seem that the enemy to fight is no longer in the external world, but within each of us. This shift of emphasis implies a revolution which is once more comparable, though in the inverse sense, to the transition from the Ptolemaic to the Copernican system, in that it shifts the center of gravity and responsibility for war from the sovereign state to the individual.

A similar process takes place in the transition from the schizo-paranoid to the depressive position, according to Melanie Klein. The abolition of the sovereignty of the state, at the moment when the state becomes an alien persecutory entity, would thus appear to represent, on the group level, the swing of the destructive pole from the object to the subject which occurs in the infantile depressive position.

The shift of the center of gravity of the war phenomenon from the state to within each individual obviously implies a need for the rise of new institutions. Expressed in psychoanalytic terms, the problem could be posed as follows: If war is a social institution whose function is that of expressing a group of processes which involve an integration of the satisfaction of auto- or heterodestructive impulses as well as of the defenses against psychotic anxieties (all of which is accomplished through the paranoid elaboration of mourning), *what characteristics should an alternative institution have which would no longer operate through the paranoid elaboration of mourning?*

To answer this question, I should like to evolve a hypothetical argument. Let us imagine for a moment a state that has abolished its judicial institutions: its courts of justice, its penal code, etc. We can assume that in a situation of this sort great anxieties would be aroused within me. I should begin to fear that the number of criminals would greatly increase, for they would no longer be restrained by the fear of punishment, and that they would arm themselves and endanger my life, the life of my loved ones, my property, in a word, all that I hold dear (persecutory anxieties). At this point I should begin to think that if I, too, did not arm myself to defend my loved ones, I should be a coward deserting his love objects instead of preserving them, if necessary, even at the cost of my life (depressive anxieties). Naturally the mental maneuvers of anxieties and defenses which I should carry out with regard to others, others would carry out in relation to me. If judicial institutions were abolished, I too should appear as a possible aggressor in the eyes of others (persecutory anxiety) who would think themselves cowards if they left their love objects at the mercy of my destructive attacks (depressive anxieties).

We may say, therefore, that judicial institutions constitute a defense against psychotic anxieties, which does not, however, function through the paranoid elaboration of mourning. *On the contrary, I believe that the law may be considered a normal elaboration of mourning.* In fact, the law also permits us to avoid the anxieties of the Internal Terrifier (in the form of an absolute universe of guilt where the mere fantasy of murder is regarded as murder) in a series of controllable dangers, for a concrete rule establishes what may or may not be done in order not to feel legally guilty. In addition to this transformation of the absolute, unpredictable, uncontrollable Terrifier into a relative, predictable, and controllable danger, there operate in the law *functions of preservation of the love object, inspired by an authentic elaboration of mourning,* in the sense that the reparation of the really injured object must be made not by a hypothetical enemy, but by the author of the injury himself, not in an absolute form, but in a form relative to the injury.

The thesis that the judicial institutions of the state act as defense organizations against psychotic anxieties represents the submerged part of the iceberg, the visible part of the iceberg being the judicial institutions themselves. That is, the real concern of the judicial institutions are not men's psychotic anxieties, but real crimes and violations of the law. In other words, laws are concerned with those who violate them and not with the psychotic anxieties of the honest citizens. Actually, however, the violators of the laws would seem to be a proof of the failure of the function of the laws. And because the law constitutes the love object of the group, a violation of the law is equivalent to a destruction of the love object and has all the aspects of a mourning. The reaffirmation of the law after it has been broken therefore has all the aspects of a reparative process as a normal elaboration of mourning.

For this reason, the punishment of the guilty (condemned by modern psychopathology, which tends to consider criminality a psychic illness) would appear to preserve its significance as a function of the judicial institution assigned to the normal elaboration of mourning. To make the state a war-inhibiting rather than a war-promoting force would evidently involve a revolution of unprecedented magnitude. This revolution would lead to the mobilization of psychotic depressive anxieties and anxieties regarding the survival of the group, analogous to the fear of the "sorcerers who kill," which is experienced by primitive peoples deprived of war.[9]

The road of pacifism foreseen by psychoanalysis, therefore, is by no means strewn with roses; psychoanalysis foresees the possibility of mobilization of psychotic anxieties and, perhaps for this very reason, it could also suggest the means to master such anxieties. The hypothesis here presented will require a great amount of reflection and research before it can be ascertained whether or not it is historically realizable.

As an introduction to this reflection and research, I should like to take up again here the story of the Prince of Homburg, as told in the poem by Kleist, and the considerations which I have already developed in this connection in *The Psychoanalysis of Nuclear War*. The story

9 We have seen that primitive tribes deprived of war disintegrate and experience, instead of the fear of being destroyed by the enemy, fantasies of being destroyed by their own sorcerers. It is difficult to predict what would happen to our society if it were radically deprived of the possibility to make war. However, while among primitive peoples colonization totally destroys the primitive culture, the rejection of war does not appear to destroy any culture.

of the Prince of Homburg in fact represents a paradigmatic exemplification of a situation of conflict between individual ethics and group ethics, *resolved in favor of the former at the moment when the latter fails in its function of preserving the group love object.* In fact we may assume that if the Prussian generals had followed the example of their ancestor, they would not have arrived at the moral alienation of Nazism.

In Kleist's poem, the Prince of Homburg is on the battlefield preparing to give the order to attack, when he is confronted by a difficult problem of choice. He knows that if he obeys the king's unwise orders, he will expose his army to defeat. He must choose between the need to obey the king, thus allowing his army to suffer defeat, and the need to lead his army to victory, thus disobeying the king and consequently violating the martial law. Homburg, as we know, chooses to disobey the king and leads his army on to victory. Transferred into the dialectic of the relations between the state and the individuals as such, Homburg's choice represents the necessity for the reversion to the subject as such of the responsibility for the preservation of his love object, when the state institutions, instead of guaranteeing the love object's safety, determine its destruction. In this manner we may affirm that the return to the subject, instead of being—as Leeds fears—a psychologistic deformation irrelevant to social phenomena, may constitute the most formidable instrument for deossifying ossified social institutions, that is, social institutions which are no longer able to fulfill their function of preserving the collective love object.

I have called the process of reappropriation on the part of each individual of his sovereignty alienated in the sovereignty of the state, *the holocratic position.* However, this reversion of the sovereignty to the subject, which has an apparently anarchic significance, is not the point of arrival but the point of departure from which to start in order to be able to deposit into the state, at one stroke, all our violence needs, guilt needs, and love-reparation needs which, integrated in the individual, constitute the individually responsible ethics. Nevertheless, the holocratic position is not aimed at denying the law but at reaffirming it as a function of preservation of our common love object.

The sovereignty of the state may in reality be defined, in the present period of history, as *an anomic situation in intergroup relations*. In contrast with this anomie, the aim of the reversion of the sovereignty to the subject through the holocratic position is to cause the current anomie of sovereign states to evolve toward a *holonomic position* in which the state, no longer sovereign, must obey the same laws as its citizens.[10]

The holonomic significance of the holocratic operation which consists in the reversion of the sovereignty to the subject as such may be clarified by the rest of the Prince of Homburg's story. Homburg, as we have seen, chose to oppose the institutions of the state in order to preserve his love object (the army). However, the climactic moment in Kleist's poem is reached when, having led his army on to victory, the general must answer charges of high treason before a court-martial. In the poem, the prince resents his situation as absurd and injust, since he is being condemned for having led his army on to victory, i.e., for having preserved his love object.

It happens, however, that the king refuses to apply the martial law. He leaves it to Homburg to decide for himself whether or not the martial law should be applied to

10 In addition to being recommended by Glover, the abolition of the sovereignty of the state was presented as desirable by A. Sullivan and others in *Tensions That Cause Wars*, edited by Hadley Cantril (Urbana, 1950).

him. At this point events take an unexpected turn. Homburg, who until then had rebelled against the martial law as a persecutory entity, suddenly changes his attitude toward it. Because he himself is now responsible for the application of the law (which now becomes for him a love object that must be preserved, in the same manner as he felt that the army had to be preserved), and with the same ethical consistency which he had shown on the battlefield when he decided to disobey the king, Homburg condemns himself to death and goes to the scaffold in a state of happy exaltation: in this manner, the subject's return to personal responsibility permits the simultaneous preservation of the army and of the law.

Homburg's story, therefore, seems to me adequate for sanctioning the necessity for the return to individual responsibility as a requisite transition to the restoration of social institutions as functions of preservation of the love objects, when the politico-social institutions fail in the performance of these functions.

The operation of reappropriation by the citizens of the violence saved by them and deposited into the state as if into a bank, though at first sight suggesting anarchy, has in reality a holonomic significance, for the reappropriation of the aggressiveness by the *legibus ligati* citizens would ultimately prevent the anomic monopolization of aggressiveness by the *legibus solutum* sovereignty of the state.

However, in wishing to abolish the monopolization and capitalization of the aggressiveness saved by the citizens, we by no means wish the citizens to become violent. That would be a regressive, prestatal situation in which all men would be *legibus soluti* and in the conditions of *homo homini lupus*.

The operation of removal of the aggressiveness deposited by the individuals into the state, the reappropriation on the part of the citizens of their alienated aggressiveness, arises precisely as a historical necessity and as an operation tending to render *legibus ligatum* every type of aggressiveness, whether interindividual or interstatal. To escape from our alienation in the state through the reappropriation of our aggressiveness which until now we have allowed to be monopolized and capitalized by the state, then, means also to realize that the aggressiveness of the state-beast which makes war is our own alienated aggressiveness. Although this is obscured by the fact that war is a state institution, *it is we ourselves who desire war, and the alienation of our aggressiveness into the state serves us simply to be able to say that it is not we who desire war but that the state forces us to make war.* In this manner, we convince ourselves that the state is responsible for war in order not to feel responsible for it ourselves. To escape from our alienation in the state, therefore, means to feel personally responsible for war, just as we feel personally responsible for interindividual crimes.

*The Omega Institution as an alternative to war and as a normal elaboration of mourning.*

As we have said, what we have called the Omega Institution (and what we now see being defined as a new judicial institution which represses the crime of war from within the groups, considering it a criminal wish of individuals rather than a function of the state) can control the persecutory and depressive anxieties which are already being controlled by judicial institutions through the normal elaboration of mourning.

The Omega Institution, therefore, may be considered a defensive organization effective against the same deep anxieties which the war institution has always allayed, or believed to have allayed, with the paranoid elaboration of mourning. A security operation of this type, however, concerns those dangers which threaten the submerged part of the iceberg, in the same manner as judicial institutions serve to control the persecutory and depressive anxieties of the citizens who do not commit crimes. But what can the institution proposed by us do in the face of real violations of the law, in the face, that is, not of the illusory Terrifier of the internal world, but of the real dangers of the external world, such as the acts of individuals who violate the laws or, of individuals who, in spite of the eventual existence of an Omega Institution (which prohibits war as an individual crime), succeed in forming a criminal association and reinstate the war institution as a paranoid elaboration of mourning?

At this point our investigation departs from the field of purely psychoanalytic research applied to political and judicial problems to make a junction with the security organizations already in operation or still in the process of developing, as far as to take into particular consideration the thesis of World Government proposed by Bertrand Russell as an urgent alternative to the pantoclastic situation.

Wishing to connect my thesis of the Omega Institution with the prospect of World Government, I shall use as a point of reference the situation regarding the child's transition from the familial group to the larger social group.

It is reasonable to believe that the laws of a state are operative on its citizens inasmuch as previously there has taken place, in our culture at least, a process of ethicization of the child carried out through the force of the familial culture. If we investigate the history of social misfits, we find, in almost every case, an affectivo-pedagogic deficiency on the level of familial culture.

What renders possible the process of socialization and

the adult person's ability to accept social authority is ultimately a certain capacity of the child to accept his dependency on the father, who is subsequently internalized as the superego, that is to say, as the internal moral law. The judicial institutions of society thus become operative and effective because they have been preceded by an internal ethical organization, formed in the child during the development of the dialectics of affective ambivalence in the relation to his parents, on whom he wishes to depend while also wishing to become independent of them.

In transposing the relation between the internal moral law and the judicial institutions of society into the political sphere (more accurately, into the relation between the Omega Institution and World Government), several thoughts come to mind. First, it is hard to think that a World Government could be formed through the union of sovereign states. Second, a World Government presupposes the abolition of the sovereignty of the states, but who will abolish it? We have seen when the United Nations was founded that each member nation was above all jealous of preserving its own sovereignty. Third, the abolition of sovereignty from above tends to arouse strong paranoid anxieties of persecution and castration and so feeds vindictiveness. This was shown by the reaction of the Chinese, the French, and several other nations to the Soviet-American agreement to limit nuclear proliferation, i.e., to monopolize it. In a way, an agreement between the major countries which would monopolize nuclear weapons could constitute an introduction to a World Government, or perhaps even a sort of World Government. However, many nations felt this as a grave threat to their sovereignty: those nations, obviously, whose leaders were most sensitive and vulnerable to paranoid anxieties.

It seems, then, that the hypothesis is not groundless

that the road to a World Government is feasible only if we make our point of departure *the abolition of sovereignty from below,* which is what I have proposed in the theoretical context and the practical implications of the Omega Institution.

A state whose sovereignty has been abolished from below (that is, through the reappropriation on the part of each *legibus ligatus* citizen of the violence alienated into the state, the latter understood as *legibus solutum*) could have, on the national level, the significance of a moralization within the group as a precondition to the acceptance of a World Government as an extranational authority, in the same manner as the moralization which takes place within the familial group is the precondition for the child's later acceptance—when he becomes adult— of the social authority as an extrafamilial authority.

The political instruments for setting in motion a series of processes tending to found the Omega Institution should not be inaccessible. The Italian Constitution, for example, already foresees the possibility of limiting its sovereignty, on the condition of reciprocity. What seems, nevertheless, very difficult is for an institution of this type to arise in the major countries directly involved in the struggle for world leadership which practically immobilizes them in their need for power.

For this reason, the Omega Institution seems to have a better chance in the so-called satellite countries, of either major power bloc, whose loss of sovereignty would not affect the balance of power of the great. The satellite countries, thus divested of their sovereignty, could eventually place themselves under the protectorate of the United Nations, to whom they could also devolve their armaments. The United Nations, in this case, would no longer be in the position of having to restrain, with inadequate means, the aggressiveness of member nations infinitely more powerful than itself but would progressively acquire the power to control aggressive states which it does not have today, its situation at present being that of a handful of policemen armed with guns, trying to control millions of gangsters armed with nuclear weapons. If by any chance the Omega operation were to succeed and if by any chance it were also to extend to states having nuclear weapons who, in the event of abolition of their sovereignty from below, would deliver their armaments to the United Nations, then the future World Government, achieved through the abolition of sovereignty from below, would have at its disposal nuclear weapons as police weapons against gangster nations, in the same manner as guns are police weapons against individual gangsters.

The Omega Institution, then, which is based on the acknowledgment of the unconscious motivations for war, suggests, through the abolition of sovereignty from below, a way to World Government that is rather different from that followed by the foreign ministers of various sovereign nations. The gravest obstacle to disarmament negotiations consists in the paranoid presupposition, more or less explicitly admitted, that if one assumes an attitude of demobilization, it is the other who will profit by it. In effect this is not improbable, but the probability of an occurrence of this sort is enormously exaggerated by the fact that in such cases one projects his own intentions or unconscious fears into the other and then perceives them as really existing in him. In this manner, the mutual guarantees requested refer to some extent to real problems but they refer to a much greater extent to psychotic persecutory anxieties which, as long as they remain unconscious and are not recognized as such, cannot be allayed by any kind of realistic reassurance. In other words, since psychotic anxieties cannot be cured by foreign ministers who can, at the most, manipulate them more or less conscientiously or skilfully, another, more efficient, method of recognizing and controlling these anxieties must be found. Since unconscious anxieties, though operative in group dynamics, actually originate in individuals, it seems that disarmament guarantees cannot be successfully elaborated by foreign ministers until *after* the anxieties and defenses which are integrated in the war phenomenon have been resolved by treatment. It does not appear, however, that this treatment could be applied individually, as many moralists and even psychoanalysts naively believe, but rather through the rise of a new social institution that would resolve the same anxieties which are resolved by the war institution as a paranoid elaboration of mourning. Now since the law, as we have seen, performs the function of defending man against persecutory and depressive anxieties, and at the same time constitutes the normal elaboration of mourning, the Omega Institution, as a judicial institution that regards war as an individual crime, would have the capacity to control—and in a more authentic manner—those anxieties which would presumably be mobilized by the abolition of war.

A highly qualified reviewer of my book, *Psicanalisi della Guerra Atomica* (*The Psychoanalysis of Nuclear War*), declared that he was disappointed by the solution I proposed to the pantoclastic prospect. I am referring to the holocratic and holonomic solution which may be considered an integrally judicial solution to the war phenomenon, a collectively consummated individual crime. The reviewer's disappointment was due mainly to his belief that the acceptance of my theses would result in such widespread occurrence of neurosis that death would almost be preferable to a life so unhappy.

Actually, the tracing of the war phenomenon to the

unconscious, that is to say, the discovery of a new significance of war after the descent to the depths inaugu-
rated by psychoanalysis, has for me the precise purpose of
a premise—the validity of which is open to discussion—
from which to begin in order to affirm the thesis of the
individual responsibilities for war. Thus it is a matter not
of a conflict between the traditionally recognized, external causes (economic, demographic, political, ideological, etc.) of war and its unrecognized internal causes,
but rather of a shift of emphasis from the former to the
latter. In turn this shift of the epicenter of war from the
outside to the inside is not, as it could easily seem, a
moralistic operation but a premise which I consider indispensable for the application of the law to war.

To maintain that war is not a strange occurrence which
is extraneous to men and which they must endure against
their will, but rather a mode of expressing one's unconscious wishes and of defending oneself against anxieties,
also unconscious, which are experienced by every individual (even the most sincere pacifists), has a depressive
significance.

However, the fact that I have shown, and in a manner
attached value to, the depressive aspects of the nuclear
situation as a process of totalization in course on our
planet—a process which corresponds to the transition
from the schizo-paranoid (part object) situation to the
depressive (whole object) situation in the early psychic
development of man—may have induced the reviewer to
confuse a diagnosis with a proposed therapy.

In effect, we may expect that the war crisis will mobilize and uncover unconscious anxieties. There is some
justification, then, for the fears expressed by the reviewer.
The abandonment of war as a paranoid elaboration of
mourning could in fact lead to the emergence of depressive situations: such a thing did happen, as we know,

among certain primitive tribes deprived of war. All this, however, pertains to the diagnosis which the psychoanalyst is induced to make.

In the frame of this diagnosis, and remaining on the level of psychiatric evaluation, I must add that in the transition from the schizo-paranoid to a depressive position I see an evolutive process, a possibility, though dramatic, of an integration of group life on a higher level of humanization.

I have made a relative re-evaluation of the world of guilt (which, in psychoanalysis, is to go a little against the current) because I believe that it constitutes the pillar on which the edifice of the individual responsibility for war may be founded. This re-evaluation of guilt involves a total remeditation of psychoanalysis in one of its essential points, both on the theoretical and clinical level. It seems to me that the point of reference for a positive re-evaluation of the problem of guilt on the clinical level may be found in one of the aspects of the countertransference, discussed at the Twenty-third Congress of Romance Language Psychoanalysts held in Barcelona in 1962. I am referring to Racker's conception that in the analyst's countertransference there are at work reparative tendencies based on the fact that, for the analyst, the patient takes the place of an infantile love object injured by the analyst's sadism. It is evident that in a position of this sort, in which the analyst feels unconsciously guilty for the patient's illness, the unconscious sense of guilt (in spite of the fact that it is illusory when confronted with the patient's real illness) plays a concrete role in determining a genuinely reparative therapeutic attitude. This indicates that even though the unconscious sense of guilt cannot in any way be taken for a point of arrival, it constitutes a prerequisite for the assumption of reparative responsibility in a relationship with a really injured object. Such an attitude of reparative responsibility would naturally be irrelevant if it did not have at its disposal the concrete technical knowledge in which the therapeutic exercise expresses itself. But the fact that to become an analyst implies, through personal analysis, a partial but profound modification of the analyst's personality indicates that the psychoanalytic therapeutic exercise, in spite of the fact that it expresses itself in a procedure which merely explores the interpersonal relationship between patient and therapist, could become an alienating situation if it did not contain the process of the assumption of responsibility (objectively illusory) which we have discussed.

The utilization of the unconscious guilt need, as well as of the unconscious violence and love needs as the basis for each man's assumption of responsibility for war as a group illness, would ultimately appear to be based on the same psychic maneuvers which express themselves in the analyst's assumption of an apparently illusory responsibility for his patient's neurosis (and especially psychosis) as an illness of the individual.

However, in contrast with what happens in the therapeutic relationship with the individual, *the purpose of the psychoanalytic disclosure of the individual responsibility for war is to prepare the ground for new social institutions which would allow the individual concretely to express his responsibility on the politico-social level.* (If it is I who am responsible, it is I who must make amends; but if I must make amends, I must have concrete political instruments through which my reparative wishes may be concretely expressed.)

If psychoanalysis is inclined to affirm that each man's sadomasochism is responsible for war, it does not do this to silence our unconscious guilt feelings for war by means of a moralistic discourse on war itself. When psychoanalysis affirms that we all share the responsibility for war and that in order to escape from the alienation into which we are led by the sovereign state, it is necessary—as Glover maintained—that the state-beast become the state-man, subject to the laws of individual morality, it lays a scientifically sound theoretical foundation for a practice destined to lead to the creation of new social institutions which would concretely express the mastering of our alienation in the sovereign state.

In saying all this, however, I do not intend to propose as therapy either depression or guilt, which unfortunately already exist autonomously as the central fact of a human event which, as it seems, must now be moved from the individual to collective life. However, I do believe that man's original depressive nucleus, though painful *in se* and *per se*, is a crucial and particularly important moment in the process of humanization, even though (and here the Freudian intuition that morality originates in the death instinct retains all of its value) it contains, at the fantasy level, a self-destructive anxiety, that is to say, the very same anxiety which the nuclear situation makes come true at the reality level. All this, however, still pertains to the diagnosis and the epicrisis of the primary depression as well as of the pantoclastic nuclear prospect.

The problem of therapy begins when we ask ourselves the question of how the relationship between the unconscious depressive anxieties and the real pantoclastic situation is to be understood.

What renders the investigation particularly complex and difficult at this point is the fact that *the real pantoclastic prospect tends to be no longer clearly distinguishable from the pantoclastic universe of unconscious guilt, understood as the Internal Terrifier.*

From this unexpected coincidence between the illusory internal pantoclastic situation and the real external pantoclastic situation, from the confusion, that is, of the Internal Terrifier with the External Terrifier arises the crisis—which I consider irreversible—of the war phenomenon and the need for an alternative social institution.

An alternative social institution, hypothesized as the Omega Institution, could serve to control psychotic anxieties in the same manner as do regular judicial institutions. However, what I envision as actually constituting the Omega Institution is not so easily described. F. Schendler has called the role assumed by the schizophrenic in his own family the "Omega role." The Omega role could be regarded as one which is lacking in adaptation and which by its specific type of maladaptation arouses conflicts in other family members. The family senses the Omega member as a severe threat; he mobilizes their unconscious fears of infanticide, patricide, and matricide. The schizophrenic is the weak link in the family equilibrium. Through him emerge the deep anxieties of the entire family and the family defends itself by expelling its own Omega member. In other words, the family member who assumes the Omega role expresses the evil that exists within the family.

Psychiatric institutions usually serve as an aid to the family in its defense against schizophrenic members. The more recent treatment methods, however, are in my opinion oriented toward the Omega role in that the deviant behavior of the schizophrenic is considered as merely symptomatic of a more basic disease that involves the entire family. Accordingly, the family is brought to tolerate the conflicts existing within it and the contribution of each member to this basic pathology is exposed and explored.

The old method of expelling the schizophrenic from the family (the typical psychiatric procedure of isolating the sick) actually constitutes a type of paranoid defensive maneuver on the part of the family who locks away its anxiety-provoking member in a "snake pit." The type of therapy that brings the family as a whole to feel equally involved in the illness of its schizophrenic member, on the other hand, utilizes a reparative procedure of the depressive type, inasmuch as the family assumes the blame as its own rather than restricting the illness to its symptomatic member.

I have consequently called the hypothetical alternative to war, which would strive toward the group's acknowledgment of its own conflicts rather than toward their expulsion into another group, the "Omega Institution." If from the psychoanalytic point of view, war may be considered a paranoid elaboration of mourning because it exports one's own violence against the love object, then the reimporting of this violence could be regarded as an alternative to war.

I should like to draw attention to the fact that as a result of the current war crisis we have had an interlude of peace, but that again, what we call peace is merely a relative equilibrium of mutual dissuasion from making war, through the accumulation of armaments. In order for the Omega Institution to be a true alternative to war, it would have to dissuade the individual citizen (not the enemy state) from having recourse to arms to export his internal conflicts onto an alien nation. In my discussion of the psychology of war, I have neglected the political aspects of war since they may be regarded as a superstructure based on a fundamentally psychotic maneuver described as a paranoid elaboration of mourning. This pathological process has its origin not in the constitution of the state but in the family group. The aim of this shift of emphasis from the politico-military institution to the intrafamilial conflict in our search for the causes of war is the recognition and the clarification of the anxieties which are mobilized at the moment when war, as an institution, enters a state of crisis and compels us to find an alternative defense mechanism.

In order to clarify the anxieties which war has served to defend against until the current era, we could refer to the "dilemma of the prisoner" as described by K. E. Boulding in his work on game theory as applied to peace research. Let us imagine the relationship between two states, A and B, in a hypothetical environment where all states practice disarmament. Since neither state has military power, neither feels threatened by the other. This is obviously the most favorable situation for both states, for both are secure and at the same time do not have to sacrifice themselves in order to stock-pile dissuasive weapons. Let us call this Position One. Now let us imagine a second situation in which A arms itself and B continues to follow a policy of disarmament, called Position Two. Considering these two positions from the standpoint of the distribution of goods existing in A and B, we may say that in Position Two, A by arming itself is in a more favorable situation than in Position One, for A can now force B to yield to it its own goods. In this manner, B finds itself in a much less favorable state than in Position One. As a result, B has no recourse but to arm itself. We thus arrive at Position Three, where both A and B are armed but where the goods are less than in Position One, for much of the wealth of both states has had to be wasted on armaments. Accordingly, Position Three is less favorable than Position One but is at least more equitable than Position Two. The important point to be investigated is why Position One, which is clearly the most favorable for both parties and which is the position adopted by most individuals, has not been realized on the collective level. In terms of individual relationships, man ceased to arm himself many, many years ago. Why is it that nations refuse to adopt a mode of relations that is both more equitable and advantageous? What are the factors that obstruct this more favorable course?

The obstacles to Position One appear to reside in the emotional rather than in the cognitive domain. We may, in fact, suppose that while the transition from Position Two to Position Three has a rational motive, the transition from Position One to Position Two is based on a feeling of mistrust rather than a desire for gain. We know that this feeling of mistrust toward another nation is analogous to the stranger anxiety appearing in the infant at the age of about eight months, as described by Spitz. The anxiety appears spontaneously, without any unfavorable experiences or threats on the part of strangers. The reason for the stranger anxiety is that the mother is absent and that the child senses his mother's absence as a loss. The stranger anxiety constitutes at an early developmental level the paradigm of the later mechanisms which we have described as the paranoid elaboration of mourning. These reflections permit us to understand why the solution to the problem of mistrust has its roots in the primary affective life of the individual. The child, by externalizing the persecutory object, enables himself to idealize the relationship to his mother. Both the stranger anxiety and the paranoid elaboration of mourning thus seem to solidify the positive identity of one's own group by forming a negative view of the alien or external group.

We could therefore say that if groups have always preferred to go from Position One to Position Three, even if Position Three is less advantageous, they have done so in order to solidify and idealize their group identity by projecting and externalizing the unacceptable, unconscious impulses which exist within the group and even within the family. The unconscious world of each member of the human family is filled with murderous impulses toward other family members, as well as with fears of retaliation. This situation is illustrated, not only by the myth of Oedipus, but also by the stories of Orestes and of Hamlet. The fear that induces groups to evolve beyond Position One to Position Two is not purely the result of problems of acquiring goods but stems from the paranoid process of projection which is basic to the formation of a group identity. The experience of killing the enemy in war serves to reinforce the needed belief that the alien group is the one who really threatens the ambivalently loved group ideal. The mutual slaughter of enemies in war constitutes, for both groups, a way of exporting the sense of guilt aroused by hostile impulses toward the group love object. This persecutory elaboration of guilt would appear to be the reason why A and B cannot trust each other, even though a situation of mutual trust would be the most beneficial to both. If we schematize our three positions in terms of fear—trust, we find that Position One equals A—trust and B—trust, Position Two equals A—fear and B—trust, and Position Three equals A—fear and B—fear.

To return to our discussion of the Omega Institution, we may describe it as a hypothetical institution based on the psychoanalytic discovery that the forces that bring about the evolution of Positions Two and Three from Position One can be found originally in both A and B, as explained by the paranoid elaboration of mourning. Accordingly, since the fear that causes Position Two to evolve from Position One is not aroused by the real threats of B to A or vice versa, the situation cannot be resolved by an alteration of the true cognitive messages that form the relationship of A and B. The infant, at the stranger-anxiety stage, does not develop fear of the stranger as a result of threatening messages emitted by the latter, but rather the fear is a result of the infant's own hostility toward the mother, so that he senses her absence as equivalent to a self-induced loss.

The Omega Institution would be an institution which would allow groups to accept the sense of loss without attributing the cause of the loss to another group. In order to prevent the evolution of Position Two from Position One, therefore, there must be an internal change in A and B. Without this, all relative changes (for example, disarmament) in the real threatening power which A and B might request, as a reassurance against their mutual fears, can never really be effective. The fact that in Position One both A and B are unarmed does not prevent the development of Position Two or Three. The Omega Institution would not serve to regulate the relationship between A and B, but rather to co-ordinate the relationship of A to its citizens as well as the relationship of B to its citizens. It would attempt to alter the structures that foster the experiencing of illusory threats in order that the latter may no longer be projected onto alien groups. The Omega Institution would serve to curb the reciprocal paranoia that creates a sense of fear in both A and B and would alter those processes which tend to force A and B out of Position One, which, as we have seen, is the most reasonable and advantageous mode of relations for both.

Now, since the schizo-paranoid foundation of the identity of the group causes the original fear of other groups on the basis of the fact that a group's identity can only be regarded in a positive way if the identity of other groups is the recipient of negative feelings, the Omega Institution aims at re-establishing this negative sense within the group's own identity. Whereas the military institution tries to dissuade the alien group through violence, the Omega Institution attempts to dissuade the members of its own group through the acceptance of guilt for their own aggressiveness. This is what has been described above as the depressive process. Only the acceptance by the group members of their own aggressiveness can lead to the recognition of the negative feelings toward the group's idealized love object. In other words, the Omega Institution would not concern itself with guaranteeing that another group does not arm itself but would operate within its own group giving visible evidence that its own group is not arming itself. In this sense, the Omega Institution would act in opposition to the sovereignty of the state and would concern itself with dissuading the citizens of each state from exporting their violence outside their borders. The Omega Institution aims at repressing aggression against another group in the same manner as aggression against one's own group is repressed. It assures that unless disturbed by pathogenic processes, both A and B desire to remain in Position One and thus it would see to it that each group remains in Position One. The Omega Institution, therefore, is an institution that works within A and B and occupies itself with preventing the development of fear toward the other.

At the moment when war enters a state of crisis with regard to its traditional function of defending the group love object, it ceases to be a method of territorial defense and becomes a crime against the love object. In this sense, the psychoanalytic discovery that the responsibility for war exists in the unconscious of each individual constitutes a necessity for a new type of legal code among the citizens of the state in which true loyalty to the state is expressed by forcing the state to remain in Position One, for in our atomic era the evolution to Position Two or Three contains the greatest threat of destruction to one's own country. If psychoanalytic findings confirm that each of us is truly responsible for war, this may in effect serve as the basis for an Omega Institution, since then the member of group A or B will no longer seek to dissuade the other by threats of violence but by a sense of mutual trust. This can come about only if each group refuses within itself to have recourse to violence. This would correspond to the usual function of the police within the group, but in this case it would be aggression against another group that would be prohibited.

Moreover, since the evolution from Position One to Position Two derives from the basic sense of fear, and not from a real external threat, the Omega Institution would seek to replace this basic sense of fear with a basic sense of trust. In order to achieve this aim, we would dissuade our own group from resorting to violence against other groups, for only in this manner can we gain the confidence of the other group. The confidence of the other group cannot be earned by our asking that it not arm itself as a precondition to our own disarmament, or by assuring it that we have no intention of aggressive action, but rather by clearly stating that our group does not desire to attack and has therefore formed within itself a system prohibiting the expression of aggressive desires which in the nuclear era would be disadvantageous to all.

It should be made clear that such action would not resolve all of the possible problems that might arise, such as the other group actually arming itself regardless of our intentions. The creation of the Omega Institution cannot, of course, completely convince the other group of our peaceful intentions or create complete confidence. Nevertheless, without an institution of this sort, which implies a structural change within both groups, the development of trust appears impossible. The Omega Institution is primarily an attempt to master the original anxieties implicit in the schizo-paranoid make-up of groups, in the same

manner as individuals in their own relationships are able
to remain in Position One. In order to better understand
the significance of the Omega Institution, we can refer
to the way in which individuals within groups are able to
abstain from violence. All states employ an aggressive institution (the police) whose task is to dissuade the citizens from having recourse to violence. In fact, criminals
who violate laws are a minority arising from the criminal
subculture. The rest would appear to be controlled by the
fear of police and of punishment. However, neither police
nor punishment could successfully prevent murder if the
citizens were not first brought to accept a specific code of
morals which is shared by all. This code is perpetuated by
the familial education and the superego. Usually familial
values supercede social mores, but in civilized nations,
loyalty to the family morality does not require the murder
of other family groups. In this manner, families are able
to live in a relative state of mutual trust. Loyalty to one's
group, however, is often still expressed through the murder of the members of other groups. But since today the
exportation of violence to a neighboring state jeopardizes
the very existence of one's own country, the time is ripe
for the creation of internal structures that would force
each state to accept the social code required for survival
in the nuclear era.

Now this social code cannot be imposed by one group
on another, in the same manner as family A cannot force
family B to adhere to A's own moral standard. And it is
only after both family A and family B have imparted a
certain moral standard to their members that the two families can enter a relationship of mutual trust. Passing from
the family to group relations, the Omega Institution
would exert its influence in the sphere of international
affairs by instituting penalties for the exportation of violence onto alien groups. It would appear that only the

formation of Omega Institutions could guarantee the promise of group A or B to remain in Position One and allow a sense of mutual trust to replace the attitude of mutual fear.

The task of the Omega Institution is to reimport the conflicts into its own group and to see that they are solved within it. It proposes to achieve this end through the promotion of the normal depressive elaboration of mourning and the elimination of the paranoid elaboration of mourning. Through the depressive elaboration of mourning, the sense of guilt for hostility against the love object can be elaborated into authentic attempts at reparation. The Omega Institution would not be able to resolve the anxieties arising from objective reasons or from actual threatening behavior of alien states; nevertheless, such an institution seems to be necessary for examining real threats without interference from irrational forces; in fact, the real threat represented by the other is directly proportional to his inability to establish an Omega Institution within its own borders.

We may affirm that the normal individual vacillates between the depressive and the schizo-paranoid position. Group life, however, has until now tended solely toward the schizo-paranoid position. It would appear that groups must reach a new stage of maturity if they are to survive. We aim to replace the paranoid position of "I must kill you because you want to kill me," which corresponds to Position Three and which has until now characterized the relations between groups, with the depressive position which states "I understand that it is not you who wish to kill me, but rather that I myself wish to kill you because I have projected into you my own destructive wishes against my love object. However, I also realize that in killing you I may kill myself, so I voluntarily prohibit killing because I understand that by killing you I can no longer assure the survival of what I love, but rather I hasten its destruction. I have established a new law that prohibits this type of aggression and this law now deserves my loyalty." Will group A believe this sort of statement from group B? Obviously, credibility will depend on the establishment of new laws, on the establishment of an Omega Institution. In this event, it is possible that A and B will so relate to each other that they can remain in Position One. Each will have to suffer an amount of calculated risk in order to initiate this new mode of relations, and certain objective proofs of trust may be required. The significant changes, however, will be brought about by the new mode of dealing with unconscious fantasies which can no longer be projected but have to be accepted as belonging to the self. The responsibility for our unconscious wishes, as taught by Freud, can become not only a therapeutic instrument but a social force leading to the creation of a new institution at a time in our history when we are precariously balanced between the prospect of destruction and the hope for survival.

In essence, the Omega Institution aims at stimulating the evolution from a psychotic to a neurotic mode of group experience. The paranoid elaboration of mourning is conducive to a split identity of the manic variety through which a part of the self is projected onto the other group, thus indicating a psychotic process. The Omega Institution, on the other hand, would bring the group to terms with its own aggressiveness.

I have already shown the relation between the function of the law and psychotic anxieties, which exists on the basis of the fact that laws allow us to control the original unconscious absolute depressive Internal Terrifier by relativizing it in concrete dangers. I should now like to return to this problem in order to discuss therapy. The best-known literary work which we could use to exemplify the re-emergence of the Internal Terrifier from the dissolution of the judicial institution is, in my opinion, Kafka's *The Trial*. This book is the best example of how the collapse of the judicial institution leads to the emergence of psychotic anxieties, both persecutory and depressive, and of how it also leads to an unconditional surrender to the Internal Terrifying Persecutor.

What we know about Joseph K. is that a trial is being prepared against him by a mysterious court of justice; his crime, however, is not revealed. He is asked to present himself before his interrogators from time to time. At first he tries to fight, but after a while he succumbs and remains at the mercy of a gigantic, monstrous judicial organization which arouses terror and a sense of impotence. (The stifling garret where the interrogations take place seems to symbolize the unconscious.) Becoming more and more isolated, Joseph K. stands before the whole city as if before a gigantic court where everyone accuses him and where each word that he utters becomes an unretractable admission of guilt. In this state of things, there are no longer any intermediaries between himself and the trial (accusation and guilt). The city, turned into a gigantic court of justice, indicates that there are no longer any judicial institutions which could interpose themselves between Joseph K. and guilt. Everything that is outside himself is the Depressive and Persecutory Terrifier of guilt. Everything is the execution of a sentence which has already been pronounced, which exists *ab aeterno* and which will last forever because the revelation of the crime ultimately becomes the autopsy of the self.

Joseph K.'s nightmare appears to be sustained mainly by the fact that his crime is never revealed; one would therefore be tempted to say that it is unconscious; at any rate, it is not revealed and it remains indefinite. Now we know that *"Indefinitum non est pertransibile."* This is why Joseph K. fails in his attempt to control the anxiety of guilt.

Accordingly, the famous legal axiom *"nullum crimen sine lege"* may, from a psychoanalytic point of view, be regarded as a demand for a concrete law which would delimit the indefinite, uncontrollable, infinite guilt—a concrete law which would establish what may or may not be done and so control the indefinite, unconscious anxieties of guilt. What I have proposed under the name of Omega Institution, therefore, would be an attempt at therapy, aimed at preventing the war crisis from exposing men to the nightmare of the Internal Terrifier.

Since the unconscious court of justice (Alexander and Staub actually speak of the unconscious as of an archaic court of justice) is a territory where, as in Kafka's *The Trial*, the crimes committed in fantasy are equivalent to crimes committed in reality and are, at the same time, unrevealed, the morbid universe of guilt proliferates in the unconscious in a truly Kafkaesque manner.

The defense against the psychotic anxieties which are associated with the universe of guilt (and which can be clearly seen, particularly in the wars of primitive peoples), however, constitutes one of the bases of social phenomena. For this reason, my thesis concerning the functions of culture, of civilization, and therefore of society agrees with Freud as regards the fact that civilization (social institutions) leads to the separation, in man, of instincts and culture, so that "every increase in civilization is repaid by man with an increase in the sense of guilt" (*Civilization and Its Discontents*). However, I also believe that the partial sacrifice of instinctual life is not a gratuitous and purposeless process. On the one hand, the sacrifice of the aggressive instincts, and their transformation into guilt, seems to be closely connected with the preservation of the love object. On the other, civilization does not signify a sacrifice only of the instincts. On the contrary, the war phenomenon represents a social institutionalization of the destructive instincts. But certain social institutions and their attending cultural phenomena seem to find their primary source in the creation of structures whose purpose, in a realistic or illusory form, appears to be essentially that of defending men against the deep primary psychotic anxieties.

The thesis of law as a normal elaboration of mourning presented itself to my mind during a remeditation of the origins of civilization as proposed by Freud in *Totem and Taboo*, which Thomas Mann once called the saga of humanity. We need not concern ourselves here with determining whether from a purely ethnological point of view, Freud's thesis, which finds the Oedipus complex in the totemic civilization, is correct or not; that is open to discussion. Freud's thoughts on totemism interest me from the viewpoint of the phenomenology of mourning. Accordingly, what interests me is the mysterious "fermentation of the soul" whereby the killed animal (which represents the father) becomes, after its death, the sacred animal, the life-and-death-giving father who must not be killed: to kill him means to violate the taboo, i.e., to violate the law. If the taboo as the original law is related to the killed, dead animal which represents the father, if the taboo is the dead one who prohibits killing, then the law is an elaboration of mourning and in particular of mourning for a love object which one has killed. The fact that the killed animal-love object becomes a life-giving entity, in addition to indicating a relation between religion and the elaboration of mourning, clearly indicates that what has been killed (destroyed) has not only been restored in its integrity but has become a source of creativity and life. Here we find the aspect of Eros as the antagonist of death: a reparative process that restores the object damaged by destructive impulses.

There is, however, another aspect which is connected with the significance of the law in relation to the Freudian hypothesis that the father who has been killed and internalized becomes the law, i.e., the internal moral law which is formed through the reversion upon the subject of the aggressiveness previously directed at the object. *But if it is the killed and internalized father who becomes the law, then the law is a normal elaboration of mourning which leads to the recovery, in the internal world, of the lost object, guaranteeing its integrity through the reversion upon the subject of the destructive aggressiveness* (the sense of guilt) and restoring its integrity through libidinal fantasies as a reparative process, when destructive fantasies arouse in us the anxiety of having damaged or destroyed it. When Freud postulates that the sons' sense of guilt for having killed the father (whether in fantasy or in reality it matters little) is the unconscious source of the law, he lays down the premises which may, in my opinion, serve as the starting point for the hypothesis of a theory of the origin of the law as a normal elaboration of mourning.

Because the problems connected with the law are intimately related to the problems of guilt, which I have already discussed, I should again like to state certain concepts referring to the law as a normal elaboration of mourning. Thus while the paranoid elaboration of mourning tries to resolve the depressive experience of mourning (guilt feelings for the death of the loved person) by unrealistically projecting into another the cause of the destruction of the love object, and while the manic elaboration of mourning seeks to avoid the pain of mourning through a process of negation, by denying, against internal or external reality, that the love object has been lost, the normal elaboration of mourning presupposes an ego sufficiently strong to be able to tolerate the pain of mourning and sufficiently confident of its reparative powers to be able to feel, through a primary belief, both illusory and realistic, into the omnipotence of the affects, that what has been damaged can be repaired. Unconsciously we feel, in fact, that our fantasies of hate can destroy what we love and that our fantasies of love can preserve or restore what we have destroyed.

The relation between the normal elaboration of mourning and the restoration of the lost object and its recovery within ourselves may be explained by the meaning of the totemic feast. Freud saw in the totemic feast a simple repetition of the murder of the primal father: a periodic return of what has been repressed. (He interprets the war phenomenon in the same manner.) Freud, moreover, explicitly compares the totemic feast to the Catholic Communion.

In my view, however, the relation we have observed between the law as a normal elaboration of mourning and the restoration and recovery of the lost love object allows us to see in the totemic feast a rite of incorporation and re-establishment within the self of the lost love object. Since in the Catholic rite the Eucharistic feast is preceded by confession, we are able to realize, if we consider these two sacraments in the frame of the elaboration of mourning, that the rite of restoration and recovery within the self of the destroyed love object (which was unconsciously killed by ourselves) is integrated in a vast context of processes ranging from the suffering caused by the sense of guilt for having killed the love object to the resolution of never killing it again and finally to gratitude for having been forgiven. Indeed it would not be possible to recover and internalize the lost love object which we have killed if it were not for an extensive ritual of reassuring propitiation owing to which we feel that the love object is no longer angry with us on account of the harm we have done it; in other words, if it were not for the feeling that, once re-established within ourselves, the love object will not take revenge on us for having killed it by killing us in turn.

Seen in the context of the situations here described, the law, connected with the recovery and the internalization of the destroyed love object, represents a formidable organization of normal defense against psychotic anxieties, depressive as well as persecutory. *Actually, more than just a defense, it would appear to represent the solution of these anxieties at the level of deep affective dialectics.*

The establishment of the superego (its pathological distortions aside) as the original law, inasmuch as it is associated with the recovery of the lost, killed love object and is, at the same time, brought about through the re-version upon the bad self of the aggressiveness previously directed against the love object, *resolves the problem of mourning avoiding either to project or to negate it.* Thus it succeeds, on the one hand, in recovering the lost object not only without denying the pain of loss (for only what has been lost can be recovered), but by actually passing through it as the requisite antecedent condition for the recovery of the object; and, on the other hand, without alienating, through a paranoid process, the bad parts of the self which are responsible for the loss of the object.[11]

[11] It is worth specifying that in speaking of mourning, loss, and recovery of the love object, we speak of fantasy processes that are for the most part unconscious, whether as object relations, anxieties, or reparative processes. Although unconscious, however, these events exert influence on a person's behavior and participate in character formation.

The question is to what extent the recovery of the original love object, as an absolute object, is possible. Obviously, such recovery is possible only at the secondary-object level and in a continuous dialectic and verification of illusion and reality.

The superego, then, may be considered the prototype of the law as a social institution whose task is the normal elaboration of mourning.

We have before asked ourselves whether the foundation of an Omega Institution which would forbid individuals to make war, regarded as an individual crime (normal elaboration of mourning), would be able to arouse in men unconscious repercussions. In order to attempt to answer this question, I should like to make use of the symbolic characters in the legend of St. George, the Virgin, and the Dragon. In the edifying version of war as a paranoid elaboration of mourning, St. George is the hero son, the virgin is the mother country threatened by an enemy-bad father represented by the dragon.

To continue to use this legend to describe the nuclear situation, let us say that St. George's sword has suddenly become an enormous stock pile of H bombs. Obviously, at this point, the roles of the characters in the legend change. If St. George still uses his H sword to slay the dragon, he also slays the virgin. The least that can happen to our hero (unless he be of the idea that *"fiat H pereat virgo"*) is that he will become the victim of a nightmare, because the Internal Terrifier is equal to the External Terrifier, that is to say, the H sword is equal to the nightmare of the dragon.

Now let us see if we can imagine how our unconscious could resonate in a new manner to a situation of this sort. Let us suppose that the virgin, the mother to be rescued, is peace (the sum total of men's concrete love objects), threatened by the dragon-war-H sword. What role shall we assign to our hero, who is a hero inasmuch as he saves the virgin? Obviously, we can no longer leave the H sword in his hands, because the H sword is now the same thing as the dragon-bad father who wishes to devour the mother. In the nuclear version of the legend, then, St.

George's sword and the dragon seem to fuse and to become one and the same thing. Accordingly, the nuclear version of the legend seems to induce us to feel more and more clearly that *peace, understood as the sum total of our concrete love objects,* is the new mother symbol and that we become the dragon if we naively continue to take refuge in the edifying symbol of St. George rescuing the virgin with his sword (now an H sword). The legend of St. George is thus on the point of disclosing its most profound psychoanalytic significance because the dragon is in reality the oral sadism of the child. And as the child experiences fantasies of destroying the mother, so we now discover that we are no longer the defenders of our country but matricides. It is in this antithesis that the antithetic significance of the paranoid and the normal elaboration of mourning may be seen. However, the transition from the first to the second type of elaboration of mourning arouses a series of ambiguities and anxieties.

Although St. George's sword is now an H sword, the prospect of no longer being able to exhibit our sword-potency to the dragon arouses in us anxieties of impotence. Since no longer to have a weapon (which is unconsciously sensed as a sexual symbol) arouses in us the fantastic fear that our mother-mother country is at the mercy of anyone, that she may be possessed by anyone, the disarmament fantasy arouses in us the anxiety that we shall cause our mother to become a prostitute and that we ourselves shall be made cuckolds of. Accordingly, in the present period of history, because of the dilemma which arises between persisting in the illusion of being able to save the virgin with the sword (even though it is now an H sword) and the feeling that we should be committing matricide if we were to use the H sword, we find ourselves in the particularly difficult situation of knowing how to preserve the capacity for objective judgment and to continue our journey avoiding both the Scylla of the anxiety of being cuckolded, should we fail to defend our mother for fear of the dragon, and the Charybdis of the fear of becoming matricides in the illusion of being heroes.

To exemplify the dilemma between the antithetic anxieties which we have described, we could make use of the story of a particularly dilemmatic hero: Hamlet, the pale prince of Elsinore.

The prenuclear situation, or, more accurately, a prenuclear situation of a war of liberation, could be easily connected with the Oedipus myth, in the classical version of St. George's legend.[12] We have, in this case, a good mother (mother-country) who is oppressed by a bad father (an enemy, the dragon who devours the virgin). St. George, like Oedipus, kills the father and rescues (marries) the mother.

In Hamlet's story, however, the events are far more complicated. Hamlet's mother is not a virgin mother; she is an adulteress who prompted her lover to kill the king, Hamlet's father. What should Hamlet do? As we know, Hamlet is the hero of doubt. The unconscious root of Hamlet's doubt, according to the most widely accepted psychoanalytic interpretation, consists in the fact that the uncle who kills the king and marries the queen is nothing but an alienated representation of Hamlet himself: that is to say, the uncle is the projection of Hamlet's wish to kill his father and marry his mother. (In some theatrical productions of the play, Hamlet's relationship with his mother is given incestuous overtones.)

The Internal Terrifier, in the form of a sense of guilt for incest and parricide, is projected into the uncle, through a sort of paranoid elaboration of mourning which trans-

---

[12] For a psychoanalytic interpretation of colonial wars of liberation, see *Psicanalisi della Guerra Atomica* (*The Psychoanalysis of Nuclear War*), by Franco Fornari (Milan, 1964).

forms Hamlet and his uncle into mortal enemies of each other.[13] In a manner, then, Hamlet's dilemma between loyalty to his father and the attachment to his mother is a repetition of the dilemma of Orestes. Orestes, however, is rescued by Athena's forgiving vote, while Hamlet's tragedy ends in a sort of panto-sacrificial rite in which Hamlet, like the soldier in war, is both the sacrificer and the sacrificed.

But apart from the fantasy meanings which it gains when traced to the unconscious, I should like to use the story of Hamlet and his dilemmatic situation to explain the unconscious repercussions connected with the ambiguities contained in the war crisis. Indeed, if one could continue to see one's country and one's ideology as the good mother, and to think of the enemy as the dragon, and of nuclear weapons as the sword with which St. George can slay the dragon, things would be quite simple.

If, however, we identify with Hamlet and are reluctant to kill the dragon-uncle (even though the ghost of the father continues to urge us to avenge him) we think ourselves cowards At the same time, if the uncle contains that part of us which wishes to kill the father in order to possess the mother (naturally not in an incestuous relationship, but as a good object which we wish to win), to kill the uncle may also mean to reject that part of the self which wishes to possess the mother, i.e., to win the love object. At this point the hypothesis could be advanced that the tragic epilogue of Hamlet's dilemma (this tragic ending is connected with the process which had made

---

[13] The paranoid elaboration of mourning which participates in the establishment of the other as enemy does not belong exclusively to the war phenomenon. It also participates in the formation of many interindividual pathological relationships. However, what is peculiar to the war phenomenon is the transformation of the paranoid elaboration of mourning into a venerable social institution.

Hamlet and his uncle enemies of each other) could have been avoided if Hamlet had recognized, in the ambiguous need for choice between loyalty to the mother and loyalty to the father, a personal dilemma of his, that is, if Hamlet, abandoning the paranoid elaboration of mourning, could have recognized in his uncle his own wish to kill his father and could also have realized that it was a wish only, not a deed! The admission that he wished to kill his father would have brought Hamlet pain for the fact that he experienced desires of this sort; he would have experienced feelings of mourning, but he would have been able to realize that his mother's adultery was only a dream, or rather a nightmare, on awakening from which he could have rectified his nightmares in the gentle face of Ophelia, his adult love object. His sexual possession of Ophelia would have realistically shown the illusory part of his destructive anxieties to be untrue, in an authentic elaboration of mourning expressed in the unconscious by the child whom he could have given life to with Ophelia. In this manner, love could have shown the persecutory and depressive anxieties to be unfounded through the fantasy that "it is not true that I kill and am being killed by the person I love; on the contrary, I engender life through love." Such an "edifying" version, so full of sense and so little psychotic, certainly would not have permitted Hamlet to become one of the greatest heroes of world literature. However, what I wished to show in referring to the story of Hamlet is that a certain possibility of choice exists between the normal and the paranoid elaboration of mourning.

The moral of the story, which seems at any rate to issue from the war crisis, is an acute situation of *dilemma between the old and the new mode of feeling loyalty toward one's love object*. According to the old type of loyalty, not to fight whatever the cost—even with nuclear weapons —to preserve one's love object constitutes the desertion of what one loves for fear of what one is afraid of. (St. George is a coward because he refuses to fight for fear of the dragon.)

According to the new type of loyalty, in which peace (the sum total of the love objects to be preserved) is the new mother symbol threatened by the dragon war, not to fight for the mother-peace against the dragon-war is to desert what we love because the need to prove that we know how to fight (as a defense against the fear of impotence) is narcissistically more important than the preservation of what we love. This is a situation that translates itself into the axiom of military fanaticism which, as we have seen, goes as far as to affirm that what is important is to fight, and not what one fights for. Explained in psychoanalytic terms, this axiom is a mechanism of defense against impotence: "The more I fight, the more I show that I am potent." But what could be hidden behind the compulsive need to prove one's potency if not the intimate, unconscious, infantile fear of impotence?

In the new myth, then, peace with all its goods to be preserved and enjoyed is the virgin threatened by the nuclear dragon. Consequently, it seems that in this new myth, not to feel bound to fight with the law (normal elaboration of mourning) instead of with the sword (paranoid elaboration of mourning) constitutes the greatest desertion and the greatest cowardice possible with regard to what we love.

The idea of the war phenomenon as a result of defenses against psychotic anxieties, rather than as the result of a conflict of interests, particularly economic, is usually met with strong resistance.

The reason for this resistance seems to reside in the

fact that since wars cause slaughter and ruins, the lack of a rational explanation, such as a conflict of interests, which would somehow justify the slaughter and ruins is apt to arouse a quantity of depressive anxieties. One of the so-called realistic ways of theorizing about war is that of the apologue of "the kick in the shins." It goes like this: "If someone kicks you in the shins, what do you do?" In this case a quarrel between individuals, which is governed by laws, is confused with war, which rather than being "a kick in the shins prohibited by law" is the "institutionalization of the kick in the shins."

Thus it happens that to speak of the illusory functions integrated in the war phenomenon ultimately results in the discussion of the illusory functions to be misunderstood as being illusory in itself, through a confusion of the object of a given discussion and the discussion itself; as if one were to confuse tuberculosis with a lecture on tuberculosis.

I have sometimes heard those who defend the thesis that war is a result of a conflict of interests, which are in turn governed by possessive impulses, illustrate their thesis with what I shall call the apologue of the quail. It tells of two men who go hunting. A quail is sighted; both hunters shoot at it, and the quail is killed. At this point arises a conflict of interests and war. Each of the two hunters is convinced that the quail rightly belongs to him; unable to come to an agreement, they begin shooting at each other, i.e., they make war.

As is usual with apologues of this type produced in support of *the realistic theory of war*, the apologue of the quail confuses a quarrel between two individuals with war. War is a social institution which states use to order the citizens to become hunters and to shoot at one another to determine who the quail belongs to, even though the citizens themselves may have no wish (consciously at least) to do so. Actually it seems that this apologue or others of the same sort are precisely what is needed to throw in relief the illusory functions of war.

In fact, if the two hunters, exasperated by their wish for exclusive possession of the quail, begin to make war, that is, begin to shoot at each other in order to kill each other, they carry out an operation that no longer has anything to do with the possession of the quail. The fact that the hunters shoot at each other signifies that, apart from the quail, they have arrived at *a fanatical position which transforms the two antagonists simultaneously into hunter and prey; each of the two hunters becomes quail for the other, substituting himself for the disputed object and submitting to the same process of killing that the object was subjected to.*

It is this transformation, then, of the two hunters into prey, their becoming simultaneously the sacrificer and the sacrificed in the death rite, that constitutes the transformation of the apologue of the quail into the war phenomenon. The possession of the quail is only the incidental cause. At this point it is obvious that the realistic factors which seemed so evident in the apologue of the quail are instead the superstructure of something much more complex and very interesting, but decidedly unrealistic; namely, the death rite.

At the most, the apologue of the quail as a theory of war signifies "to be mutually transformed into quail in order to determine who the quail belongs to." Now it does not seem to be a result of professional distortion to call the mode, so described, of selecting the owner a psychotic process in comparison with other modes of competition for ownership which are more realistic. Thus those who uphold the realistic theory of war as promoted by conflicts of interests *very often tend to confuse the real existence of conflicts of interests with the psychotic mode of resolving them.*

Hamlet's story as paradigmatic of the difficult choice between loyalty to the father (the sovereignty of the state), which leads to the desertion of the mother (peace), and loyalty to the mother (peace), which leads to the desertion of the father (sovereignty of the state), may be adequate to make us understand the double desertion—each of which is anxiety arousing—which we are apt to commit in the nuclear situation.

In fact, if we remain loyal to the sovereignty of the state which leads us to war as the institutionalization of the paranoid elaboration of mourning, we desert peace as the preservation of earthly goods.

If instead we choose loyalty to the mother-peace as the receptacle of our love objects, we feel that we are deserting the father who, like Hamlet's father, instigates us to avenge his honor, even at the cost of destroying his love object (his wife). One of the most conspicuous results of the change in power politics, which is a consequence of the nuclear age, in fact seems to be that the struggle between states no longer acts as a preservation of the love object (because nuclear weapons destroy it), but rather expresses our desire the more to exhibit our potency as a defense against the fear of being impotent the more potent we are: hence a vicious circle which grows bigger and bigger until we understand the illusory and infantile character of the impotence anxiety. In the current period of history, perhaps more than ever, the impotence complex makes us fear, as it did Hamlet, that loyalty to the mother is cowardice and that "conscience does make cowards of us all."

For my part, I believe that the prevalence of the functions that pursue the preservation of the love object, over the impotence anxieties-fears (as a purely narcissistic function of the self), is a typical trait of a man's maturity. I believe, moreover, that this type of behavior belongs to the type described by Money-Kyrle as humanistic.

I would, then, like to call humanistic those who, in the nuclear era, feel that war is no longer an instrument of defense of, or loyalty toward, what they love, but on the contrary a betrayal and a desertion of every love object, theirs as well as others'.

Peace is the good mother threatened by war as the bad father; accordingly, desertion of peace (the mother) and obedience to war (the bad father) are typical of the authoritarian personality. Persons of this type react to the prospect of renouncing war as to something that arouses in them the fear of losing an instrument of potency. Authoritarians would appear to experience anxiety not at the prospect of their love object being destroyed, but rather at the prospect of not having at their disposal an instrument with which to possess their love object. Dominated by this fear, therefore, they feel castrated at the prospect of being no longer able to make war. They are not interested in enjoying their love object, but rather they fear that if they were disarmed, their love object would be possessed by others.

Humanists and authoritarians exist within each group, each political party, each nation, each class, each major state, any ideological or religious group; and the two anxieties from which these two characters originate exist within each man.

Now that every individual sees the enormous importance that the prevalence of one or the other type of anxiety or of one or the other type of defensive character structure can have at the level of decision-making, especially in international politics, it seems that the new frontier[14] no longer separates one ideology from another, one class from another, one country from another, one political party from another, one church or one army from another. The new frontier runs within each ideological group, each class, each country, each political party, each major state, and, finally, within each man. This new frontier will be the scene of brave battles which will perhaps decide the issue of our survival.

[14] The theory of the new frontier, as I have tried to outline it here, would therefore imply the need for a new process of splitting at the moment when the process of totalization leads to the danger of confusion and therefore of inefficiency and paralysis. However, the concept of splitting associated with the delimitation of the new frontier is obviously not a return to the process of paranoid elaboration of mourning, which is traceable to a process of splitting off of the bad parts of the self and of their expulsion into the other. The humanistic type of character in fact rests on the normal elaboration of mourning; the humanist's opposition of the authoritarian occurs not in a splitting into friend and enemy, but in a new dialectic between the healthy and the sick man which, even before it is expressed on an external frontier, is expressed on an internal frontier that runs within each man. As a literary simplification of the mode in which the operating of the new frontier may delineate itself concretely, I should like to cite the film *Fail Safe*. Whoever has seen this movie will remember that each of the two major states (America and Russia) is split into two groups, authoritarians who feel that to trust the enemy—so that nuclear war may be avoided—is a betrayal, and humanists for whom betrayal consists in not trusting the sincerity of the enemy. Notably, in this film the heads of the two major states are humanists, while the authoritarians are non-military intellectuals.

# EPILOGUE

The presentation of my paper at the Twenty-fifth International Congress of Romance Language Psychoanalysts was followed by a debate in which many members of the Congress participated. Among these were André Green, Bofil, Madame Spira, Alberoni, Abadi, Madame Clancier, Luquet, Barande, and Dalibard.

I tried to answer the arguments, obviously dedicating myself more to the criticisms, objections, and questions that had been advanced than to the very numerous and at times fervid approbations. I wish to take up again some of the arguments here in the hope that what was simply a sketch of a debate may lead, through publication in this volume, to further exploration and discussion.

During the debate Professor Alberoni attempted to individuate—along the guidelines of the Kleinian discoveries—a more specific original collective than the mother-child duad. When he considers the mother-father couple (as it is experienced on the fantasy level by the child in the form of the paternal penis inside the mother, or in the form of a combined parental figure) as a primary collective which is originally felt as such and as one object by the child; when he proposes to us the emergence of Oedipus in relation to the child's need to extract from the combined parental figure (conceived as an original fantasy collective and as originally frustrating) a single preferential and gratifying object, he proposes to us, so to speak, a *primitively sociological conception of Oedipus.*

In the story of Oedipus—as it has been told to us in the Greek myth—the primitive fact is not parricide and incest, but rather the criminal parental couple who has condemned the newborn Oedipus to death. Thus it could be said—adhering to the myth—that Oedipus experienced in his cradle the infanticidal intention of his parents, united against him in the combined parental figure.

I fully agree with Alberoni's hypothesis that in the individual who must adjust to it, society could cause the mobilization of psychotic anxieties. Moreover, this hypothesis can be verified clinically in microgroups whose dynamics have been studied by group psychotherapy. Bion and others have noted a situation of this type, and I have been able to confirm it personally through the supervision of a group psychoanalysis conducted by Dr. Napolitani.

On the other hand, there surely are reality functions in group life connected with sociocultural, economic, political, and other situations that are interwoven with the symbiotico-narcissistic situation I have tried to derive from the analysis of the ceremonial of mourning—which is itself a typical and normal social experience. Evidently the paranoid elaboration of mourning among primitive peoples does not at all imply that they are unable to verify the dead body as a reality datum.

It is true that it is possible to consider the group experience in many ways, just as one can do with the human experience in general. If I have tried to consider the group's strange criteria of truth in relation to the symbiotico-narcissistic position, it is because this position—which is obviously regressive but not abnormal in group life—finds its most clamorous realization in the war phenomenon. This in turn radically reverses the problem of the mobilization of psychotic anxieties to which the individual finds himself exposed when he begins his relationship with the group. The brutality of primitive peoples' initiation rites may well lead to the mobilization of profound anxieties, but the initiation into war, which coincides with such rites, constitutes at the same time the defense against these anxieties, to the extent that war offers a concrete possibility of destroying—in a way which is both magic and realistic—the anxiety-arousing imagos that have been projected from the group onto the enemy.

Alberoni also had reservations about Róheim's statement regarding the projection of the maternal imago onto one's own group. It seems to me that one cannot deny this affirmation and at the same time uphold the thesis of the original collective, the thesis based on the combined parental imago that Alberoni has proposed to us. In both cases one postulates, in group formation, the externalization of fantasy imagos on the group.

The shadow of infanticidal intentions over Oedipus' cradle—a theme that is connected with the unconscious repercussions of the demographic factor of war as deferred infanticide—is related to the argument of Dr. Abadi, who brought us the valuable testimony of South American psychoanalysis. I was very much struck by his thoughts on the relation between war and the psychotic elaboration of the themes connected with birth and matricide. In my own experience I have not found clinical evidence to support the fact that at birth the infant develops fantasies of matricide except in a generic schizoparanoid elaboration of the original experiences of anxiety. Nevertheless, I have been able to observe on the mother's side certain occurrences that may be considered parallel to the fantasy vicissitudes of the infant, as related to us by Dr. Abadi.

In collaboration with professors Malcovati and Miraglia

I have, in fact, had the opportunity to study the fantasy content of the anxieties that are mobilized in the mother at the moment of childbirth. I have been able to observe that during labor the mother experiences, temporarily but very acutely, primary anxieties of the paranoid and depressive type. Specifically, in the dilating period of labor, the mother's anxieties refer mainly to persecutory fantasies of being injured and destroyed by the child. During the expulsory part of labor, on the other hand, typical depressive anxieties connected with the fear of injuring and destroying the baby are mobilized in the mother. These occurrences may be compared to what Dr. Abadi has said about the infant's side of it, in regard to the paranoid and depressive dynamics that are structured in the war phenomenon.

Madame Clancier presented a clinical case in which dream fantasies of war were particularly implicated in the mechanism of omnipotent sadistic control over the frustrating object. On the methodological level, this situation is connected with the problem of using dream fantasies of war as material from which certain evidence can be extracted to serve as an introduction to a discussion of the tracing of the war phenomenon to the unconscious.

In *The Interpretation of Dreams*, Freud taught us that we are psychologically responsible for our dreams, and he clearly stated that whoever denies this will not be able to understand anything about psychoanalysis. Every day we observe in our clinical work that in dreams political or military authorities become parental images. What we usually do in our work is precisely to trace the dream world to the subject's wishes. Through such a tracing, Hitler's image appearing in a dream becomes a reality receptacle of a dreamer's parental object, to the point where this object may be rediscovered as the fantasy repercussion of the dreamer's destructive impulse.

This is the reason why the wonderful description of Richard's case, which Melanie Klein has given us in her *Narrative of a Child Analysis*, may be regarded as the best preparatory reading for the psychoanalytic theory of the war phenomenon. If Hitler is seen not only as a real historical entity, but also as Richard's bad father and at the same time as Richard's projected sadism, the problem that confronts us is how to know what we are supposed to make of these psychoanalytic discoveries. We find here all that is essential for tracing the war phenomenon to the unconscious. Concerning *the implication of the war phenomenon in the unconscious of the individuals*, what confronts us is not, then, a methodological problem but a fact of empirical observation. We observe in our unconscious what Ugo Foscolo[1] has called "the native raving of battles" that is in every man. This is not, however, something newly discovered by psychoanalysis. The specifically psychoanalytic discovery is that this "raving of battles" constitutes a "raving" activity in the clinical sense because psychotic anxieties and processes of projection into the enemy of both the representations of one's parental objects and the representations of the self visibly participate in the establishment of the other as enemy.

It is a fact of empirical observation that in preconscious fantasies the war phenomenon is often used by the subjects, even in time of peace, to express unconscious fantasy vicissitudes. Is it a problem of language here, of expression, in the sense of a dream semantics, or does this expression contain a decidedly dynamic significance?

Before speaking of the methodology of applied psychoanalysis we must, I think, take a fairly definite position with regard to this problem. If we say that we are facing a problem purely of dream semantics, we assume the re-

[1] Italian poet of the late eighteenth–early nineteenth century. (Translator's note.)

sponsibility of denying—we psychoanalysts!—any dynamic significance of the unconscious in the life of men. What is more, we risk taking a position that finally removes all dynamic significance from the general phenomena of transference and causes the transference itself to become a purely metaphoric expression.

An important question was posed to me at the Congress regarding the limits within which the psychoanalytic investigation may be exercised. At the risk of oversimplification let me state that *territory open to psychoanalysis may be found in every situation in which transference phenomena take place.*

The social phenomenon, as Freud and Róheim have shown, is a privileged sector for the massive activation of transference situations. The difficulty encountered in evidencing the transference processes in the realm of social phenomena may reside precisely in the symbiotico-narcissistic position which renders arduous the simultaneity of identification and neutrality in the observer. For the moment, as Madame Kestemberg pointed out in 1963 at the First International Congress of Group Psychotherapy in Milan, group psychoanalysis seems to constitute the most important tool, from the methodological point of view, for the exploration of collective life. The dynamic situations offered us in group psychotherapy, in reference to certain typical roles that are played in therapeutical groups, seem to confirm rather than deny the constant participation in social life of the mechanism of paranoid elaboration of mourning, as a mechanism more peculiar to collective psychology than to individual psychology.

On the other hand, as regards my thesis of the individual responsibility for war, I think that, even from the methodological point of view, it may be strictly based on the individual psychoanalytic investigation, that is, on the investigation of *the individual modes of living the collective experience,* which we encounter every day in the clinical practice.

I do not think that psychoanalysis can describe war in all of its reality; but it can, and I think must, describe the ways in which war is unconsciously experienced by individuals. In a general formulation, then, it could be said that psychoanalysis may study the social facts as screen structures, upon which the individuals continuously carry out transference processes. It seems to me, therefore, that what Durkheim said of the social reality conceived "as a thing" may be understood and integrated by psychoanalysis in the sense that the social phenomenon constitutes something which has a reality of its own but upon which the individuals continuously operate transference processes.

The thesis of the individual responsibility for war, then, may be based on the reality of the transferences in which the individual modes of collective experience express themselves.

It is therefore tragic that in our era these responsibilities, though demonstrable from the point of view of the psychoanalytic science as the science of the human unconscious, do not as yet have at their disposal social institutions which would permit these individual forces to be integrated into the social reality. *Psychoanalysis may, therefore, denounce this lack as a dangerous social vacuum, as a situation of anomie.*

It is worth recalling that among some primitive peoples, a situation of this type has already been realized. Among certain African tribes, for example, when a man dreams of having sexual intercourse with another man's woman, he goes the following day to the family of the woman he possessed in the dream, to make reparation in the form of gifts. As Fanon told us, these tribes take the unconscious seriously.

We find here a situation that agrees with the theme of the guilt for unconscious fantasies, of the possibility of socialization of this guilt, of its nature, its limits, its ambiguity, its inevitability, its unauthentic participation in the war phenomenon, etc. All of these problems are closely involved with our discipline.

Dr. Barande justly asked what would be the possible concrete results of the proposed solution. First of all, I should not wish my thesis to be confused with a simple pacifist position, understood as a preference for peace rather than war. All men are in general convinced of wanting peace. It is precisely psychoanalysis, however, that disillusions men by uncovering unconscious tendencies that imply both a desire for war and a sense of guilt for this desire.

My thesis takes as its starting point the historical observation of the crisis of war with the advent of the nuclear era. The nuclear situation has thrown us into a condition analogous to that of the Kanachi tribes deprived of war. This means that there is no need for us psychoanalysts to become—as Barande suggested—the sorcerers who kill. As we shall see further on, our culture is already living a situation of this sort and is already beginning to become aware of it. Since it throws the war institution into jeopardy, we may foresee that the pantoclastic prospect will fatally lead to a re-emergence within the groups of destructive anxieties that until now could be silenced by exporting the aggressiveness to the outside.

It seems, therefore, that we may expect an increase in the level of drama in the communal life within groups and perhaps a generic depressive tendency which would in its turn enter into a dialectic antithesis with the old position of paranoid elaboration of mourning.

Lanternari's researches have shown that among the primitive tribes deprived of war, in addition to the depressive evolution Elaine Metais has written of, there exist others. In these cases the depressive evolution is avoided through warlike myths in which the dead ancestors are fantasied to rise from the dead and to lead their tribes in a war of liberation against the whites. The nuclear bomb, however, is not a melancholiac or paranoid myth, but a concrete destructive reality which permits us (and in a way forces us) to verify the paranoid and depressive myths in terms of reality.

Dr. Barande's stimulating question has forced me to advance a more specific, and at the same time paradoxical, answer: The most probable result of the realization of my thesis could be its militarization; that is to say, I think that my thesis has a capacity for arousing impassioned approvals as well as equally impassioned rejections.

When psychoanalysis treats a neurosis or a psychosis, it provokes a transference neurosis or psychosis. In the same manner, it may be foreseen that if the course of action which I have proposed for curing war has a psychoanalytic character, *there is a great possibility of its provoking a transference war.*

The hypothesis that any attempt to follow a pacifist course of action is apt to and perhaps even must provoke a transference war was suggested to me by the countertransference reactions at the Congress. I must say that during the meetings I felt very keenly the approval of the members of the Congress and did not give much consideration to their reservations. But after a day or so—without anything having changed in reality—I found myself in a totally opposite position. In fact, I felt the reservations very strongly, while the approvals faded into the background. It was as if my feeling of having won a battle had suddenly changed into a feeling of being defeated by an impossible task. It then became evident that in my unconscious fantasies I had gone to the Congress as if to a war in which I was both victor and vanquished. It occurred to me that it was perhaps necessary to place both myself and the Congress "on the couch," even if on my side this could have an aggressive significance toward the Congress itself. The Congress thus appeared to me as a sociological reality in which I found myself deeply involved.

The concrete experience at the Congress, as a sociological experience that had translated itself into my emotional responses of victory-defeat, could then find concrete social evidence (the approvals or rejections of the members of the Congress) in which to rationalize itself. But the awareness of the fantasy contents of my emotional response allowed me to trace, in the contributions to the debate as a whole (above and beyond their specific content), a certain militarized, or, to use a word of Greek derivation, polemical movement.

It was then obvious that Dr. Green's contribution to the debate, in which my paper had been called the most important work on the subject since Freud's *Civilization and Its Discontents,* had an idealizing significance which transformed my theses into a banner for the battle against the removal of psychoanalysis into scientific neutrality. Some of the other contributions to the debate, on the other hand, as, for example, Dr. Dalibard's (who maintained that one cannot speak of the nuclear catastrophe until it has been experienced) became a persecutory attack against this idealization: an attack which seemed to originate in the fact that my supporting the humanist position as opposed to the authoritarian one was sensed by Dr. Dalibard as a threat to analytic neutrality, in turn idealized as normative of our discipline.

At this point the Congress, *as experienced by me,* was

on the verge of militarizing itself through the formation
of two subgroups, each of which was apt, through an epistemological splitting, to take a partial truth and use it to
fight another partial truth (the thesis of the responsibility
for our unconscious used against the methodological concerns and the methodological concerns used against the
thesis of the responsibility for our unconscious).

Concerning the general significance of the epistemological splitting and of its militarization, my thoughts are
based not only on what happened at the Congress but
also on clinical group experience.

I am referring to my work in group supervision in the
Psychotherapy Department of the Psychiatric Clinic of
the Milan University. My intention was to investigate
group dynamics in a group formed of psychiatrists who
were at an advanced stage in their psychoanalytic training and were beginning to treat psychiatric patients in
the clinic.

After a period in which my task was to speak from time
to time on the technique of psychoanalytic treatment in
a pedagogic way, I decided to stop doing this in order to
try to mobilize a certain anxiety through a calculated frustration. I was proposing in this manner to observe the
ways in which each psychiatrist under supervision controlled his own anxieties. I noted then that following
some anxiety reactions—which could be recognized as relating to the frustration of the wish to be nourished by
my words (food)—each member of the group adopted a
different attitude. Some became passive, while others became decidedly active. When a given clinical material was
presented by one of the members, the other members'
participations in the discussion revealed a clear tendency
to splitting in their manner of understanding the clinical
material.

Thus I have called epistemological splitting that process

through which each member approached the clinical material, extracting from it a partial aspect which was then set against the others. This peculiarity seemed to me typical of group supervision, as contrasted with individual supervision. I have observed another typical situation which is parallel to the epistemological splitting, namely, that the members who became more active were also those who tended to use *one aspect of reality to deny another.* Later it was possible to show that the "partial aspects" of reality which were polemically maintained were in reality associated with the dominant defense mechanism of each participant's personality.

The dominant defense mechanisms of each group member's personality were decisive in the intuition as well as in the choice and use of technical and scientific notions which characterized our work. At a certain point I had the feeling that if I did not intervene to interpret the mechanisms involved in group dynamics (independently from the specific content of the various interventions), the group's technical efficiency could have greatly deteriorated, to the point where in the end the group itself could have disintegrated. Against this background, my function as a supervisor, which was that of a leader of a microgroup, had the possibility either to augment or to reduce the processes of splitting and militarization, depending on whether I intervened as a pedagogue—supporting, for example, one member's partial truth in preference to others—or analyzed the group dynamics; that is to say, depending on whether I assumed a pedagogic or an analytic function.

We may therefore ask ourselves whether this might serve as a model which could be transposed to the sociological field in general. For the moment I think that this cannot be either denied or affirmed. It may be supposed, nevertheless, that if the battles that took place in the psychoanalytic sphere—battles which pertain to the sociology of psychoanalysis—could have been acted out in sessions of group psychoanalysis, their militarization could have been softened and perhaps rendered more profitable for the development of our discipline.

It is evident, at any rate, that psychoanalysis cannot replace history—psychoanalysis is itself a part of history. But at the moment when history forces national communities to coexist, psychoanalysis, by showing the unconscious motivations for war, can make a contribution to the study of the general human modes of experience which make coexistence possible. After all, the presence and significance of psychoanalysis at a given moment in the history of Western culture cannot be considered an accident, even though it could become necessary for some psychoanalysts to turn into sociologists in order to bring psychoanalysis in contact with new methodologies which would render it operatively more fruitful.

I realize that to compare the normal arguments which take place at every scientific Congress to bloody battles between nations seems an oversimplification. However, since arguing arises from the process of epistemological splitting (through which the individual extracts a partial aspect from a given truth and deludes himself that by fighting and denying another's truth he supports his own), we can understand why Freud said that if scientific problems began to interest men at large, violent battles would break out in the name of science. It seems, then, that the quest for truth does not render man free of his strivings.

This psychoanalytic conclusion, though apparently pessimistic, nevertheless contains an insight which can be *the best antidote to the dogmatization which reveals itself to us as a typical mechanism of militarization of culture.* This insight would appear to have the same therapeutic significance as the discovery that the psychoanalytic treatment of neurosis or psychosis leads to the transference neurosis or transference psychosis. This is perhaps the best method of approach for avoiding the paranoid elaboration of mourning, for it renders the psychoanalyst conscious of the paradoxical fact that, in a certain sense, it is the cure itself that sets in motion the ill one wishes to cure.

Transporting this specifically and peculiarly psychoanalytic discovery to the social level, it may be affirmed that the psychoanalyst who wishes to use psychoanalysis to "cure" war must accept the responsibility for the mobilization of that very ill which he wishes to cure. If the psychoanalyst proposes certain tentative cures for the war illness, understood essentially as the manifest result of unconscious psychotic maneuvers, he must be fully aware that he is running the risk of being considered a sorcerer who saves and/or destroys, as Dr. Barande has suggested. We know, moreover, that this has been the fate of many innovators in human history; not only of the mystico-religious ones, but also of scientific innovators from Galileo to Freud. I am not, however, calling for martyrdom, but merely pointing out that certain risks are an unavoidable part of our profession. This is simply because we form a neutral screen for the transferences of the persons whom we analyze and to whom we explain, from time to time, precisely that they make us become saviors or destroyers, in order to hand back to them their potential for love or hate. If the psychoanalytic tool were to operate in the social field, we should have to expect complications which, however, would not be totally unforeseeable in a psychoanalytic perspective.

The legitimate expectation of *a transference war,* which would probably occur in the event one wished to "cure" war, could then give to a discovery of this sort a specific character which would hardly be accessible to a non-analytical approach.

Given the current historical situation in which the war crisis has also brought with it the crisis of the ideology-forming processes (or rather, of the dogmatization of political myths), psychoanalytic research could acquire a particular function in revealing the nature of the schizo-paranoid processes that lie beneath what can be called the groups' general tendency to form in a Manichean way.

I know full well that to do this means to deprive men of their illusions and I, for one, am not inclined to dispel illusions because I believe that they perform an essential role in their dialectic with reality. But now it is evident that, with the advent of the nuclear era, war itself, this "grand illusion," has entered a state of crisis with regard to its function of a dispenser of illusions.

One realizes that it might be unpopular for psychoanalysis to claim the right to qualify as psychotic the process of idealization which controls the formation of ideologies in groups. In the face of this attitude, the same rebellion is to be expected which would be encountered on the clinical level if one should wish to unmask a delusional activity, qualifying it as such to the subject who is experiencing it. Psychoanalysis, which was in the position to discover the meanings and the profound realities which lie behind the dereal appearances of a delusion, can be all the more in a position to discover, and in a certain sense to validate, on a different level, the meanings and the intimate human realities which lie behind the ideologies.

Our task, therefore, is not to jeopardize the ideologies and war because history seems to have already taken care of this. This task, in other words, has been historically fulfilled by the war crisis which is connected with the pantoclastic nuclear prospect. Actually, the necessity of changing the relations between groups cannot be either denied or affirmed by psychoanalysis. This necessity will be dealt with by the cogent historical conditions in the nuclear era. Psychoanalysis does not propose to suggest that the tasks of our era are the tasks of survival because this appertains after all to the wishes of men. Psychoanalysis can, however, try to individuate the means through which survival may be better ensured.

So if the process of ideology-formation leads to a conservative process which expresses itself in the motto *fiat justitia pereat mundus,* psychoanalysis can show that this process arises through an illusory hope of preserving one's love object, an illusory hope which, as we have seen, finds its origin in a manic elaboration of mourning or loss in general. In other words, the rise of an ideology would appear to be connected with the fundamental dynamics and the deep-seated processes which condition the human ego to found itself on a love object or rather on a sort of incapacity of man to accept the loss of the formative love object (the mother). To reiterate Róheim's thesis, an ideology would appear to arise from a sort of intimate human need to try to regain in an illusory form what can no longer be kept in a concrete form. Hence the essential relation between ideology and mourning which was underlined by Money-Kyrle.

Here we find ourselves face to face with a singular need of man which is closely bound to the necessity of defending oneself against the experience of loss as a depressive experience, namely, the need for illusion. From this need arises a continuous tension along with a continuous dialectic between the illusory and the real. This continuous tension and continuous dialectic is the field of the psychoanalytic verification in its everyday experience of the dialectic between the internal and external world, between fantasy activity and reality; and this, I believe, is the most essential contribution of psychoanalysis to a general theory of knowledge which would seem to find in the social field one of its specific fields of application and verification.

In this perspective we may grasp, in my opinion, the difference between a conception of the nature of the war phenomenon seen as, for example, the result of economic conflicts and ultimately of class struggle—and therefore of a real conflict of interests—and a conception of war seen as a psychotic process which—beyond any concrete conflict of interests—develops as the result of the paranoid elaboration of mourning. I should like to clarify my thought at this point, affirming that in the war phenomenon there really exists a continuous tension and a continuous dialectic between the real conflict of interest and the psychotic conflict. Now, even if we disregard the not at all unfounded theory of Bouthoul—according to which the economic functions of war reveal themselves as purely functions of destruction of economic goods rather than functions of acquisition of economic goods—psychoanalysis can show that even on the level of real conflicts of interests, which are expressed in the class struggle, psychotic processes interfere which can decide, at a given moment, the character and the more or less realistic aspects concretely assumed by the class struggle.

Are psychoanalysts "the sorcerers who kill"? The transformation of a magic entity which protects into a magic entity which kills (the transformation feared by Barande as a possible result of a pacifist system that would deprive men of war) reveals itself in the current period of history to be closely connected with the nuclear war as absolute war which would prevent the dialectic between reality and illusion.

It could also be said, however, that a situation of this sort is not fatally destined to evolve toward the apathicomelancholiac situation of the Kanachi tribesmen, who expected that they would be killed by their own sorcerers. In the film *The Battleship Potemkin*, we see the revolution break out at the exact moment when the sailors, having received rotten meat to eat, externalize upon the officers the persecutory phantasm to be destroyed. At that moment, in other words, in a particular integration of fantasy and reality, the officers become the mother who kills because she serves poisoned food, while the good maternal imago, the mother-good fairy, in a dimension that is both illusory and real, will fill a new symbol of group identification: namely, the socialist revolution.

If, however, we think for a moment about Stalin and the history of the socialist revolution, we realize that, through Stalinism, the paranoid elaboration of mourning resurfaces within the revolution itself, when reality contradicts the idealized expectations. The revolution (the good mother, the revolution attained and enjoyed by the revolutionaries-sons) deteriorates, and the incapacity to accept the suffering for this deterioration as a mourning produced by the same sons who are nourished by the mother brings Stalin to project the guilt onto his brothers, and the revolutionaries themselves are deported to Siberia.

Thus Stalin's trial will repeat, within the group, their anxiety of being destroyed by their own sorcerer. The history of men, a singular integration of phantasms and reality, seems, then, to be guided by *a mysterious repetition of what has already been*, a repetition related to the very essence of the transference as discovered by Freud.

The theory and practice of the transference neurosis, as a re-emergence of neurosis in the curative process itself, seems to have a relation to what Sartre has called counter-finality. We have seen on the historical level the equivalent of what is, on the clinical level, the transference neurosis. Thus Christianity rises as a redemptory myth of liberation from guilt; its advent, however, leads to the exacerbation of the world of guilt. The French Revolution affirms itself in the name of liberty, equality, and brotherhood; its advent leads to Bonapartism. The Soviet Revolution seeks to prevent the domination of man by man; its advent leads to the exacerbation of domination in the form of Stalinism, and so on and so forth. One would be tempted to think, therefore, that when man wishes to fight against evil, if he chases it out the door he must expect to see it come back through the window. This observation, though pessimistic, could be very valuable if true.

Let us return now to the hypothesis that if one wishes to "treat" war, one must expect a "transference war." To show how useful a similar working hypothesis could be in the political field, I am going to develop some hypothetical considerations, applying them, in imagination, to concrete situations.

It may be supposed that, if the hypothesis that the fight against man's domination by man could determine the re-emergence of a "transference domination" (Stalinism) were among the predictions of the Marxist theorists, the Russian revolutionary leaders could have realized this and so could have better tolerated the depressive anxieties deriving from the observation of the deterioration of the revolutionary ideals. They would have been in a position to avoid the projection of their guilt feelings onto loyal servants of the revolution. Such an awareness could also have reinforced the ego of the revolutionaries themselves, permitting them to tolerate depressive feelings, and diminishing the tendency to fanatic dogmatization and the compulsion to elaborate mourning paranoically, in the form of Stalinism, within the revolution.

If I here propose as desirable the acceptance of depressive anxieties (which seem inevitable if one abandons the paranoid elaboration of mourning), it should also be clear that such a proposition—which in effect corresponds to the humanistic type as described by Money-Kyrle—does not in any way intend to idealize depressive suffering as opposed to paranoid suffering. The acceptance of depressive suffering as the capacity to tolerate anxiety in general is aimed at creating the possibility of new integrations between fantasy and reality, between the internal and the external world.

In fact if one admits that the deterioration of the ideals of the revolution does not happen at the hands of "the enemies of the revolution" but inevitably takes place in the process of putting the revolutionary ideals into practice, then the control of the anxieties, both paranoid and depressive, becomes the indispensable condition for dealing with the problem of deterioration and reparation in terms of reality.

If one accepts this formulation, he must also admit that the crisis of the paranoid elaboration of mourning with regard to the so-called "enemies of the revolution" leads to a diminution of the fanatic component implicit in every revolution. This arouses anxieties relating to the weakening of one's own impetus, sensed as dedication to the revolution itself as a love object. This would lead to depressive anxieties due to the fact that the de-dogmatization of the modes of living the political experience may arouse a sense of guilt connected with the fantasies of desertion of one's love object.

In this context, the idealization of consumption, which seems to constitute the dogma of the bourgeois society that is pursued in a fanatical manner through the myths of production, would seem to strive to deny, through compulsorily offering consumer goods, the persecutory phantasm of a mother who allows her children to starve. Clinically, this corresponds to the attitude of certain anorectic or bulimic patients who refuse food or eat enormous amounts of it, not because of a lack of appetite or an actual need for food, but in order to defend themselves against the anxiety of an illusory starvation produced precisely by the fantasy of a mother who allows one to starve. The relativization of the myth of production performed by many humanistic types would therefore appear to be sensed as the danger of the emergence of a persecutory object which is then elaborated and projected into the phantasm of a socialist society as a society of starving ragamuffins.

Thus the interference of psychotic anxieties weakens the capacity concretely to assess reality and an enormous amount of wealth is used to construct nuclear weapons which, paradoxically, serve to the poor and the rich, to the starving and bulimic nations to control deep and psychotic persecutory anxieties.

Against the background of psychotic anxieties, the real militarization of the relations between nations augments the psychotic level of the relations themselves, resulting in a more and more unverifiable entanglement of phantasms and reality. Owing to this entanglement, the verification of what is illusory and what is real in the problems which are on the verge of causing humanity to destroy itself becomes more and more difficult. On the practical level and on the level of political preferences, it is fairly easy to identify with one's group and perhaps, in the best of the hypotheses, to opt for the starving, weak nations; but the process of militarization of the relations between groups threatens at this point to render such preferences inane.

At the historical moment when humanity, driven by its deep psychotic anxieties, is apt to perish in the attempt to identify with phantasms in order to destroy phantasms, the most important task of man seems to have become a rigorous application of the reality principle to one's own choices as a continuous dialectic integration between the illusory and the real—in a new dialectic between the sane man and the man who is mentally ill.

Finally, I would like to touch on a general theoretic problem which may, on the one hand, relate to the meeting between psychoanalysis and the other sciences of man and, on the other, to aggressiveness and the death instinct.

The very fact that we are alive somehow leads us to deny the death instinct as if it were a question of denying certain disquieting realities out of a debt of gratitude toward the mother, who has denied them with her love. This is perhaps why mourning (a fantasy denial of love and of its partly realistic and partly illusory function of giving life to libidinal objects), and especially war as paranoid elaboration of mourning, could be the privileged terrain for observing certain disquieting evidences of the death instinct. *As loss of the love objects that satisfy the needs, mourning would appear to leave man face to face with absence, as a dramatic image of his own annihilation; that is to say, face to face with the emergence of the death instinct.*

The paranoid elaboration of mourning would therefore seem to be connected with what Freud has called "the biological excuse for war." It must be noted, however, that this is not the psychological excuse. In a merely predatory animal, the paranoid elaboration of mourning would be unthinkable. This is because the animal's relation to its prey is not complicated by the mysterious fantasy formation with which man's affective ambivalence distorts his relation to his original love objects. Such a fantasy formation does, in fact, seem to be the singular prerogative and original folly of man. Since war has occurred without fail thoughout the history of *Homo sapiens*, this does not seem to be due so much to his being a predatory animal as to the fact that his predatoriness is primarily directed against his love object. Paradoxically, war thus seems to be a madness of love rather than a madness of hate.

For this reason, on a merely predatory, biological level, the increase in available consumer goods does not seem to mitigate the war phenomenon. On the contrary, it could even exacerbate it.

Among primitive peoples the first accumulations of economic goods, of wealth, are not aimed at saturating man's predatoriness but are destined to be sacrificed to the dead ancestors-gods. This indicates how the archaic foundations of the political economy itself are intimately associated with the elaboration of mourning. The very myth of original sin, which our culture received from the Hebraic culture, as a bite of the apple-breast that angered God-mother, indicates to what an extent the sense of guilt for an illusory cannibalism reigns in the original madness of man, connected with the fantasy distortion of the possession and loss of the primary love object.

If, then, the war phenomenon is not so much connected with the congenital predatoriness of man as with the fantasy complication of his ambivalent relation to the primary love object, the problem of understanding, and eventually of curing, the war phenomenon becomes a human and therapeutic task. One could even say, with Glover, that the war phenomenon is itself a therapeutic attempt—an attempt to face phantasmic anxieties through the translation of the psychotic dimension in terms of reality.

The attempt of psychoanalysis to unmask and recognize the war phenomenon as a psychotic phenomenon seems therefore permissible at a moment when history itself, as the history of the nuclear era, induces men to awaken from the grand illusion. At this point war itself—as absolute war—exposes men to experiencing as realistic anxieties those same psychotic, i.e., illusory, anxieties which until now war was able to mask and illusorily to resolve.

Beyond all pessimism and all optimism, then, the psychoanalysis of war proceeds in the investigation of certain unconscious realities with the specific intention of showing the illusory functions of war at the moment when life on earth is in danger of perishing in man's attempt to destroy phantasms in order to save phantasms.

# ADDITIONAL READINGS

ARON, R., *Les Guerres Enchaîne*, Paris, 1951.

——, *Paix et Guerres Entre les Nations*, Paris, 1962.

ARROW, K. J., *Social Choice and Individual Values*, New York, 1951.

ATKINSON, J. D., *The Edge of War*, Chicago, 1960.

BAKER, P. N., *The Arms Race*, London, 1958.

BARNET, R. J., *Who Wants Disarmament?*, Boston, 1960.

BARTLETT, F. C., *The Study of Society*, London, 1939.

BERKOWITZ, L., *Aggression: A Social Psychological Analysis*, New York, 1962.

BERNARD, L. L., *War and Its Causes*, New York, 1944.

BION, W. R., "Group Dynamics: A Review," in M. Klein, et al., eds., *New Directions in Psycho-Analysis*, London, 1955.

BONAPARTE, M., *Myths of War*, London, 1947.

BOULDING, K. E., *The Image*, Ann Arbor, 1956.

——, "National Image and International Systems." *Journal of Conflict Resolution*, 1959.

——, "The Need for Study on the Psychology of Disarmament" in *Our Generation Against Nuclear War*, 1964.

BOURTON, J. W., *Peace Theory: Preconditions of Disarmament*, New York, 1962.

BOUTHOUL, G., *Les Guerres: Éléments de Polémologie*, Paris, 1951.

BRENNAN, D. G., *Arms Control, Disarmament, and National Security*, New York, 1961.

CANTRIL, H., ed., *Tensions That Cause Wars*, Urbana, 1950.

———, and BUCHANAN, W., *How Nations See Each Other: A Study in Public Opinion*, Urbana, 1953.

CHRISTIANSEN, B., *Attitudes Toward Foreign Affairs as a Function of Personality*, Oslo, 1959.

CHURCHMAN, C. W., *Prediction and Optimal Decision*, New York, 1961.

CLARKSON, J. D., and COCHRAN, T. C., *War as a Social Institution: The Historian's Perspective*, New York, 1941.

COHEN, J., *Human Nature, War, and Society*, London, 1946.

COMFORT, A., *Authority and Delinquency in the Modern State*, London, 1950.

DAVIDSON, W., KOLKSTEIN, M., and HOHENEMSER, C., *The Nth Country Problem and Arms Control*, Washington, 1960.

DAVIE, M. R., *The Evolution of War*, Port Washington, New York, 1968.

———, *La Guerre dans les Sociétés Primitives*, Paris, 1931.

DEUTSCH, M., "A Psychological Basis for Peace," in Q. Wright, W. M. Evan, and M. Deutsch, *Preventing World War III*, New York, 1962.

DOLLARD, J., *Frustration and Aggression*, New Haven, 1939.

DOUGHERTY, J. E., *Arms Control and Disarmament: The Critical Issues*, Washington, 1966.

DUNN, F., *War and the Minds of Men*, New York, 1950.

DURBIN, E. F. M., and BOWLBY, J., *Personal Aggressiveness and War*, London, 1939.

EDWARDS, W., "The Theory of Decision Making." *Psychological Bulletin*, 1954.

FALK, R. A., and MENDLOVITZ, S. H., *The Strategy of World Order: Toward a Theory of War Prevention*, New York, 1966.

FANON, F., *The Wretched of the Earth*, New York, 1963.

FLÜGEL, J. C., *The Moral Paradox of Peace and War*, London, 1943.

———, *Population, Psychology, and Peace*, London, 1947.

FORNARI, F., *Psicanalisi della Guerra Atomica*, Milan, 1964.

——, ed., *Dissacrazione della Guerra*, Milan, 1969.

FRANK, J. D., "Breaking the Thought Barrier: Psychological Challenge of the Nuclear Age." *Psychiatry*, 1960.

——, "Human Nature and Nonviolent Resistance," in Q. Wright, W. M. Evan, and M. Deutsch, *Preventing World War III*, New York, 1962.

FRAZER, J. G., *The Golden Bough*, New York, 1959.

FREUD, S., *Totem and Taboo*, The Standard Edition of the Complete Psychological Works of Sigmund Freud, translated from the German under the general editorship of James Strachey in collaboration with Anna Freud, London, 1953, Vol. XIII.

——, *Thoughts for the Times on War and Death*, Standard Edition, Vol. XIV.

——, *Why War?*, Standard Edition, Vol. XIV.

——, *Group Psychology and the Analysis of the Ego*, Standard Edition, Vol. XVIII.

——, *Civilization and Its Discontents*, Standard Edition, Vol. XXI.

FRISCH, D. H., ed., *Arms Reduction: Program and Issues*, New York, 1961.

GLAGOLEW, I., and GORYAINOV, M., "Research Communication: Some Problems of Research." *Journal of Peace Research*, 1964.

GLOVER, E., *War, Sadism and Pacifism*, London, 1946.

GOLDHAMMER, H., "The Psychological Analysis of War." *Sociological Review*, 1934.

HENKIN, L., ed., *Arms Control: Issues for the Public*, Englewood Cliffs, 1961.

HUNTINGTON, S. P., ed., *Changing Patterns of Military Politics*, New York, 1962.

IRVING, J., and KATZ, D., "The Reduction of Intergroup Hostility: Research Problems and Hypotheses." *Journal of Conflict Resolution*, 1959.

JACQUES, E., "Social Systems as a Defense Against Persecutory and Depressive Anxiety," in M. Klein et al., eds., *New Directions in Psycho-Analysis*, London, 1955.

JAMES, W., "The Moral Equivalent of War," in *Memories and Studies*, New York, 1911.

JONES, E., *The Life and Work of Sigmund Freud*, New York, 1957.

JORDAN, N., "International Relations and the Psychologist." *Bulletin of Atomic Scientists*, 1963.

KAHN, H., *Thinking About the Unthinkable*, New York, 1962.

——, *On Thermonuclear War*, Princeton, 1960.

KELMAN, H. C., ed., *International Behavior: A Social-Psychological Analysis*, New York, 1965.

KLINEBERG, O., *Tensions Affecting International Understanding*, New York, 1950.

——, *The Human Dimension in International Relations*, New York, 1964.

KLUCKHOLN, C., "Anthropological Research and World Peace," in T. M. Newcomb and E. L. Hartley, eds., *Readings in Social Psychology*, New York, 1947.

LASSWELL, H. D., *Psychopathology and Politics*, New York, 1930.

——, *World Politics and Personal Insecurity*, New York, 1935.

LÉVI-STRAUSS, C., *Totemism*, Boston, 1963.

McNEIL, E. B., "Psychology and Aggression." *Journal of Conflict Resolution*, 1959.

MALINOWSKI, B., "An Anthropological Theory of War." *American Journal of Sociology*, 1941.

MARK, M., *A Social Psychology of War and Peace*, New Haven, 1942.

MASSERMAN, J. H., ed., *Violence and War*, Vol. VI, *Science and Psychoanalysis*, 1963.

MEERLOO, J. A. M., "La Psychiatrie Face à la Guerre et à la Paix." *Médicine et Hygiène*, 1963.

METAIS, E., "Les Sorciers Nous Tuent." *Cahiers Internationales de Sociologie*, 1963.

MONEY-KYRLE, R. E., "The Development of War." *British Journal of Medical Psychology*, 1937.

——, "Psychology of Propaganda." *British Journal of Medical Psychology*, 1941.

——, "Some Aspects of Political Ethics from the Psychoanalytical Point of View." *International Journal of Psychoanalysis*, 1944.

——, *Psychoanalysis and Politics*, London, 1951.

——, "Social Conflict and the Challenge to Psychology." *British Journal of Medical Psychology*, 1948.

MURPHY, G., *Human Nature and Enduring Peace*, Boston, 1945.

NEF, J. U., *War and Human Progress*, Cambridge, 1950.

NIELSON, S., ed., *Psychology and International Affairs: Can We Contribute?* Proceedings of the XIV International Congress of Applied Psychology, Copenhagen, 1962.

PEAR, T. H., ed., *Psychological Factors of Peace and War*, New York, 1950.

PENROSE, M., ed., *The Pathogenesis of War*, London, 1963.

RASER, J. R., "Learning and Affect in International Politics." *Journal of Peace Research*, 1965.

REIK, T., *Ritual: Four Psychoanalytic Studies*, New York, 1946.

RÓHEIM, G., "War Crime and the Covenant." *Journal of Criminal Psychopathology*, 1943.

——, "Projection and the Blood Feud." *Journal of Criminal Psychopathology*, 1943.

——, "War and the Blood Feud." *Journal of Criminal Psychopathology*, 1943.

——, "Crime in Primitive Society." *Journal of Criminal Psychopathology*, 1944.

——, *The Riddle of the Sphinx*, London, 1934.

SHERIF, M., et al., *Intergroup Conflict and Cooperation: The Robbers Cave Experiment*, Norman, Oklahoma, 1961.

——, and SHERIF, C. W., *Groups in Harmony and Tension*, New York, 1963.

SPITZ, R., *The First Year of Life*, New York, 1965.

STRACHEY, A., *The Unconscious Motives of War*, London, 1957.

TOLMAN, E., "Drives Toward War" in Q. Wright, ed., *A Study of War*, Chicago, 1942.

WALLACE, V. H., ed., *Paths to Peace: A Study of War, Its Causes and Prevention*, New York, 1957.

WALSH, M. N., "Psychoanalytic Studies of War." *Philadelphia Association of Psychoanalysis Bulletin*, 1962.

WALTZ, K. N., *Man, the State and War: A Theoretical Analysis*, New York, 1959.

# INDEX